RETURN

OF THE

BISON

ROGER L. DI SILVESTRO

RETURN
OF THE
BISON

A STORY OF SURVIVAL, RESTORATION,

AND A WILDER WORLD

MOUNTAINEERS
BOOKS

 **MOUNTAINEERS BOOKS** is dedicated to
the exploration, preservation, and enjoyment
of outdoor and wilderness areas.

1001 SW Klickitat Way, Suite 201, Seattle, WA 98134
800-553-4453, www.mountaineersbooks.org

Printed in the United States of America
Distributed in the United Kingdom by Cordee, www.cordee.co.uk
26 25 24 23   1 2 3 4 5

Copyeditor: Melissa Ousley
Design and layout: Jen Grable
Cartographer: Lohnes+Wright
Cover photograph: *Bison in Badlands National Park* (istock/franckreporter)
Sources for map on page 6: Committee on the Status of Endangered Wildlife in Canada, "Plains Bison and Wood Bison: COSEWIC Assessment and Status Report 2013"
and Alaska Department of Fish and Game

Library of Congress Control Number: 2023931932

Mountaineers Books titles may be purchased for corporate, educational, or other
promotional sales, and our authors are available for a wide range of events. For information on special discounts or booking an author, contact our customer service at
800-553-4453 or mbooks@mountaineersbooks.org.

Printed on FSC-certified materials

ISBN (paperback): 978-1-68051-583-1
ISBN (ebook): 978-1-68051-584-8

An independent nonprofit publisher since 1960

MIX
Paper from
responsible sources
FSC
www.fsc.org   FSC® C005010

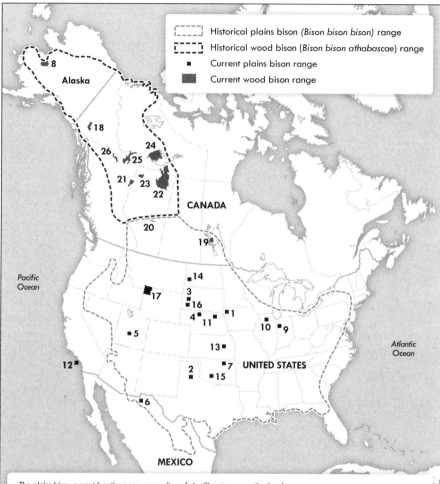

Historical plains bison *(Bison bison bison)* range

Historical wood bison *(Bison bison athabascae)* range

■ Current plains bison range

■ Current wood bison range

The plains bison current locations are a sampling of significant conservation herds.

United States & Mexico

1 Broken Kettle Grasslands Preserve, Iowa
2 Caprock Canyons State Park, Texas
3 Custer State Park, South Dakota
4 Fort Niobrara National Wildlife Refuge, Nebraska
5 Henry Mountains, Utah
6 Janos Biosphere Reserve, Chihuahua, Mexico
7 Joseph H. Williams Tallgrass Prairie Preserve
   (The Nature Conservancy/TNC), Oklahoma
8 Lower Yukon/Innoko Rivers herd, Alaska
9 Kankakee Sands (TNC), Indiana
10 Nachusa Grasslands (TNC), Illinois
11 Niobrara Valley Preserve (TNC), Nebraska
12 Santa Catalina Island, California
13 Tallgrass Prairie National Preserve (TNC), Kansas
14 Theodore Roosevelt National Park, North Dakota

15 Wichita Mountains National Wildlife Refuge, Oklahoma
16 Wind Cave National Park, South Dakota
17 Yellowstone National Park, Wyoming, Montana & Idaho

Canada

18 Aishihik herd, Yukon
19 Chitek Lake, Manitoba
20 Elk Island National Park, Alberta
21 Etthithun herd, British Columbia
22 Greater Wood Buffalo National Park,
   Alberta & Northwest Territories
23 Hay-Zama herd, Alberta
24 Mackenzie herd, Northwest Territories
25 Nahanni herd, Northwest Territories & British Columbia
26 Nordquist herd, British Columbia

Contents

Introduction: *Back from the Brink* 9

CHAPTER 1
In the Beginning 18

CHAPTER 2
When Science Favors Extinction 37

CHAPTER 3
Where Buffalo Roam, Again: Early Restoration 53

CHAPTER 4
American Bison Step Out of the ER 71

CHAPTER 5
Private Herds: Hopes, Aspirations, Roads to Recovery 89

CHAPTER 6
Tribes: Finding Home 108

CHAPTER 7
Lost Herds: Mexico and Canada 125

CHAPTER 8
The Way of the Wisent 146

CHAPTER 9
The Last Refuge 167

CHAPTER 10
Building a Future for Bison 192

Acknowledgments **219**
Notes **221**
Bibliography **239**
Resources **245**
Index **251**

AUTHOR'S NOTE

Common names for plants and animals are inexact throughout the world, so I use *buffalo* and *bison* interchangeably to
avoid the monotony of a single term. *Bison* was originally a
Greek noun meaning "ox," while *buffalo*, in the context of
bison, is derived from the word that early French explorers
used for bison—*bœuf*, which also means "ox." English colo-
nists anglicized the name to buffalo in the early 1600s, at
least 140 years before the founder of modern scientific tax-
onomy, Carolus Linnaeus, put the label bison on the New
World animal. The use of *buffalo* has fallen out of favor among
some nomenclature enthusiasts who believe *buffalo* should be
reserved for certain African and Asian ungulates (but they
raise no objection to calling a burrowing rodent a prairie
dog). Nevertheless, *buffalo* carries the pungency of tradition, as
it was used by pioneers and explorers and appears throughout early written accounts of American history; it is also
widely used today by Indigenous people.

INTRODUCTION
Back from the Brink

The bison looms large in human prehistory—it was a vital prey animal throughout Europe and into Russia and North America. Stone Age Europeans depicted the species widely in cave paintings dating back 40,000 years or more, probably part of animalistic religious rites from an epoch when perhaps all humans felt spiritually linked to wildlife. It was one of the animals whose meat, bone, and hide made possible humankind's journey into Europe, across Russia, and into the Americas. Unlike many of its ancient contemporaries, the bison was a survivor. While mammoth and mastodon disappeared, along with the Neanderthal people who hunted them, bison lived on, outlasting the ice ages.

The bison is emblematic of another vanished era, America's Old West, which harbored one of Earth's last wildlife spectacles, an ecological extravaganza almost unmatched anywhere during the past two hundred years. Plains and prairies often swarmed with bison, elk, pronghorn, deer, and wild sheep that in turn attracted and fed grizzly bears, wolves, and mountain lions.

The buffalo was a special symbol among the people of the Old West, too. For the Plains Indians, it meant survival in the form of meat and items crafted from hide, horn, and bone, making bison essential. For pioneers, it was a different story. The buffalo represented a force of nature that could destroy fences and compete with cattle for grass, and so the buffalo had to go. For the military, it represented the mainstay of many Plains Indians, another obstacle to Manifest Destiny's concept of progress, and so the bison had to go—and by and large, it did.

Bison may outrun a fast horse, but they couldn't outrun the impacts of modern history, which is why in the United States, untallied millions of bison withered to a few dozen in less than a century, symbolizing another verity of human life—we can wreak total destruction on wildlife when we're unbridled by laws, regulations, and an ethic that encompasses all species. No other large mammal has sunk so low in number and revived as a species. But the bison *is* showing signs of recovery, even in Europe, where poachers once cut the native population to about fifty animals, all captives behind zoo bars.

THE AMERICAN BUFFALO—WHICH OCCURS AS TWO SUBSPECIES, THE FAMIL-iar plains bison and the slightly larger wood bison of western Canada and parts of Alaska—once haunted prairies and woodlands, meadows and moun-tainsides from northern Canada into Mexico and from the Rocky Mountains to the Atlantic Seaboard. They were so common in what is today upstate New York that pioneers had a hard time putting up cabins—bison rubbed against the frames almost as soon as they were erected, knocking them out of line. We can trace the animal's once-extensive range in today's geographic names—Buffalo, New York, springs to mind, but there are also towns called Buffalo in Iowa, Kentucky, Minnesota, Missouri, Ohio, Oklahoma, South Carolina, South Dakota, Texas, Wisconsin, and Wyoming. Minnesota has a Buffalo Lake, Illinois a Buffalo Grove, Texas a Buffalo Gap, and Iowa a Buffalo Center. Nebraska has a Buffalo County, as do South Dakota and Wisconsin, and Saskatchewan has Buffalo Narrows.

Europe's distinctive bison species, the wisent, stands taller than the American thanks to longer legs. Of two Old World subspecies, only the lowland wisent survives today. Poachers shot the higher-ground Caucasian wisent into extinction in the 1920s. Because the wisent was nearly extinct by modern times, what we know about wild bison comes mostly from studying the North American plains buffalo.

Before agriculture and cities took over the bulk of American bison habi-tat, the animals traveled in migratory herds so large that on cold winter days you might have located out-of-sight buffalo by the fog their exhalations created above them. Their numbers made an impression on early European chroniclers of the West. "While feeding, they are often scattered over a great extent of country, but when they move in mass, they form a dense and almost impenetrable column, which, once in motion, is scarcely to be impeded," according to an 1833 account. "Their line of march is seldom interrupted even by considerable rivers, across which they swim without fear or hesita-tion, nearly in the order that they traverse the plains. . . . These animals have been seen in herds of three, four, and five thousand, blackening the plain as far as the eye could view. At night, it is impossible for persons to sleep near them who are unaccustomed to their noise, which, from the incessant lowing and roaring of the bulls, is said to resemble distant thunder."

One measure of the bison's numbers, and of the slaughter that took place in the West, was the increasing haul of bone collectors, who traveled the prairies in wagons gathering up bison skeletal remains for use as fertilizer and in refining sugar. In 1872, these scavengers shipped 568 tons of bison bones on the Atchison, Topeka, and Santa Fe line; in 1873 they shipped 1,372 tons, and in 1874, 3,457 tons. Along the Northern Pacific Railroad, collectors conveniently gleaned bones for a hundred miles on either side of the track; in 1885 a single firm shipped 200 tons from Miles City, in eastern Montana Territory. Fertilizer companies in Michigan paid eighteen dollars a ton for crushed bones, twelve dollars a ton for uncrushed.

In the years before slaughter and fences, bison followed their food with the seasons, seeking plains, prairies, and meadows where they could feed on grasses and sedges. Some herds climbed to higher elevations in summer and descended in winter, as elk, wild sheep, and some deer do today. When buffalo crowded into an area by the thousands, each downing about thirty pounds of grass daily, they could crop vegetation to the ground.

Given their numbers and the amount of food and water they consumed, buffalo packed a powerful ecological wallop. Their grazing, and the seeds that lodged in their fur, influenced the type of vegetation that flourished in their wake, which impacted the grasshopper species and other insects on a given prairie, in turn affecting the types of bird species found there.

In winter, when head and forequarters were insulated with long, shaggy hair, bison would face into the wind, swinging their heads into accumulating snow to uncover vegetation. Wandering across snowbound landscapes, they cleared paths that were beneficial to less powerful animals, such as deer, pronghorn, and wolves. While grazing, they cut openings that served as refuges for birds needing shelter from stinging wind.

Bison created microhabitats by rolling in dust patches or muddy spots, perhaps to get rid of biting insects, perhaps to cool themselves with mud, perhaps for other, unknown, reasons. This wallowing created shallow but lasting pits or depressions that filled with water during spring rains, creating temporary ponds useful to other species in dry prairie habitat. Even buffalo hunters would bathe in wallows and drink from them, practices recalled with the grim distaste of experience by Frank Mayer and Charles Roth in *The Buffalo Harvest*. You can still find wallows from centuries past where the plow has not erased them, such as in the Kansas Flint Hills. They continue to serve as breeding ponds for amphibians and as ephemeral water sources for birds and smaller mammals as well as thirstier plant species. Bison also left their mark in another way: many of today's state and interstate highways, and many railroads, follow routes etched by buffalo as they moved, year by year, century by century, from feeding ground to feeding ground—well-worn trails, some of them two feet deep.

Bison cows and their offspring grouped together in maternal herds. Bulls left when about three years old, leading either solitary lives or gathering with other bulls. During breeding season, from midsummer to early fall, young bulls, seeking mates, rejoined the females but usually found an older male already herding with the cows and ready to defend his position.

When bison herds were plentiful, breeding bulls brought prairies to rumbling life, challenging one another with bellows and roars that could carry for more than three miles. Pawing the earth, a group of fifteen or twenty bulls in combat could send up dust clouds visible across miles of plains. Dominant older bulls tended to mate first, usually during the opening month of breeding season. Younger bulls might mate later.

Calves were born in spring, most of the cows in a herd giving birth within a tight time frame—at Yellowstone National Park today, for example, 80 percent of calves are born between April 25 and May 25—a strategy that helps make the young less vulnerable to predators. Cows usually wean their calves within eight months, but some continue nursing for up to a year, the cows kicking and butting their offspring away as the calves grow large enough to be a drain on maternal energy.

The earlier in the calving season a buffalo was born, the higher its social rank was likely to be as an adult. As early birth probably reflected the breeding of the healthiest, most dominant bulls with the most physically fit cows, higher rank for the early born may have reflected both birth order and better genes. In any event, calves, like scions of some royal lineage of the plains, tended to inherit their parents' rank, with bulls and cows maintaining separate dominance hierarchies.

From late spring to early summer, cows and calves were predator magnets. Wolves, especially packs with greater numbers of large males, also attacked old, declining bulls. Sometimes wolves took hours to complete a kill, surrounding a buffalo, ripping at vulnerable spots, rendering the prey helpless by cutting the tendons of the hind legs, closing in for the kill, tearing away meat and eating before the bison was dead. One observer wrote of watching wolves kill a bull in 1859 near today's Salina, Kansas:

> [A]bout a dozen brown and white wolves [were] arrayed in a circle around one of the largest buffalos I had ever seen. . . . They did not rush upon the buffalo in a mass, but calmly waiting until his heels were towards them, several of them sprang like darts from the circle and fastened to his flanks or hams and as the buffalo turned to confront these, others would seize upon the vulnerable parts. . . . Nor did they seem the least hurried about it. Some, tired by their violent efforts, withdrew a short distance and sat down on their haunches with their tongues lolling out to watch and rest. In a few moments they returned to the attack and others dropped out to rest. Thus by this system of relief, they kept up the contest with a certainty of overcoming their foe however strong.

Because of their size, aggressiveness, and herd instinct, healthy bison generally were able to protect themselves against wolves. Calves ran to cows for defense, and cows to bulls, which when healthy and robust could combat almost any predator, with the possible exception of the grizzly bear. Early observers reported that cows and bulls often formed an outward-facing circle around vulnerable herd members to ward off predators, but generally they avoided serious conflict by running away, with cows and calves in the lead and the pugnacious bulls in the rear. If enemies drew too close, the bulls would turn and fight.

The tendency to follow the leader sometimes betrayed a herd, making it easier for Plains Indians on foot to encircle and spook the animals, driving them into a makeshift fenced pathway leading over a cliff, a preferred hunting method before Native Americans acquired European horses. Once the horse and the rifle came to the plains, and later the railroad, the bison was doomed. By 1800, mounted Plains Indians were killing an estimated 200,000 to 400,000 bison yearly, enough to contribute to a population decline. As early as 1804, Lewis and Clark reported that bison were scarce around the permanent villages of farming Indians along the Upper Missouri River, suggesting that horse-mounted Indians had wiped out bison regionally.

The most relentless slaughter began when trade in bison hides exploded in the early 1800s. The killing expanded after the Civil War, which—wrote Frank Mayer, himself an 1870s bison hunter, in his memoir, *The Buffalo Harvest*—supplied the nation with a cadre of eager riflemen:

> At the close of any war there are bound to be thousands of young men who find peacetime pursuits too dull for their adventure-stirred lives. Maybe that was truer after the Civil War than at any other time. I know how I felt. I was restive. I wanted out. Fortunately for us then we had what you don't have now: we had a frontier to conquer. It was a very good substitute for war.
>
> And on this frontier, old mountain men who drifted in and kept brass rails and cuspidors of crude saloons in high polish, told us there were literally millions of buffalo. They didn't belong to anybody. If you could kill them, what they brought was yours. They were walking gold pieces, the old timers said, and a young fellow who had guts and gumption could make his fortune.

The buffalo hunters who were trying to convert bison into gold, a strange alchemy, destroyed the herds all across the plains. Market hunters rapidly depleted herds in Kansas and Nebraska, then in Texas, and finally in Montana and the Dakota Territory. The bison cooperated in its own destruction. Under attack from gunfire, a herd might mill around aimlessly until killed to the last animal. Or, if a hunter was adept at staying hidden and a good enough shot to kill almost instantly with one bullet—no muss, no fuss, no bawling alarm calls—a buffalo herd might graze calmly while picked off one by one. Hide hunters called this efficient slaughter a "stand." One famed rifleman, Vic Smith, who estimated he killed about 5,000 bison a year during the 1870s and early 1880s, once shot 107 at a single stand in a single hour. Shooting could be so constant that gun barrels became too hot to fire and would have to be allowed to cool off before the work could proceed.

AFTER LARGE BISON HERDS HAD BEEN WIPED OUT IN THE SOUTHERN AND central parts of the animal's range, the last big herd made its final stand in what are today Montana and North Dakota. When the North Pacific Railroad arrived there in 1883, it brought market hunters into the area in droves, and they killed off bison wherever they found them. Indians, too, contributed to the species' destruction. The agent of the Lakota (Sioux) reservation in the Dakota Territory allowed the Indians in his charge to go off the reservation for one last hunt in mid-1883. The Indians, and some white hunters, swooped down on a herd of about ten thousand and killed all but about one thousand. The agent said the hunt benefited the Indians, but at least one Badlands observer disagreed, calling the foray "a blood-lustful debauch of two days, masquerading as a hunt in the name of necessity. . . . in which 600 [the count was probably 1,000] mounted Sioux Indian warriors were deliberately encouraged to destroy their own sustenance, to draw their own teeth, that they might easier be held to their reservations." He added that the hunt was "particularly reprehensible not only because of its more than questionable purpose, to starve the Indians into submission, but because none knew better than the Government that it was a slaughter of the sole surviving herd of the species in America."

The following year, hunters piled their gear into wagons and went out on the plains expecting to hunt more buffalo. When they found only rotting flesh and bleaching bone, they presumed the bison had gone elsewhere, Canada perhaps, and would be back. A few years passed before the hunters admitted to themselves that they'd destroyed the incalculable herds. Within the next few years, small, harried, isolated bands of bison were hunted down and wiped out, in large part by ranchers who wanted to eliminate competitors for their cattle's grass range. Nothing remained of wild herds but perhaps a few dozen buffalo in Yellowstone National Park.

Down to the very end, governments made little effort to save the bison from market hunters. William T. Hornaday, a leading naturalist and bison advocate in the late 1800s and early 1900s, lamented the blatant neglect that pushed the bison toward extinction: "The business-like, wholesale slaughter, wherein one hunter would openly kill five thousand buffaloes and market perhaps two thousand hides, could easily have been stopped forever. Buffalo hides could not have been dealt in clandestinely, for many reasons, and had there been no sale for ill-gotten spoils the still-hunter would have gathered no spoils to sell." The means for saving the bison were readily available; the will simply was not there.

Nevertheless, some Americans lamented the passing of the bison and of the Old West. A nostalgic trace of evidence left by one such person, apparently an anonymous writer for the *New York Times* in 1907, reflects the sense of loss in a poem called "Passing of the Prairie":

> They have tamed it with their barrows, they have broken it with plows;
> Where the bison used to range it someone's built himself a home;
> They have stuck it full of fence posts; they have girded it with wire,
> They have shamed it and profaned it with an automobile tire;
> They have bridged its gullied rivers; they have peopled it with men.
> They have churched it, they have schooled it, they have steepled it—Amen!
> They have furrowed it with ridges, they have seeded it with grain,
> And the West that was worth knowing, I shall never see again.
>
> They have smothered all its campfires, where the beaten plainsmen slept,
> They have driven up their cattle where the skulking coyote crept;
> They have made themselves a pasture where the timid deer would browse;
> Where the antelope were feeding they have dotted o'er with cows;
> There's a yokel's tuneless whistling down the bison's winding trail,
> Where the red man's arrow fluttered there's a woman with a pail
> Driving up the cows for milking; they have cut its wild extent
> Into forty-acre patches till its glory is all spent.
>
> I remember in the sixties, when as far as I could see,
> It had never lord nor ruler but the buffalo and me;
> Ere the blight of man was on it, and the endless acres lay
> Just as God Almighty left them on the restful seventh day;
> When no sound rose from vastness but a murmured hum and dim
> Like the echoed void of Silence in an unheard prairie hymn;
> And I lay at night and rested in my bed of blankets curled
> Much alone as if I was the only man in all the world!
>
> But the prairie's passed, or passing, with the passing of the year,
> Till there is no West worth knowing, and there are no pioneers;
> They have ridded it of dangers till the zest of it is gone;
> And I've saddled up my pony, for I'm dull and lonesome here,
> To go westward, westward, westward till we find a new frontier;
> To get back to God's own wilderness and the skies we used to know—
> But there is no West; it's conquered—and I don't know where to go.

This book does not chronicle the destruction of the bison, a story that has been told thoroughly in many volumes. Rather, it begins where other books on bison history usually leave off, in the 1880s, when the bison was a vanishing shadow on two continents. Chronicling roughly the past 140 years, this volume shows how the species is edging toward recovery, thanks to, and sometimes in spite of, efforts to preserve it, beginning in an era when knowledge of wildlife and its needs was rudimentary.

Today, conservation biologists are struggling across the globe with the challenges of protecting herds of large, nomadic, willful species—from bison to giraffes, and from elephants and rhinos to wildebeest and African Cape buffalo. What these scientists uncover about the conservation of bison—the first large mammal subjected to recovery efforts—will provide clues for protecting these other species from systematic destruction. If you've ever suffered at the thought of losing these fellow earthlings, the story of the bison offers an element of hope for you and for them.

CHAPTER 1

IN THE BEGINNING

The Dakota Badlands, September 20, 1883: Twenty-four-year-old Theodore Roosevelt, fewer than two decades from becoming president of the
United States, is doing a faux Indian war dance around the bloody carcass of
a bull bison he has shot and killed. His guide, a local man named Joe Ferris,
watches in astonishment and relief. Tough enough to eke out a living in the
Badlands ranch country, Ferris has been put through the wringer as Roosevelt's guide. He has spent the past three weeks on horseback in pursuit of
bison that fled at the approach of the hunters, having been shot at so often
that most of them carried bullets in their bodies. Riding the prairie through
days of rain, even sleeping out on rainy nights without a tent, Ferris had
begun to think he might die of exhaustion before the relentless Roosevelt
killed a buffalo. When Roosevelt concluded his exuberant dance, he handed
Ferris a magnificent tip of $100, further amazing the guide.

THROUGHOUT MOST OF HIS LIFE, ROOSEVELT—DESCENDED FROM ONE OF
New York City's wealthiest families—was an avid sport hunter. In his youth
he shot birds of all kinds, including songbirds for his personal museum.
His yen for shooting attracted him to the Dakota Badlands, which lay in
the region where some of the last of the wild bison outside of Yellowstone
National Park were making their final stand. Roosevelt was determined to
kill one before the animals were all gone. This fixation made Roosevelt part
of a trend among sport hunters. William T. Hornaday—chief taxidermist

for the National Museum in Washington, DC—wrote about this trend in his 1889 book *The Extermination of the American Bison*, which was based on his landmark 1887 report for the museum: "A buffalo is now so great a prize, and by the ignorant it is considered so great an honor (?) to kill one, that extraordinary exertions will be made to find and shoot down without mercy the 'last buffalo.'"

Only four years after his hunt, Roosevelt would help found the Boone and Crockett Club, which organized hunters to fight on behalf of wildlife and its habitat. The club led the struggle to defend the last wild bison—and their refuge in Yellowstone National Park—from the destructive development plans of such entities as the railroad industry. Nevertheless, it is little short of a miracle that bison and other dwindling species survived not only the onslaught of uncontrolled hunting and widespread habitat loss but also the practices of early wildlife advocates. Park administrators, for example, thought that predators were an evil that should be exterminated to make the world safe for deer, elk, and other game species, an idea negated by modern research. They were supported in this viewpoint by conservationists such as Theodore Roosevelt, who as president of the United States wrote in 1905 that in Yellowstone "the cougars are noxious because of the antelope, mountain sheep, and deer which they kill; and the Superintendent has imported some hounds with which to hunt them." Many sport hunters initially opposed hunting seasons and bag limits even as game species dwindled.

Roosevelt thoroughly exemplified the ambiguous state of wildlife conservation during a period critical to bison survival. Hunting in Idaho in spring 1889, a little below the Montana border and twenty-five miles west of Yellowstone National Park, he discovered fresh bison tracks, trailed the animals, and found them feeding in a glade fringed with timber—a cow, a calf, and a yearling. These buffalo, almost certainly from Yellowstone, would have numbered among the specific animals the Boone and Crockett Club endeavored to save. Moreover, shooting bison as they left the protective boundaries of the park, or even driving them out of the park into Idaho, was a well-known practice among poachers.

Another cow and calf joined the first animals as Roosevelt watched, sure a bull was bound to turn up. He pondered the moment: "Mixed with the eager excitement of the hunter was a certain half melancholy feeling as I gazed on these bison, themselves part of the last remnant of a doomed and nearly vanished race. Few, indeed, are the men who now have, or evermore shall have, the chance of seeing the mightiest of American beasts, in all his wild vigor, surrounded by the tremendous desolation of his far-off mountain home."

Afraid the cows might run off, Roosevelt grew increasingly edgy. Then, to his relief, a bull appeared at the edge of the glade, head outstretched as he scratched his throat against a young tree, shaking its branches. Roosevelt aimed behind the bull's front leg, seeking heart or lungs, and fired. "At the crack of the rifle all the bison, without the momentary halt of terror-struck surprise so common among game, turned and raced off at headlong speed. The fringe of young pines beyond and below the glade cracked and swayed as if a whirlwind were passing, and in another moment they reached the top of a very steep incline, thickly strewn with boulders and dead timber. Down this they plunged with reckless speed." Roosevelt found the dead buffalo fifty yards beyond the edge of the forest: "a splendid old bull, still in his full vigor, with large, sharp horns, and heavy mane and glossy coat; and I felt the most exulting pride as I handled and examined him; for I had procured a trophy such as can fall henceforth to few hunters indeed."

Roosevelt's pursuit of vanishing species dated at least to the mid-1880s, when he was establishing two ranches in the Dakota Badlands along the Little Missouri River. After hearing that an old hunter had killed a cow elk—a member of a species then nearly extinct in the region—about twenty-five miles from one of Roosevelt's ranches, he hastened to the kill site. There he tracked down a bull elk and promptly shot it, elated that it was "probably the last of his race that will ever be found in our neighborhood."

But he went further than merely killing bison for sport. Roosevelt endorsed ideas then widely accepted by a nation stoked on the concept of Manifest Destiny—the belief that the United States was meant to sweep over and settle the entire stretch of continent that lay between Canada and Mexico. "While the slaughter of the buffalo has been in places needless and brutal," he wrote, "and while it is to be greatly regretted that the species is likely to become extinct, and while, moreover, from a purely selfish standpoint many, including myself, would rather see it continue to exist as the chief feature in the unchanged life of the Western wilderness; yet, on the other hand, it must be remembered that its continued existence in any numbers was absolutely incompatible with any thing but a very sparse settlement of the country; and that its destruction was the condition of precedent upon the advance of white civilization in the West, and was a positive boon to the more thrifty and industrious frontiersmen." Bison, he added, competed with cattle for grass, and so must go. But there was another reason for their extinction. "Above all, the extermination of the buffalo was the only way of solving the Indian question. As long as this large animal of the chase existed, the Indians simply could not be kept on reservations, and always had an ample supply of meat on hand to support them in the event of war; and its disappearance was the only method of forcing them to at least partially abandon their savage mode of life. From the standpoint of humanity at large, the extermination of the buffalo has been a blessing."

And yet in the same book, only a few pages earlier, he declared, "The extermination of the buffalo has been a veritable tragedy of the animal world. . . . It may truthfully be said that the sudden and complete extermination of the vast herds of the buffalo is without a parallel in historic times."

In the hands of such men lay the fate of the bison and other hunted species at the close of the nineteenth century. Not content with killing jeopardized wildlife, Roosevelt produced an outpouring of books about his hunting experiences. His first, *Hunting Trips of a Ranchman*, resulted in his meeting George Bird Grinnell, one of the great leaders of the wildlife-conservation movement that was developing in the 1880s. As editor of *Forest and Stream* magazine, an influential voice for the protection of wildlife and other natural resources, Grinnell would guide Roosevelt down a path to wildlife advocacy.

GRINNELL WAS BORN IN BROOKLYN, NEW YORK, ON SEPTEMBER 20, 1849. His distinguished family tree included five colonial governors. His father served as the key Wall Street agent for Cornelius Vanderbilt, ruler of the New York Central system of railroads and founder of the Vanderbilt family line that would become synonymous with wealth and power during America's Gilded Age.

In 1857, when Grinnell was seven or eight years old, his family built a house on Manhattan's west side in an area called Audubon Park, overlooking the Hudson River north of where Columbia University stands today. This move from Brooklyn initiated a change that would have lasting effects on

George Bird Grinnell. The family had purchased the site of the new home from Lucy Audubon, the widow of artist John James Audubon, who had died six years earlier after earning worldwide acclaim for his life-sized paintings of every known bird species native to the United States. Lucy, remaining in the Audubon home, ran a small school in which Grinnell enrolled. Her influence on him must have been profound. Roughly thirty years later, he would found an organization for the protection of birds that is still today a preeminent advocate for wildlife and habitat, the National Audubon Society.

As a youth, Grinnell attended a military school in Ossining, a Hudson River town about twenty miles upriver from Manhattan. In 1866, he started at Yale, where he received a bachelor of arts degree in 1870 after four academically undistinguished years. With the ink on his diploma barely dry, he left for an expedition across Kansas, Nebraska, Wyoming, and Utah the following summer, accompanying one of the leading paleontologists of the time, O. C. Marsh, on a six-month fossil-hunting foray.

That trip was the first of a series of annual journeys west. In 1874, he signed on as a naturalist for George Armstrong Custer's exploration of southwest Dakota Territory's Black Hills, a mountain range that rises above the plains and extends into Wyoming. The federal government set it aside by treaty for Plains Indians, who regarded it as both sacred and a source of game when other areas were lacking sufficient wildlife to sustain tribes. The expedition discovered gold in those hills, and miners flooded into the area, triggering the last of the Indian wars in the northern plains. Two years later, Custer invited Grinnell to join a campaign against tribes in eastern Montana Territory. Grinnell, busy with his work in osteology at Yale's Peabody Museum, could not spare the time. Had he been able to do so, he might have sown the earth with his own bones at Little Bighorn during Custer's Last Stand, June 25, 1876. Instead he lived to receive a doctorate in osteology and vertebrate paleontology in 1880 and to take a leading role in wildlife conservation during its infancy.

As early as 1873, Grinnell voiced the need for bison protection even though the animals were then "still often sufficiently numerous to blacken the plains." He could see that "their days are numbered, and unless some action on this subject is speedily taken not only by the States and Territories, but by the National Government, these shaggy brown beasts, these cattle upon a thousand hills, will ere long be among the things of the past."

Grinnell's first experience with Yellowstone came in 1875, when he accompanied an expedition under Colonel William Ludlow, the army's chief engineer of the Department of Dakota, who was surveying park resources and the potential for building wagon roads. Grinnell's report on the area's wildlife was well received and signaled the dangers that park wildlife faced. In the cover letter that accompanied his report to Ludlow, he wrote, "It may not be out of place here, to call your attention to the terrible destruction of large game, for the hides alone, which is constantly going on in those portions of Montana and Wyoming through which we passed. Buffalo, elk, mule-deer, and antelope are being slaughtered by thousands each year, without regard to age or sex, and at all seasons. . . . Females of all these species are as eagerly pursued in the spring, when just about to bring forth their young, as at any other time."

Though wildlife was then abundant in the West, Grinnell made the case that many species were vulnerable: "It is estimated that during the winter of 1874–75 not less than 3,000 elk were killed for their hides alone in the valley of the Yellowstone, between the mouth of Trail Creek and the Hot Springs. If this be true, what must have been the number for both Territories? Buffalo and mule-deer suffer even more severely than elk, and antelope nearly as much. . . . It is certain that, unless in some way the destruction of these animals can be checked, the large game still so abundant in some localities will ere long be exterminated."

His expectations proved prescient. In 1880, P. W. Norris, the park superintendent, estimated that about six hundred bison roamed Yellowstone. In 1885, the number was about two hundred. In response to the decline, Superintendent D. W. Wear wrote in his annual report to the Secretary of the Interior, "I would most earnestly call your attention to the entire inadequacy of the laws to provide punishment for violations of the regulations for the protection of the Park."

In the summer of that year an energetic, voluble nature enthusiast came to Grinnell's office at *Forest and Stream* to discuss one of the magazine's book reviews—hardly a prophetic beginning for a meeting that would engender a force for wildlife protection that reverberates to this day. Theodore Roosevelt had just concluded publication of *Hunting Trips of a Ranchman*, a book about his experiences in the Badlands that a *New York Times* reviewer said would "take a leading position in the literature of the American sportsman."

Grinnell, in the July 2, 1885, issue of *Forest and Stream*, took a different view, one more in line with a comment about the West made by Austrian sport hunter and writer William A. Baillie-Grohman: "There is, I suppose, no country in the world on which so much has been written, based on less personal experience." This matter of personal experience—Roosevelt had spent a total of barely six months in the West—undermined Grinnell's enthusiasm for the book. In his review, Grinnell pointed out that "Mr. Roosevelt is not well known as a sportsman, and his experience of the Western country is quite limited." He added, "We are sorry to see that a number of hunting myths are given as fact, but it was after all scarcely to be expected that with the author's limited experience he could sift the wheat from the chaff and distinguish the true from the false."

Roosevelt visited Grinnell to talk about the editor's reaction to *Hunting Trips*. Grinnell would later recall that they "talked freely about the book, and took up at length some of its statements." Roosevelt proved open to criticism. Grinnell, nine years Roosevelt's senior, recognized that the young hunter had reported on the West and its wildlife "faithfully and accurately" but had suffered "the youthful—and common—tendency to generalize from his own observations and to conclude that certain aspects of nature were always and in all places as he had found them in one place. Moreover, he was inclined to accept as fact some statements made in books, and others by men with whom he had talked, who were either bad observers or careless talkers."

The discussion segued to the subject of hunting in the West. Grinnell said, "I told him something about game destruction in Montana for the hides, which, so far as small game was concerned, had begun in the West only a few years before that, though the slaughter of the buffalo for their skins was going on much longer and by this time their extermination had been substantially completed." Grinnell did not record Roosevelt's response, but discussions during subsequent visits, in Grinnell's opinion, gave Roosevelt "his first direct and detailed information about this slaughter of elk, deer, antelope, and mountain-sheep. No doubt it had some influence in making him the ardent game protector that he later became."

During the next two years, Roosevelt and Grinnell became friends. After Grinnell launched the Audubon group through *Forest and Stream* magazine to work for bird protection, he and Roosevelt agreed to create an organization to promote big-game conservation. In December 1887, they gathered together a selection of wealthy eastern hunters for a dinner meeting to discuss the decline of big game—such as bison, elk, grizzly bears, and deer—throughout the nation, primarily because of habitat destruction and the marketing of meat, hides, and other products. This problem was a desperate one for avid hunters. If the game vanished, they feared, then hunters bereft of game would soon become extinct too. Nor would they be able to pass on hunting traditions to their children.

From these concerns sprang the Boone and Crockett Club, named after Daniel Boone and Davy Crockett, who in Roosevelt's mind epitomized knowledge of wilderness lore. It was the first US organization created explicitly to influence conservation legislation, and it would prove a powerful force for bison survival. Charter members included a contingent well familiar with Yellowstone, among them Grinnell; Arnold Hague, who'd served the park as a geologist; and Archibald Rogers, owner of a ranch near the park where several other members had stayed, including Owen Wister, a well-known journalist and author of the novel *The Virginian*. In 1889, Captain Moses Harris, shortly after he resigned as acting superintendent of the park, joined the club, setting a precedent for former park administrators to join when they went out of service. His membership ensured that the park took a leading place in the club's political agenda.

The club elected Roosevelt president in January 1888, determined to protect game and its habitat: "The preservation of forests and of game go hand in hand. He who works for either works for both." Club members also agreed with tenets, espoused by Roosevelt, that hunting was singularly important to creating sturdy citizens, "a vigorous and masterful people. The rifle-bearing hunter, whether he goes on foot or on horseback, whether he voyages in a canoe or travels with a dog-sled, must be sound of body and firm of mind, and must possess energy, resolution, manliness, self-reliance, and capacity for hardy self-help. In short, the big-game hunter must possess qualities without which no race can do its life-work well; and these are the very qualities which it is the purpose of this Club, so far as it may be, to develop and foster."

To be eligible for membership, Roosevelt required that an applicant had to have "killed with the rifle in fair chase, by still-hunting or otherwise, at least one individual of one of the various kinds of American large game," including "bear, buffalo (bison), mountain-sheep, caribou, cougar, musk-ox, white goat, elk (wapiti), wolf (not coyote), prong-horn antelope, moose, and deer." In language characteristic of his time, Roosevelt wrote, "The club is emphatically an association of men who believe that the hardier and manlier the sport is the more attractive it is, and who do not think that there is any place in the ranks of true sportsmen either for the game-butcher, on the one hand, or, on the other, for the man who wishes to do all his shooting in preserves, and to shirk rough hard work."

Roosevelt was clear about where he thought the problem of wildlife destruction lay. It was not, in his view, the sport hunter who wiped out game. He made this point in later years, too, such as in his 1905 book *Out-door Pastimes of an American Hunter*: "The professional market hunter who kills game for the hide, or for the feathers, or for the meat, or to sell antlers and other trophies; the market men who put game in cold storage; and the rich people, who are content to buy what they have not the skill to get by their own exertions—these are the men who are the real enemies of game." Subsistence hunters, who killed to feed themselves and their people, rarely threatened species survival, because they did not kill much more than they needed for food. Sport hunters arguably hunted for a few trophies and some meat. Market hunters, however, killed without limit, because their goal was maximum profit.

When the Boone and Crockett Club was founded, the concept of protecting natural resources was still new. Until then, the federal government's main role in land management had revolved around giving away federal holdings for developments such as railroad lines and homesteads. The club supported wildlife protections, such as hunting seasons and limits, even though the question of which government entities had responsibility for wildlife was still unanswered. The club also was instrumental in passage of the 1891 federal Forest Reserve Act, which authorized the president to create timber reserves that protected forests on public land from being sold or homesteaded. Presidents Grover Cleveland, Benjamin Harrison, and William McKinley subsequently set aside forest reserves protecting a total of 45 million acres. The club's work for forest protection supported its advocacy for better protection of Yellowstone National Park, a key factor of which was protection for bison. The first reserve set aside by President Harrison under the act was the 1.25-million-acre Yellowstone National Park Timberland Reserve.

CREATION OF THE BOONE AND CROCKET CLUB CONVERGED WITH A NEARLY simultaneous development at Yellowstone that would have profound effects on bison recovery: the park came under military control, putting an army officer in charge as acting superintendent. This change in administration from civilians to military officers had been in the air for more than a decade. Colonel William Ludlow, the army engineer who led the 1875 Yellowstone expedition that introduced Grinnell to the park, had urged this shift after he saw troubling examples of vandalism in the park. In his report he wrote:

> *The geysers, in the slow process of centuries probably, have built up miracles of art, of an enduring though brittle material, that can be ruined in five minutes by a vandal armed with an ax, and nearly all the craters show signs of the hopeless and unrestrained barbarity of many of their visitors. It cannot fail to fill the mind with indignation to see the utter ruthlessness of these sacrilegious invaders of nature's sanctuary. To procure a specimen of perhaps a pound weight, a hundred pounds have been shattered and destroyed, and always in those places where the most cunning art has been displayed, and the ruin produced is correspondingly great. Upon our arrival in the [geyser] basin, we found several persons already encamped, and a whisky-trader snugly ensconced beneath his 'paulin, spread in the shelter of a thick pine. The visitors prowled about with shovel and ax, chopping and hacking and prying up great pieces of the most ornamental work they could find; women and men alike joining in the barbarous pastime.*

Ludlow also was concerned about the fate of Yellowstone wildlife, only three years after the park's creation. In his report, he lamented the damage to elk:

> *Hunters have for years devoted themselves to the slaughter of the game, until within the limits of the park it is hardly to be found. I was credibly informed by people on the spot, and personally cognizant of the facts, that during the winter of 1874 and 1875, at which season the heavy snows render the elk an easy prey, no less than from 1,500 to 2,000 of these, the largest and finest game animals in the country, were thus destroyed within a radius of fifteen miles of the Mammoth Springs. From this large number, representing an immense supply of the best food, the skins only were taken, netting to the hunter some $2.50 or $3 apiece; the frozen carcasses being left in the snow to feed the wolves or to decay in the spring. A continuance of this wholesale and wasteful butchery can have but one effect, viz, the extermination of the animal, and*

that, too, from the very region where he has a right to expect protection, and where his
frequent inoffensive presence would give the greatest pleasure to the greatest number.

His prescription: "The cure for these unlawful practices and undoubted evils can only be found in a thorough mounted police of the park. In the absence of any legislative provision for this, recourse can most readily be had to the already existing facilities afforded by the presence of troops in the vicinity and by the transfer of the park to the control of the War Department. Troops should be stationed to act as guards at the lake, the Mammoth Springs, and especially in the Geyser Basin."

Ludlow's advice was ignored until the enactment of a federal law in 1883 that authorized the Secretary of War to send troops to protect Yellowstone if the Secretary of the Interior requested military aid. The Interior Secretary asked for help three years later, and Captain Moses Harris, a Civil War Medal of Honor winner and now acting superintendent of Yellowstone, led a troop of the First Cavalry into the park on August 17, 1886. In very short order, Harris had his soldiers confiscating tools, firearms, and purloined materials from park vandals, including animal hides and logs. He soon had guards posted at key tourist attractions to keep visitors from defacing geysers.

Conservationists such as John Muir, who would found the Sierra Club in 1892, were pleased with the military takeover, but local residents were divided over it. Some actively supported the military intervention, providing information on poaching activities, though often secretly. One citizen who wrote a note offering evidence added a warning: "Keep my name still if your man ketch them. I have horses here on the range and if they should find me out they wood run them off." Another similarly begged, "You will pleas keep this *perfectly secret* if they should find out that I have given you any information [I] would be in danger of my life as there is some tough cases up here." Others saw it as federal intrusion into their private lives. The *Livingston (MT) Enterprise* editorialized that "military rule in time of profound peace is distasteful to the American people under any conditions." Some residents opposed the army's efforts to keep people from grazing livestock in the park and from cutting park trees for building material and firewood. On this last point the Department of the Interior tried to compromise, letting residents from surrounding towns remove deadwood under federal permits that limited where and how much wood could be carried out.

To ensure protection of the sprawling park, the army set up a series of guard stations, extending from near the northern boundary in an irregular line to the southern boundary. Each station was garrisoned by a sergeant and two or three privates who lived in a log hut stocked with supplies in early October, to last until mid-June. During winter, the men from each station strapped on snowshoes or skis and patrolled assigned sections of the park in search of poachers. The stations also offered shelter and supplies to scouts and patrols sent out from the fort.

And still, poaching continued. In 1886, Acting Superintendent Moses Harris complained that hunters were setting forest fires to drive wildlife out of the park so they could shoot it. He also estimated that only one hundred Yellowstone bison survived. Outside the park, uncontrolled hunting had reduced bison to a few groups of stragglers scattered widely across the plains. In 1887, William T. Hornaday estimated in his federal report on the bison slaughter that only about 85 buffalo survived in the United States outside of Yellowstone National Park. Various people held another 256 in captivity. "Of the eighty-five head still existing in a wild state," Hornaday wrote, "it may safely be predicted that not even one will remain alive five years hence." Yellowstone would soon become the bison's last chance at survival.

During the next few years, little changed. Grinnell explained the legal problems in an 1891 issue of his magazine, *Forest and Stream*: "As it is now, the Park is placed under the care of the Secretary [of the Interior], and he is authorized to make rules and regulations for its government; but as no penalties are provided, there is no way in which such regulations when made can be properly enforced. . . . All that now can be done is to turn the offender out of the Park, and thus give him an opportunity of returning and renewing his malicious acts."

In 1892—during a period when the park was receiving about five thousand visitors yearly—Captain George S. Anderson took over as acting park superintendent. Twenty years earlier, he had ridden with his troops across the plains of Kansas for six days without losing sight of bison. "At times," he wrote, "they pressed before us in such numbers as to delay the progress of our column, and often a belligerent bull would lower and shake his shaggy head at us as we passed him a few feet distant." Now the last of the bison were in his hands, and he was determined to stop the wildlife devastation that threatened the species' survival. Anderson estimated that the park held about four hundred buffalo in 1892. In his report to the Secretary of the Interior, he wrote, "The great value placed upon them by sportsmen and taxidermists makes their protection difficult, but I devote my best energies to it." As he saw it, the problem of wildlife protection went beyond bison: "There is gradually settling about the park boundaries a population whose sole subsistence is derived from hunting and trapping. . . . Live elk, deer, antelope, and bears are caught and sold; the various fur-bearing animals are trapped for their pelts, and hunting parties are guided into the best game region." He suggested that Congress impose penalties on violators and establish park boundaries—the borders of the protected site had still not been defined twenty years after the park's creation. Anderson also set his sights on the most deadly poacher of all, Edgar Howell, a sometime sheepshearer from Cooke City who claimed to have killed eighty park bison, accounting for nearly 25 percent of the herd. Howell's career was about to end, and with it the heyday of Yellowstone poachers, heralding a turning point in the history of bison and the battle to save them.

ON MARCH 14, 1894, US ARMY SCOUT FELIX BURGESS GLIDES ON cross-country skis over deep snow along the southern edge of Yellowstone National Park's Fern Lake. Beyond the lake rise snow-covered foothills, long slopes cloaked in pines and aspens. With Burgess is a man recalled by history only as Private Troike. Both are under orders to patrol this area in the east-central region of the park, on the lookout for Edgar Howell, whom Anderson believes is operating there. Anderson's suspicions are based on rumors emanating from Cooke City, Montana, which abuts the park's eastern border, and on tracks that military patrols have spotted in the snow.

The sun, lying low in the morning sky, casts long shadows across the snow. After days of luckless searching, Burgess and Troike encounter a set of ski tracks that lead them northwest of Fern Lake to a primitive camp highlighted by the macabre feature of six bison heads wrapped in gunnysacks and hung on the branches of a tree, protected there from the attention of scavengers but not from the surveillance of park authorities. Clearly, the wildlife poacher has no idea that he himself is being hunted, or he would have been more surreptitious, would have cleared out entirely.

These heads, from illegally shot animals, are worth hundreds of dollars each in a time when a ranch hand or urban laborer earns perhaps fifty dollars a month. They represent the lethal work of a backcountry denizen steeped in the lore of wilderness survival and capable of superlative feats of stamina. Traveling across snow-encrusted barrens and iced-over lakes and streams on homemade skis, the lone poacher transports his supplies and bloody loot on a homemade toboggan that weighs around 180 pounds. However certain he must feel about the security of his camp against intrusion, Burgess and Troike know he will not leave these valuable heads, acquired through strenuous effort and deprivation amid the dangers of a wild land, unguarded for long. He must be nearby.

They soon find another trail of ski tracks that leads them to a newly built shelter where the poacher has been lodging. He has not gone far from his makeshift home: shortly after their arrival in the camp, they hear several rifle shots.

They follow the gunfire, well aware that here, in the remote reaches of Yellowstone, meeting head-on with an armed poacher skilled in the use of weapons could turn deadly with the speed and thunder of a gunshot. Within twenty minutes, as they ski hidden among lodgepole pines, they spot the rifleman at least two hundred yards ahead of them on the north bank of Pelican Creek. He has taken a heavy toll of park bison, slaughtering five more after driving them into deep snow, rendering them helpless. He is skinning one of his victims.

Fearing that the poacher will slip away, melting into the wilderness, if he catches sight of the trackers, Burgess rushes alone across the open grassland that separates him from his quarry, counting on a high wind to mask the sound of his skis. Luck is on his side more than he hopes: The poacher is accompanied by a dog hidden from Burgess's view, lying next to one of the bison. A warning bark from the dog would alarm the outlaw into checking for impending danger, but apparently the dog doesn't detect Burgess's presence. It never barks, leaving its owner so lost in thought that he doesn't perceive the scout closing in, gun drawn. Recognizing the poacher as Edgar Howell, Burgess announces his arrival with a shout: "Howell, throw your hands up." At this moment, Howell becomes the first poacher that park patrollers have caught red-handed. Still, he doesn't put up a fight—he may recognize that the gun indicates an inauspicious moment for challenging authority. More likely, he doesn't feel a need to flee. He's been down this road before and knows full well that park officials have no authority for punishing him or any other violator of park rules and regulations. But this time, Howell might prove too confident for his own good.

At the time of Howell's arrest, a reporter for *Forest and Stream* magazine is visiting the park. Emerson Hough telegraphs the magazine's editor, George Bird Grinnell, about the arrest and subsequently interviews Howell, a natural braggart who tells the reporter his methods for evading park staff and conducting his poaching operation:

> *It is the simplest thing in the world. When the snow begins to fall in September and October, we wait until a nice snowstorm has set in, and then taking a saddle horse and two or more pack horses, we start for the Park and travel fast. After reaching the ground we have previously selected to hunt over, we make a long detour and cross our tracks perhaps ten miles from camp so as to ascertain whether the soldiers are following our trail or not. If no other tracks are seen we go back to camp feeling safe, for we know that the new snow will obliterate all tracks before dawn. We then secure enough elk to load our pack horses and are soon on our way out of the Park.*

Howell boasts that he sold twenty-two bison heads in one winter to a Montana taxidermist for up to $125 each and that he sold one green (freshly skinned and untreated) head to a New Yorker for $275. During the height of bison hunting, a hide sold for only two or three dollars.

Edgar Howell is in the guardhouse at Fort Sheridan, but Captain Anderson holds little hope that he can mete out any meaningful punishment for the killing of the eleven bison that Burgess and Troike found in and around Howell's camp. Anderson has confiscated Howell's equipment, including wagons and horses, but he knows that confiscation has little effect because Howell's friends will soon claim they loaned the goods to him, and Anderson will have to yield the items to the claimants, who will give them back to Howell. Anderson has dealt with these circumstances time and again. A poacher even broke into the stable where his confiscated horses were being held and stole them, one of "the many instances of this kind that have arisen in the course of the year, and they afford a very discouraging picture," Anderson reported in 1892.

An indignant Grinnell seizes on the Howell story as a means for revealing the inadequacy of federal protection of Yellowstone, editorializing in his magazine:

> The man Howell, who has just been arrested, has destroyed property belonging to the Government—that is, to the people—which was worth from $2,500 to $5,000; yet if we may judge the future by the past, he will be allowed to go on his way practically without punishment. If he had committed a similar act anywhere else—if he had destroyed Government horses or mules or grain or supplies of any sort to this extent—he would have served a long time in prison. So long as these lewd fellows of the baser sort . . . know that they will not be punished for their invasions of the Park, ten regiments of troops could not protect it against their raids.

Anderson holds Howell for as long as he can but in a few days has to set him free. Grinnell unleashes a particularly searing concoction of bile on Congress, which he blames for this state of affairs: "The occurrence calls public attention again and most forcibly to the criminal negligence of which Congress has been guilty for all these years in failing to provide any form of government for the Park, or to establish any process of law by which crimes against the public committed within its borders can be punished." This weak protection of Yellowstone's natural resources is rooted in the legislation that President Ulysses S. Grant signed on March 2, 1872, turning some 2 million acres of forests, mountains, valleys, and thermal features such as geysers and hot pools in northwest Wyoming (with parts overlapping into Montana and Idaho) into the world's first national park. The law carried a serious flaw—it neglected to authorize punishment for those who violate park rules. Grinnell editorializes in *Forest and Stream* that poaching, if allowed to continue because of lax laws, means "it will not be long before the last [bison] shall have been shot down. It is for the people to say whether or no [sic] they desire this."

Reporting by Hough in *Forest and Stream*, along with Grinnell's editorials urging readers to write their elected officials in support of legislation protecting the park, sparks national outrage against poaching. The people soon make it clear that they do not desire the slaughter of the last bison, sending members of both houses of Congress hundreds of letters and petitions demanding protection for the park. The swaggering blatancy of Howell's activities enrages a public just waking to the idea that market hunters are wiping out the last vestiges of the nation's wildlife heritage—from bison to deer to passenger pigeons. Anderson says his hands are tied by the law, or lack of it. Interviewed by Hough for *Forest and Stream*, Anderson, immediately after Howell's apprehension, explains:

> *I have ordered Howell's tepee and supplies burned. His arms and outfit will be confiscated, and I will sock him just as far and as deep into the guard-house as I know how when I get him, and he won't get fat there, either. That is all I can do under the regulations. I shall report to the Secretary of the Interior and in due course the Secretary of the Interior will order me to set the prisoner free. There is no law governing this Park except the military regulations. There is no punishment that can be inflicted on this low-down fellow.*

Public outcry soon gives a voice to the bison and other Yellowstone creatures, and Congress takes action. Among those who, in 1894, share Grinnell and Roosevelt's convictions is Republican John Lacey, a former Civil War officer elected to the US House from Iowa in 1888. Lacey is an avid birder and a Boone and Crockett Club member who has visited Yellowstone. In a speech in the US House of Representatives in 1900, he will say, "I love the people who love birds. The man or the woman who does not love birds ought to be classed with the person who has no love for music—fit only 'for treason, stratagem, and spoils.'" He would one day be lionized by William T. Hornaday as "the first American congressman to become an avowed champion of wild life," the first to make issues of conservation "peculiarly his own." Lacey is galvanized by the Howell incident and primed to take action. In an 1896 speech to the American Forestry Association, he will declare how he felt about the bison slaughter: "The extermination of the buffalo is too recent and too shameful to speak of excepting in the highest terms of indignation." No doubt he feels the same way in 1894. As head of the House Committee on Public Lands, and backed by Grinnell and Roosevelt, he promptly introduces legislation setting punishments for Yellowstone violators, from woodcutters to rock collectors to wildlife poachers. The National Park Protective Act passes the Senate first, on April 23, 1894, barely a month after Howell's arrest. The House passes the bill a few days later. On May 7, President Grover Cleveland signs it, making violators of the Department of the Interior's Yellowstone regulations subject to fines up to $1,000 and two years in prison and assigning a magistrate and US deputy marshals to the park to hold violators responsible.

Anderson subsequently reports, "The act of May 7, 1894, seems to have had a most healthy effect upon the poachers who surround and prey upon the Park." Hunters on the east, north, and south sides have "nearly or quite ceased troubling it." A key problem on the west side is a lack of state law in Idaho to protect bison. Anderson's investigation of rumored poaching convinces him "that this last remaining herd is in danger of extinction." His solution to the threat is to try to pen the bison in winter and feed them.

Meanwhile, poachers are going unarmed into Yellowstone and stampeding bison across the boundary into Idaho, where the gunmen can shoot them legally. In 1896, hunters kill ten bison along the Idaho border in a three- or four-month period. George Anderson estimates the surviving bison at not more than fifty, perhaps as few as twenty; he also has learned that the bison will not use a winter pen. The idea of penning is abandoned in 1897, and in following years bison numbers continue to rise and fall, hovering always around fifty. To balance the losses from poaching, Lacey secures a $15,000 appropriation to bring eighteen head of new breeding stock from private herds to Yellowstone.

By the early 1900s, the fight to save the bison has progressed but has not been won. Several factors make protecting the park's natural resources challenging. Park boundaries are not surveyed until 1903, so the army cannot easily determine the point at which a hunter becomes a poacher by crossing into the park. Also, the soldiers charged with protecting park wildlife are not trained to function as game wardens and sometimes poach for their own profit; one enlisted man conspires with two poachers to drive bison out of the park so they can be legally shot, and others traffic in the sale of elk teeth, then popular among members of the Benevolent and Protective Order of Elks. Finally, local poachers are more familiar with the terrain and are more skilled at survival in the mountains than are the troops.

Nevertheless, strides have been made in park preservation with enactment of the National Park Protective Act. Even Howell has capitulated: after the robbing of a stagecoach in the park in 1897, Colonel Samuel Young, the acting superintendent, hires Howell as a scout to track down the robbers, which he does, earning a $150 reward. Howell continues working as a scout, patrolling the park's western boundary to protect bison there during state hunting seasons.

But the campaign to save the bison has only begun. It moves into a new phase when Roosevelt and Grinnell welcome into their cadre of fighting conservationists a man who will prove, arguably, the fightingest of them all: William T. Hornaday. In a sense, the stronger protections that John Lacey crafted for Yellowstone marked a beginning for bison recovery. But Hornaday sees that, at the twilight of the nineteenth century, wildlife are still treading a narrow ridge between extinction and recovery. In 1915, looking back at the period surrounding 1900, he will write:

> *Slaughter was the order of the day. The sportsmen who advocated game protection, and secured the enactment of protective laws, were animated by a desire, not to stop killing, but to preserve today in order to kill more abundantly tomorrow. It is well within the bounds of truth to state that even down to 1890, wild life preservation in America was little more than a pleasing dream, a shadow without substance. Excepting the Yellowstone Park, there were not then in existence any large game preserves in which killing was totally prohibited. Everywhere, without a single exception, wild game was being killed far faster than it was breeding.*

CHAPTER 2

WHEN SCIENCE FAVORS EXTINCTION

On September 24, 1886, William T. Hornaday, in his incarnation as the chief taxidermist of the National Museum in Washington, DC, arrives by railroad in Miles City, a cattle town in southeastern Montana Territory. He's on an assignment from mammalogist Spencer F. Baird, head of the nation's primary scientific agency, the Smithsonian Institution. Hornaday's task centers on a potentially impossible quest for bison, on par in difficulty with the search for the Holy Grail.

In a recent survey of the Smithsonian's wildlife collection, Hornaday discovered that "the Museum was actually without presentable specimens of this most important and interesting animal." Baird concluded that the museum must have new specimens of the continent's largest land mammal, and Hornaday has checked with various denizens of the West—military officers and scientists with experience on the nation's distant prairies and plains—about where he might find buffalo. The consensus of the experts is *nowhere*, outside of Yellowstone National Park. However, in April 1886, Hornaday receives word from an army officer in Huntley, Montana Territory, that he might find bison hiding in ravines along streams about ninety miles north of Miles City, in the wilderness surrounding Montana's Sand Creek, Big Dry Creek, and Little Dry Creek.

About two miles south of Miles City, a military installation straddles the banks of the Yellowstone River. Fort Keogh, named for an officer killed with Custer at the Battle of the Little Bighorn in 1876, is conveniently located for Hornaday's purposes, as he will rely on the army for help toting his gear and, if he's lucky, his wildlife specimens across a distant wilderness. At the fort in late September 1886, Hornaday buys massive amounts of goods, including a ton of oats for horses the party will ride and for mules pulling supply wagons borrowed from the army.

Hornaday's goal, formulated for him by Baird, is to "collect at all hazards, in case buffalo could be found, between eighty and one hundred specimens of various kinds, of which twenty to thirty should be skins, an equal number should be complete skeletons, and of skulls at least fifty." Collecting the skulls should be easy. Over vast reaches of the northern bison range, which at the time extends roughly from the border with Canada to the Platte River in central Nebraska and from the Rocky Mountains to central Dakota Territory, Hornaday will write, "the traveler may even now ride for days together without once being out of sight of buffalo carcasses, or bones. Such was the case in 1886 in the country lying between the Missouri and the Yellowstone, northwest of Miles City. Go wherever we might, on divides, into bad lands, creek bottoms, or on the highest plateaus, we always found the inevitable and omnipresent grim and ghastly skeleton, with hairy head, dried-up and shriveled nostrils, half-skinned legs stretched helplessly upon the gray turf, and the bones of the body bleached white as chalk." Theodore Roosevelt discovered the same evidence of widespread slaughter when he rode on a hunt from western Dakota Territory across part of Montana and into Wyoming, as described in his 1885 book, *Hunting Trips of a Ranchman*: "No sight is more common on the plains than that of a bleached buffalo skull, and their countless numbers attest the abundance of the animal at a time not so very long past. On those portions where the herds made their last stand, the carcasses, dried in the clear, high air, or the mouldering skeletons, abound."

Surrounded by a bison graveyard and on a mission of death, William T. Hornaday will soon become one of the nation's most ardent advocates of wildlife protection, particularly of bison and birds, animals mercilessly slaughtered for commercial markets. But at this moment in 1886, he is the perfect man to lead an expedition designed to kill every bison the expedition locates. He's had plenty of experience with this sort of thing.

Hornaday was born December 1, 1854, on a farm outside Plainfield, Indiana, a few miles southwest of Indianapolis. His family moved to Iowa when he was three, driven out of Indiana by drought and cholera. Iowa still provided habitat for a few straggling elk, bison, and gray wolves. By the time Hornaday was fourteen years old, both his parents had died, and his siblings had moved away or died, with one brother a victim of the Civil War. After selling his family's twenty-acre farm and other goods, he was cared for by supportive uncles. Fascinated with wildlife and an able marksman with a rifle, he took up taxidermy in his teens and landed a job with Ward's Natural Science Establishment, a museum in Rochester, New York, where he polished his taxidermy skills. When only in his twenties, he talked the museum proprietor, Henry Augustus Ward, into sending him on collecting expeditions to the Caribbean, the Everglades, Africa, and Asia. He killed notable numbers of exotic species. For example, during his two-year Asian sojourn he collected forty-three orangutans. In 1882, this resume landed him a job as a taxidermist at the National Museum and, finally, as leader of the Montana expedition.

Assisted by a student from the University of Kansas and by three local cowboys he has hired as guides and hunters, Hornaday spends nearly three months searching for scattered groups of bison in some 1,000 square miles of Montana wilderness. The hunters endure rough camps, some with access to water only from putrid springs. The region is surrounded on three sides by "wild and rugged butte country, and its sides are scored by intricate systems of great yawning ravines and hollows, steep-sided and very deep, and bad lands of the worst description." He tracks bison across "a succession of rolling hills and deep hollows, smooth enough on the surface, to all appearances, but like a desert of sand-hills to traverse. The dry soil was loose and crumbly, like loose ashes or scoriae, and the hoofs of our horses sank into it half-way to the fetlocks with every step. But there was another feature which was still worse. The whole surface of the ground was cracked and seamed with a perfect net-work of great cracks, into which our horses stepped every yard or so, and sank down still farther, with many a tiresome wrench of the joints. It was terrible ground to go over."

They survive a blizzard toward the end of the hunt. One participant, setting out on the long ride to Fort Keogh to request a supply wagon to pick up the expedition and its goods, decks himself out in "two undershirts, a heavy blanket shirt, a soldier's blouse and overcoat, two pairs of drawers, a pair of soldier's woolen trousers, and a pair of overalls." He also wears "three pairs of socks, a pair of *low shoes* with canvas leggings, and . . . his feet tied up in burlaps. His head and hands [are] also well protected." Nevertheless, during several days on the trail, he suffers frostbite.

BY THE END OF THE ASSIGNMENT—THE HUNTERS RETURNED TO MILES CITY on December 20—the expedition had slain twenty-two bison, to which can be added three more killed during a spring expedition that Hornaday led and abandoned the previous May because the bison were shedding their winter coats, making them poor museum specimens. The tally for both hunts was ten old bulls, a young bull, seven old cows, four young cows, two yearling calves, and one three-month-old calf. In addition, the hunters collected skins and skeletons of antelope, mule deer, white-tailed deer, coyotes, prairie dogs, jackrabbits, dozens of sage grouse, and "specimens of all the other species of birds and small mammals to be found in that region at that season."

One of the last bison shot was an eleven-year-old bull that thrilled Hornaday. "After a short chase my horse carried me alongside my buffalo, and as he turned toward me I gave him a shot through the shoulder, breaking the fore leg and bringing him promptly to the ground. . . . He then stood at bay, and halting within 30 yards of him I enjoyed the rare opportunity of studying a live bull buffalo of the largest size on foot on his native heath. I even made an outline sketch of him in my note-book. Having studied his form and outlines as much as was really necessary, I gave him a final shot through the lungs, which soon ended his career."

He added, "I was delighted with our remarkably good fortune in securing such a prize, for, owing to the rapidity with which the large buffaloes are being found and killed off these days, I had not hoped to capture a really old individual. Nearly every adult bull we took carried old bullets in his body, and from this one we took four of various sizes that had been fired into him on various occasions. One was found sticking fast in one of the lumbar vertebrae."

The acquiescence with which nineteenth-century scientists such as Hornaday faced pending extinctions is perplexing today, but they came from an age when one of the naturalist's key roles was collecting specimens. John James Audubon killed almost every bird depicted in his collection of life-sized paintings of US bird species. So did bird artist Alexander Wilson.

Collecting birds and eggs was standard operating procedure for almost every ornithologist, particularly to fill the specimen drawers of leading museums. Perhaps the sheer abundance of wildlife during much of the nineteenth century made even experts reckless, unable to believe that human activities could wipe out millions of bison, pronghorn, deer, and elk and billions of passenger pigeons.

But Hornaday's bison hunts were not freighted entirely with dead animals. In mid-May 1886—during the first days of the cancelled spring hunt—Hornaday made an unexpected acquisition. Riding the range about eighty miles north of Miles City on forays lasting two to four days away from the base camp, Hornaday searched for bison with George Hedley, a taxidermist friend and avid hunter from Medina, New York. One afternoon, when the taxidermists were traveling with Irwin Boyd, a local guide hired by Hornaday, and with an army private called Moran, the quartet came over a hill and were surprised to see a bull bison calf, its fur the reddish color of a buffalo only a few weeks old, alone in a hollow between two buttes. Shortly after spotting the calf, the hunters saw three bison cows running hell-bent across a distant hillside. The calf also tried to run, but was soon overtaken by the riders. He fought when they tried to capture him, butting the men and kicking a mule. Nevertheless, the men roped him, and the calf ended up riding back to camp on a horse with Hornaday. A few days later, Hornaday ended the hunt but was determined to come back in autumn, setting the stage for the hunt that began in September.

Meanwhile, the calf, now dubbed Sandy, traveled by train to Washington, DC, where Hornaday fed him cow's milk. The calf had grown to almost three feet tall at the shoulder by July, when he made a fatal mistake, eating a massive amount of damp clover that caused him to bloat from a foamy, gaseous buildup in the rumen, the largest of a bison's four stomachs. This bloating cut off the calf's breathing, causing it to suffocate. In cattle, bloating can kill in as little as half an hour. But the orphaned calf was subsequently immortalized, becoming part of the bison panorama that Hornaday was crafting at the National Museum.

Sandy may have helped give rise to an idea that Hornaday proposed to Baird in March 1887 to create a national zoo populated with live, rather than dead, animals. Baird proved visionary enough to endorse this latest brainstorm, but he died unexpectedly. Hornaday and his national zoo might have been aborted there and then. However, the assistant secretary of the Smithsonian, G. Brown Goode, who took over as acting secretary, supported Hornaday's plan. He created a Department of Living Animals of the National Museum and sent Hornaday on a short train jaunt into the West to collect specimens. He came back with fifteen living animals, including deer, prairie dogs, and a badger. The animals were put into makeshift pens on the mall outside the towering, redbrick Victorian edifice known as the Smithsonian Castle.

As people became aware of the zoo—the nation had only about ten zoos at that time, several of them little more than crude menageries—donors began providing specimens, including such treasures as black bears and a jaguar from Texas. Perhaps the jewel in the zoo's crown was four bison from Nebraska—a breeding pair and their two calves, one male and one female. Hornaday became inspired with the idea of breeding bison at the zoo. But in September 1887, Samuel Langley became secretary of the Smithsonian. More engineer than biologist—he was particularly interested in inventing a fixed-wing flying machine, though his experiments failed—he soon clashed with Hornaday over the taxidermist's plans for establishing a permanent zoo along Rock Creek Park in northwestern Washington, DC.

At this time, Hornaday also was working diligently in the museum's exhibit hall, mounting the bison he had brought back from the Montana Territory, including the massive bull and little Sandy. One day in March 1888—as he worked to complete the mounts for their public opening that month—drapery put around the exhibit to hide it from view was pushed aside and in strode none other than Theodore Roosevelt, a vigorous young man not yet readily recognized, for he would not become a hero of the Spanish-American War until 1898, governor of New York until 1899, and president of the United States until 1901, though he was already an influential wildlife advocate. After the greetings usual among people meeting for the first time, Hornaday and Roosevelt talked about bison, the exhibit, and the decline of game animals—interests that would prove the basis for a durable liaison.

Shortly after this meeting, Hornaday broke with Langley following a series of disputes over plans for the national zoo and who should run it—Hornaday thought he should, and Langley thought not. Hornaday resigned, and he and his wife packed up and moved to Buffalo (!), New York, where his friend George Hedley was selling real estate and thought Hornaday should join him. So Hornaday turned from conservation to real estate development and prospered, until a runaway financial crisis swept across the nation in the mid-1890s. As the real estate business died, he was forced to turn to writing nature stories for magazines to generate income. His worries must have been profound, but they soon would be resolved. In 1896, Roosevelt would come to his rescue in a stunning way, uniting the two wildlife advocates on behalf of innovative bison restoration.

LONG BEFORE THEY WORKED TOGETHER, HOWEVER, ROOSEVELT AND HORnaday shared perspectives on species restoration, recognizing that wildlife conservation required protective laws in a time when animals were hunted and killed without legal, moral, or ethical constraint. Hornaday made this point as late as 1913, when new game laws were opposed by hunters in places like New York State's Adirondack Mountains, which offered prime deer hunting at a time when overhunting had nearly extirpated the animals. With characteristic certainty, Hornaday wrote, "The big game that is hunted and killed outside the game preserves, and outside of such places as New Brunswick and the Adirondacks, can *not* be saved—until *each species* is given perpetual protection."

Roosevelt, in yet another book about hunting, turned the issue into what today would be called a culture war, stressing that wildlife protection "can only be achieved by wise laws and by a resolute enforcement of the laws. Lack of such legislation and administration will result in harm to all of us, but most of all in harm to the nature lover who does not possess vast wealth. . . . It is foolish to regard proper game laws as undemocratic, unrepublican. On the contrary, they are essentially in the interests of the people as a whole, because it is only through their enactment and enforcement that the people as a whole can preserve the game and can prevent its becoming purely the property of the rich, who are able to create and maintain extensive private preserves."

In his 1887 book, *The Extermination of the American Bison*, Hornaday focused on bison as an example of the threat posed by uncontrolled hunting, which had nearly destroyed the vast herds down to the last individual—just as it would wipe out the passenger pigeon and New England's heath hen and nearly exterminate deer, wild turkeys, elk, and other hunted species. The reason, wrote Hornaday, was a lack of strong legal protection, state or otherwise, for wildlife: "Had proper laws been enacted, and had either the general or territorial governments entered with determination upon the task of restricting the killing of buffaloes to proper limits, their enforcement would have been, in the main, as simple and easy as the collection of taxes." He added, with typical vigor and venom, "The destruction of the buffalo was a loss of wealth perhaps twenty times greater than the sum it would have cost to conserve it, and this stupendous waste of valuable food and other products was committed by one class of the American people and permitted by another with a prodigality and wastefulness which even in the lowest savages would be inexcusable."

Protecting the habitat of vanishing creatures such as the bison also proved to be a major challenge. The Boone and Crockett Club had to fight a desperate battle to keep railroad lines from crossing Yellowstone National Park, a critical threat to local bison that would have been catastrophic. This fight helped establish the club as an ardent and influential voice for wildlife and resulted in an early habitat-protection law.

The high-stakes battle began in 1892, two years before passage of Representative John Lacey's park-protection act. By 1892, the politically powerful railroad industry had repeatedly sought permission from Congress to put a track across the northern part of the national park. Mining companies and land developers joined with market hunters and poachers in supporting the railroads, arguing that the park should be put back in control of the states as a constitutional states' rights issue. The park, these factions contended, robbed workers of jobs while providing a remote playground for the rich. The factions actively blocked park protection: over the years, Missouri senator George Vest had pushed legislation for stronger park protection six times through the Senate, but the legislation was always killed in the House, where railroad proponents amended park bills to allow a train line.

The rail industry, its allies, and its lobbyists had a bill introduced in the House in 1892 that would have returned 622 square miles in the northern reaches of Yellowstone Park to the public domain. This area was noted for its populations of big-game animals, including bison, which attracted the interest of the Boone and Crockett Club. Once the land was severed from the park, the Northern Pacific Railroad planned to build a train line across it from Cooke City, Montana, to Gardiner, Montana. This development was a concern for the club. Historically, passengers often would shoot bison and other game from trains chugging across the plains, taking a toll on wildlife and leaving the bodies to rot.

At this juncture, Senator Vest, the conservationists' firmest congressional ally in fights on behalf of Yellowstone, decided to cut a deal. He accepted an amendment from Wyoming senator Francis Warren—who had served as the state of Wyoming's first governor before spending thirty-seven years in the Senate amid rumors of corruption—to remove the area coveted for the rail line on the assumption that better protection of the southern part of the park would make up for the loss. The Secretary of the Interior expressed a contrary opinion, saying that the bill "would be detrimental to all the purposes for which the Park was set apart."

Roosevelt and Grinnell charged into this battle, perhaps the worst crisis Yellowstone had faced up to that time and a prelude to the fight over penalties for park vandals. The Senate passed the railroad legislation bisecting Yellowstone, leaving the park's fate in the hands of the compliant House. In 1891, Grinnell warned, "If one such railroad franchise is granted, it will result in the practical abandonment of that region as a forest and game reserve." He launched a persistent and strongly worded campaign against the House bill, including a series of ten articles in *Forest and Stream* called "The Standing Menace." He turned the series into a pamphlet that he promised to send to all readers for free so they could distribute it widely. The pamphlet included a letter from Theodore Roosevelt, who was then gaining national renown for trying to clean up the federal government as a member of the Civil Service Commission. Roosevelt called upon "all public spirited Americans [to] join . . . in the effort to prevent the greed of a little group of speculators, careless of everything save their own selfish interests, from doing the damage they threaten to the whole people of the United States."

Once the bill passed the Senate, in February 1893, a lobbyist for the bill telegraphed key Montana Democratic members of the US House of Representatives, urging them to pressure the Speaker of the House to take action to pass the bill. Grinnell secured a copy of the telegram, which showed a vested special interest pulling strings behind the scenes, and printed it with an editorial targeting the Speaker, who backed off from the legislation, killing it. The railroads continued their efforts, but two years later gave up in the face of growing public opposition.

THE RAILROAD'S SURRENDER IN YELLOWSTONE WAS A CONSERVATION VIC-tory, but the Boone and Crockett Club couldn't continue to protect bison and other wildlife by fighting such ad hoc wars in the absence of laws designed specifically to protect wild animals. The history of failures to enact laws to protect bison illustrates this point boldly.

The first federal attempt to enact a law to protect bison from unlimited slaughter was introduced by Arizona Territory representative R. C. McCormick on March 13, 1871. The law would have banned the killing of bison on US public lands—which at that time encompassed much of the West—except for using the meat for food or for preserving the hide. Anyone convicted under the law would be fined $100 for each animal killed, with half the fine to be paid to any informer. The proposed bill died without action.

A resolution introduced into the Senate almost a year later, on February 14, 1872, by Senator Cornelius Cole of California—who would outlive most early bison advocates, dying in 1924 at the age of 102—showed more promise, as it was agreed to unanimously. It directed the Committee on the Territories to "inquire into the expediency of enacting a law for the protection of the buffalo, elk, antelope, and other useful animals running wild in the Territories of the United States against indiscriminate slaughter and extermination, and that they report by bill or otherwise." Two days later, Senator Henry Wilson of Massachusetts—who in years past had introduced bills that freed slaves in the District of Columbia and permitted African Americans to join the Union army, and who would become President Grant's vice president in 1873—introduced a bill that would have restricted buffalo hunting on public lands. On April 5, Representative McCormick gave a speech in the House on the need for bison protection and the next day asked to have remarks regarding bison protection entered into the *Congressional Globe*, the legislature's official collection of debates from 1833 to 1873, when it was superseded by the *Congressional Record*. No action resulted from any of these endeavors.

Action again seemed imminent in March 1874, when Illinois's freshman representative, Greenbury Fort, stepped up with a bill to prevent "the useless slaughter of buffaloes within the Territories." The House Committee on the Territories reported the legislation to the House with a recommendation for passage. The bill imposed strict limits on the killing of bison and would have made it "unlawful for any person, who is not an Indian, to kill, wound, or in any way destroy any female buffalo of any age, found at large within the boundaries of any of the Territories of the United States." The bill ran afoul of the language allowing Indians to kill buffalo cows, with some elected officials wanting the language removed. Eventually it passed through both houses, but President Ulysses S. Grant let it die via pocket veto. Other bills like it were batted between the House and Senate for the next two years, and all went nowhere.

Finally, on March 20, 1876, Representative Fort introduced a bill to tax bison hides, but it never made it out of committee and merely disappeared into the legislative haze. Hornaday commented on it in *The Extermination of the American Bison*: "This was the last move made in Congress in behalf of the buffalo. The philanthropic friends of the frontiersman, the Indian, and of the buffalo himself, despaired of accomplishing the worthy object for which they had so earnestly and persistently labored, and finally gave up the fight. At the very time the effort in behalf of buffalo protection was abandoned the northern herd still flourished, and might have been preserved from extirpation."

As for state and territorial attempts to protect bison, Hornaday maintained that territorial laws "vaguely and feebly intended to provide some sort of protection for the fast-disappearing animals." Colorado enacted one of the first game laws, "passed in 1872, which declared that the killers of game should not leave any flesh to spoil." But Hornaday held a jaundiced view of such legislation: "The western game laws of those days amounted to about as much as they do now; practically nothing at all. I have never been able to learn of a single instance, save in the Yellowstone Park, wherein a western hunter was prevented by so simple and innocuous a thing as a game law from killing game."

Hornaday was outraged not only by the loss of the bison but also by the economics of that destruction. He calculated that a federal tax of fifty cents on every bison hide sold in the markets would have paid for mounted police to enforce laws protecting buffalo. Moreover, the bison could have been used, he suggested, to clothe, shelter, and feed American Indians on reservations. "After the United States Government began to support the buffalo-hunting Indians with annuities and supplies," he wrote, "the woolen blanket and canvas tent took the place of the buffalo robe and the skin-covered teepee, and 'Government beef' took the place of buffalo meat." He concluded, "Therefore, while we no longer have to pay for an annual campaign in force against hostile Indians, the total absence of the buffalo brings upon the nation the entire support of the Indian, and the cash outlay each year is as great as ever."

States in the 1890s did begin enacting wildlife-protection laws designed to restore dwindling game species, however. Initially, hunters opposed statutes that, for example, banned the use of jacklights and dogs, the two most deadly tools for hunting deer, a quarry then almost exterminated across the United States. In New York State, Adirondack hunters opposed reductions in season limits and regulations that prohibited killing deer for use as food during prolonged hunts. Eventually, as species began to rebound in the wake of protection, sport hunters became accustomed to bag limits and other restrictions. The laws and statutes were important as legal measures but also as signs of changing attitudes toward wildlife, on the part of human society.

By 1900, a major shift was taking place in wildlife legal protections. Its harbinger was Iowa representative John Lacey. He sided with a member of the Royal Society of Canada who said, "There is, perhaps, no fact in the natural history of America which brings such reproach on civilized man as the reckless and almost total destruction of the bison." Lacey himself said, "The most pitiful story in the history of all animal life is Prof. William T. Hornaday's report on the extinction of the American bison. The mania for slaughter seems to have affected everyone."

Lacey's central interest was birds, which were being slaughtered for meat markets and the millinery trade by the millions. At the dawn of the twentieth century, women were wearing hats decorated with entire mounted song-birds and with plumes from birds such as snowy egrets, killed by the tens of thousands even during nesting season. Lacey wanted to stop the shipments of dead birds from distant states to fashion centers such as New York City. The bird cause became a movement in the 1880s, stimulated when Grinnell launched his Audubon Society to marshal troops of volunteers to lobby for federal bird protection. The fundamental legal question, however, was whether the federal government or the states had control over wildlife. The general consensus was that wildlife fell under the administration of the states, even though the states could not uniformly protect birds or other animals slaughtered for various interstate commercial markets.

Lacey sought a way to open the door for federal wildlife protection. He was something of a lone wolf, howling for bird protection in the desolate wasteland of an uncaring Congress. "At that time, few large men in public life took the woes of wild life seriously," wrote Hornaday in a eulogy for Lacey after the representative's death in 1913. Lacey did take the woes of wildlife seriously, alarmed by what modern technology was doing to birds and other wild animals. "The unlimited power to travel and kill should be also bounded by the limitations of the law," he said. "The necessity for protection increases as the powers of man to kill have increased. With the bloody breech-loader, and abominable automatic gun of the present day, exterminating is an easy thing."

Eventually, Lacey found the portal he needed for advancing a federal role in wildlife conservation. He used the US government's right under the Constitution to administer interstate commerce. With that legal opening, he introduced and shepherded through Congress a bill that prohibited the transport across state lines of "any wild animals or birds" killed in violation of state statutes. This legislation marked the federal government's first foray into wildlife protection, and was signed into law by President William McKinley on May 25, 1900. The Lacey Act of 1900, and Lacey's subsequent work on treaties with Canada and Mexico to protect migratory birds, set precedents that, decades later, would allow such powerful wildlife legislation as the Endangered Species Act, the Marine Mammal Protection Act, and the Bald Eagle Protection Act, which also protects golden eagles. Had the Lacey Act of 1900 been enacted in 1880, some large bison herds might have been protected, and bison conservation would not have started in the desperate straits that it did, leading to conditions that still hinder bison management today.

THE INNOVATIVE ERA THAT HERALDED THE ARRIVAL OF THE TWENTIETH CENtury, along with increasingly science-based conservation, stimulated a new idea in wildlife restoration. Rather than merely protect habitat and let wildlife recover without further help, bison advocates began promoting plans to reintroduce bison to former habitat.

Representative Lacey was at the forefront of this movement, too. On April 10, 1900, in support of his bill to set aside a preserve for bison, he submitted comments to the House Committee on Public Lands. He lamented that "the United States government has tardily attempted to preserve some of the wonders of nature on the continent. The word 'extinction' does not quite literally apply to the bison, but we have arrived at a point where nothing but heroic treatment will prevent the animal from joining the dodo, the great auk, and the mammoth."

Lacey wanted the federal government to play a role in reintroducing bison to native habitat on which they'd been wiped out: "If no one were now willing and able to try the experiment of restoring a sufficient number of these animals to insure them from total extinction, it would be the duty of a great government like ours, regardless of expense, to do whatever could reasonably be done to that end." He pointed out that current estimates of bison numbers put the species at no more than four hundred animals on the entire continent and added:

> The failure to act now in this matter will be fatal. We believe that the government should make this experiment. It ought to be made, even if it had to be made entirely at public expense, but under the plan proposed by this bill the government will not expend a single dollar. The land to be used for the purpose is public land. It belongs to the people. The whole people of the United States are concerned in saving our nation from the reproach of allowing the entire extinction of the American bison. Our children's children would curse us, and they ought to, if we do not prevent this reproach on the American people from being consummated.

The idea of reintroducing bison to a preserve on public land of course won the endorsement of Theodore Roosevelt, who became president of the United States in 1901 after the assassination of President William McKinley at the Pan-American Exposition in Buffalo, New York. When Roosevelt gave his fourth annual message to Congress on December 6, 1904, he became the first president in US history to single out the importance of creating national refuges for wildlife: "I desire again to urge upon the Congress the importance of authorizing the President to set aside certain portions of the reserves or other public lands as game refuges for the preservation of bison, the wapiti, and other large beasts once so abundant in our woods and mountains and on our great plains, and now tending toward extinction."

The reserves to which Roosevelt referred had been created by presidential decree in the wake of the Forest Reserve Act enacted by Congress in 1891—actually, by an amendment to the General Revision Act. This rider authorized the president to make forest reserves from "any part of the public lands wholly or in part covered with timber or undergrowth, whether of commercial value or not." The reserves, under this law, were protected from logging, mining, trespassing, and hunting. Needless to say, this powerful legislation was not favored by loggers, miners, hunters, and, presumably, trespassers. Consequently, Congress in June 1897 passed the Forest Service Organic Administration Act, opening forest preserves to logging, mining, and grazing. Nevertheless, millions of acres were set aside in these reserves. Roosevelt and Lacey saw them as potential habitat where bison could be released.

ON APRIL 3, 1905, ROOSEVELT—AT THE START OF HIS SECOND TERM AS president—boarded a train in New York City, the Roosevelt Special, which would take him and his presidential entourage two-thirds of the way across the nation to Fort Sill in central Oklahoma Territory, a rugged landscape of grassland, timber, and ancient, worn-down mountains older than the dinosaurs. His plan was to disappear into the wilderness to hunt coyotes, which he called wolves. Chased on horseback with a pack of greyhounds, the coyotes averaged about thirty pounds, arguably not a worthy adversary for the much larger dogs, horses, and men determined to run them down.

Roosevelt participated in the hunts with his usual gusto and rejoiced at seeing one man dive from his horse and wrestle a fleeing coyote to the ground. But Roosevelt wasn't only on the Oklahoma plains to commit mayhem on wildlife. He had a secondary plan—he also was looking for a site where a herd of bison could be restored to the wild. The federal government had never before engaged in a plan to reintroduce any wildlife species to former habitat. By the time Roosevelt finished his tour of the region surrounding Fort Sill, he was ready to launch the experiment, sure he had found the perfect place for releasing bison: the grasslands lying within the

Wichita Forest Reserve, interspersed among the worn, red-rock roots of once-towering alpine peaks.

Gathering the animals and releasing them would require the leadership of half a dozen influential people, including, predictably, Roosevelt, Grinnell, Lacey, and Hornaday. It would also inspire the creation of yet another wildlife advocacy group, with the Hornaday stamp all over it. By the time Roosevelt was harassing coyotes on the Oklahoma plains, Lacey already had secured federal funding for the purchase of bison for release on a national preserve, and Hornaday was as hot on the track of vanishing bison as ever he'd been in Montana nearly two decades earlier, but this time he wanted them alive and well.

CHAPTER 3

WHERE BUFFALO ROAM, AGAIN: EARLY RESTORATION

Plans for releasing bison into Oklahoma's Wichita Mountains had actually started to transform from dream to policy as early as autumn 1894, not long after the Boone and Crockett Club scored its coup with Representative John Lacey's National Park Protective Act. As tree leaves in New York City burnished to orange and gold, Theodore Roosevelt began pushing the idea for a major zoo to be located in the wilds of the Bronx, where animals could be exhibited in large outdoor enclosures in meadows and woods. Roosevelt was following the trail blazed by his father, one of the founders of the American Museum of Natural History, but TR was looking to amass a collection of living animals. This endeavor was the sort into which aspiring zoo director William T. Hornaday, then relegated to flipping real estate in Buffalo, would unhesitatingly hurl himself. To top it off, Roosevelt wanted his proposed zoo to include a bison-breeding program and to release surplus animals into former habitat, another aspiration Hornaday would find irresistible.

George Bird Grinnell, on the other hand, for once signaled opposition to a Rooseveltian plan. TR believed zoo bison would be able to feed on native Bronx grasses growing along a stream in a proposed enclosure. Grinnell was dubious, suspecting that woodland grasses would not be appropriate for this prairie native. He thought the Boone and Crockett Club should focus on stronger game laws. However, Roosevelt had powerful allies backing his plan: club member Madison Grant, though a New York attorney, was widely respected for his expertise in zoological subjects and helped Roosevelt by lobbying local civic agencies to approve the zoo plan; Andrew Green, who had provided funds for the American Museum, threw in his support; and mammalogist Henry Fairfield Osborn, curator of the American Museum, helped raise funds. While Grinnell busied himself with urging the club to discuss the zoo concept and to vote on whether to approve it, Roosevelt forged ahead. By spring 1895 he had formed the New York Zoological Society.

A year later, Hornaday testified before Congress on the need for a special wildlife preserve—a national bison range—where the beleaguered animals could be sheltered from the onslaught of poachers and allowed to breed. Roosevelt, of course, agreed with Hornaday's views and admired his expertise with wildlife, zoos, and museums, so it was no surprise that Roosevelt offered him the directorship of the nascent zoo, sweetening an already sweet deal by promising to let Hornaday develop exhibits and breed bison without hinderance. Roosevelt also offered Hornaday a substantial salary. Hornaday accepted the position and spent the next thirty years building and running a zoo that remains one of the largest in the nation.

Late in 1897, the zoological society approved a development plan, and in November 1898, the zoo opened. Among the zoo's features was a 20-acre paddock for buffalo that were donated by private citizens. However, Grinnell's fears about forest grasses proved correct: the bison sickened and died. The zoo acquired more, and Hornaday had the native grasses rooted out and ensured that the bison were properly fed.

The zoological society's scientists soon produced a report outlining the need for national wildlife refuges and alluding to long-term plans for bison. Roosevelt, in 1901, became president of the United States, an ascension that gave him tremendous clout in terms of conservation issues, such as bison restoration. From 1901 to 1908, he pursued conservation from the White House with unprecedented vigor, creating the first national wildlife refuge and then adding fifty more; quadrupling the size of the national forest system, from 50 million to 200 million acres; and successfully urging Congress to create five more national parks. He shepherded the creation of today's US Forest Service. In 1908, he assembled a White House conference on conservation that included the governors of several states and the heads of various national organizations concerned with natural resources. The meeting resulted in the appointment of thirty-six state conservation commissions and the formation of the first National Conservation Commission, assigned to create a guide for future conservation measures by completing the first inventory of US natural resources. Clearly, President Roosevelt was the right advocate for bison reintroduction.

Meanwhile, in 1904, Ernest Harold Baynes, whose origins are shrouded in the haze of history, visited banker and railroad baron Austin Corbin's 25,000-acre Blue Mountain Forest and Game Preserve in New Hampshire, where Baynes was so moved by the sight of a herd of about 160 bison that he became an instant advocate, determined to ensure that the species survived his own profligate era. He immediately published articles in periodicals across the nation about what he had seen, and he urged the federal government to establish permanent herds. His chief concerns about the few existing private herds were that they could be wiped out by catastrophic disease and that herds might be sold off when their individual owners died. He contacted various influential people and organizations. President Roosevelt told him to keep up the good work, with the result that on December 8, 1905, Baynes joined Hornaday and a dozen other bison advocates in the New York Zoölogical Park Lion House to create the American Bison Society, with Hornaday as president, Baynes as secretary, and TR, shortly afterward, as honorary president. On the day the group organized, only two bison herds were under federal jurisdiction—a handful of animals at the National Zoo and the ever-waning-and-waxing Yellowstone herd. The society's central goal was to put bison herds on federal lands, where management could be more consistent than on private lands, helping to ensure the species' survival.

The society soon lobbied Congress on behalf of a recommendation Hornaday had made even before the society was created—fund a federal bison preserve. This advocacy resulted in a 1907 congressional appropriation of funds sufficient to fence an 8,000-acre bison enclosure on the Wichita Forest Reserve (now the Wichita Mountains National Wildlife Refuge) in central Oklahoma, a site chosen by Theodore Roosevelt during his coyote pursuits. Hornaday sent J. Alden Loring, the New York Zoölogical Park's assistant curator of mammals, to Oklahoma to assess which part of the area Roosevelt had recommended offered the best bison habitat. Loring returned with a detailed report that pinpointed an area in the reserve. Hornaday then agreed to freight fifteen bison to the forest reserve. An astute observer in 1907 might have asked where these bison would come from. Answer: the New York Zoölogical Park (a.k.a. the Bronx Zoo). The astute observer might then have asked, How did the zoo acquire them, given that wild bison survived only in Yellowstone, where they were too rare to supply even so low a number as fifteen?

The answer to that question is somewhat convoluted. It begins with a handful of citizens who took it upon themselves to collect and save bison in private herds. Some did it to preserve an element of American Indian culture, others from a fascination with bison, and yet others with commercial plans in mind. Perhaps one or two of the collectors were motivated by a combination of these impulses. In any event, beginning in the 1870s, about half a dozen men, independently of one another, captured and sheltered eighty-eight wild buffalo. Virtually all of today's plains bison, other than those of Yellowstone, are descended from those eighty-eight.

ONE OF THOSE HALF DOZEN MEN WAS A PEND D'OREILLE OR KALISPEL INDIAN named Samuel Walking Coyote. (Several versions of the Walking Coyote story have been told through the years; see chapter 7 for another variation.) He had begun living with the Flathead Indians in what is now western Montana and had married a Flathead woman. In summer 1872, he trekked across the Rockies to join the Blackfeet for a season of bison hunting. He stayed with them into spring 1873 and married a Blackfoot woman. He then packed up and took her with him on a return trip to the Flathead Reservation and his first wife. By then he was worrying about his fate among the Flatheads, who did not allow even adopted members to marry outside the tribe. Moreover, the Jesuits who were working on the reservation to convert Indians to Catholicism were opposed to polygamy, which was common among Plains Indians.

During the journey home, Walking Coyote acquired eight bison calves. He claimed that they wandered into his camp, apparently orphaned or separated from their mothers during a hunt. They willingly followed his horses, and Walking Coyote concluded that the Flatheads and the Jesuits might forgive his marital transgressions if he brought them bison. All but two of the calves survived the trip, which included an arduous crossing of the Rockies. However, the Flatheads were not mollified and gave Walking Coyote and his new wife a beating, for which he also blamed the Jesuits. He held on to his bison, which were culturally important to all Plains Indians. Within a few years the calves matured and more calves were born. By 1884, Walking Coyote owned thirteen bison, but they were rambunctious, and he tired of caring for them.

At this point, Charles Allard and Michel Pablo—two local ranchers with Indian mothers—offered to buy the animals, and Walking Coyote accepted $2,000 in gold for his herd. Allard's parents established a ranch at the south end of Flathead Lake, and Allard and Pablo located their bison herd on this ranch, giving them a close link to the Flathead Indian Reservation. They continued to maintain the herd and in 1893 augmented it with twenty-six bison from Kansas rancher Charles "Buffalo" Jones, which provided an influx of genes from the southern end of bison range.

When Allard died suddenly in 1895 following surgery for a knee injury, the herd, which then numbered three hundred animals, was divided evenly between Pablo and the Allard family. Allard's wife sold her share to Charles Conrad, a wealthy businessman from Kalispell, Montana. Allard's daughters and one of his two sons sold theirs to Howard Eaton, a Wyoming rancher who had run a horse ranch near Medora, Dakota Territory, when Roosevelt lived there. Eaton then donated the bison to Yellowstone. Allard's other son sold his share to a Missoula judge, who eventually passed them on to the owners of the 101 Ranch in Oklahoma. Pablo held on to his bison until 1906, when the federal government announced that it would open much of the Flathead reservation to white settlement. Seeing his ranchland slip from his hands, Pablo offered to sell his bison to the US government. Roosevelt asked Congress to appropriate money for the purchase, but the legislature refused, and Pablo sold his herd, which totaled more than seven hundred animals, to Canada over the next few years, sending the last shipment in 1912. Bison advocates in the United States never got over the sense of loss and resentment that stemmed from congressional failure to buy these bison, which were thought to be purebred and composed the largest herd in the United States. Sunday newspapers across the nation ran a feature article about the Pablo bison in the midst of the shipments, recounting the risks and dangers to herders, handlers, horses, and the bison themselves, many of which died during transport:

And this is all done to make room for the white man—the man with the plow and the hoe, whose conquest of the soil has swept the red men, the buffalo and other wild game before him like mist before the wind. The settler, in the great battle of development, needed more land to conquer. The Flathead reservation offered an enticing field for his activities. But there was not room for the red man's buffalo and the white man's cattle; perforce the bison had to make way for the munching cow, the toiling horse and the ravenous sheep and swine of him who was coming to transform the untamed wilds into an Arcadia of homes, farms and ranches. The grazing range of the buffalo was to become the feeding ground of domestic animals, so the bison were sold for a paltry sum and men were hired to capture and ship them into the country of the purchases, the Canadian government.

Meanwhile, in what today is the state of South Dakota, a French Canadian trapper, Frederic Dupree, also had an Indian connection when he became the owner of bison calves. He was married to a Lakota woman and raising cattle west of Pierre when his son Pete came home from a bison hunt with five calves he had roped. Fred and Pete didn't pay much attention to the calves and their subsequent offspring, letting them mingle with their cattle and sometimes offering a buffalo for a local barbecue. When Pete died in 1898, he owned perhaps eighty bison. His brother-in-law, as executor of Pete's estate, sold the bison to another rancher, James "Scotty" Philip, who had come to the United States from Scotland in 1875, when he was sixteen. After a checkered career that included illegal gold prospecting in the Black Hills, he and two partners started the Minnesota and Dakota Cattle Company, which sold thousands of head. When Philip died in 1911, his fenced ranch near Fort Pierre was home to around four hundred bison. By then the animals had increased in value due to interest from both government agencies and private citizens. Philip's two sons solved some financial problems they encountered in 1914 by selling off three dozen bison to the State of South Dakota and various private collectors, including the owners of the 101 Ranch, and to William Randolph Hearst, who founded the Hearst publication empire. The thirty-six animals sold to South Dakota ended up in Custer State Park, which in the years ahead would become the home of a large bison herd.

Despite these sales, Scotty Philip's herd still numbered around 250 animals, which had been moved to a ranch in northeastern New Mexico under the management of Philip's son-in-law, Andy Leonard. Leonard came up with a plan to dispose of the bison, harkening back to an era that the world had forsaken but that attracted the participation of several influential men from across the United States: a major bison hunt. Presumably these partially domesticated animals were not a challenge to chase. The hunt slaughtered about two hundred of them, and the rest were sold off.

James McKay—born and raised in western Canada, where he became adept in both political and wilderness skills—worked to conserve bison. He was a seasoned outdoorsman who served as a Hudson's Bay Company postmaster and clerk from 1853 to 1860, when he quit to start his own businesses, which included transporting freight and mail and running a stagecoach from Winnipeg to Edmonton. He also outfitted and guided hunters and travelers, priding himself on getting people to their destinations on time regardless of bad weather or other difficult conditions. One photograph suggests he was a mountain of a man, with a large, dark-bearded head on a massive body crammed into a vested suit. Once, while guiding Hudson's Bay Company executive Sir George Simpson, he waded through streams and muskegs with Simpson on his shoulders.

McKay's facility with Indian languages earned him the trust of local tribes, and he helped them negotiate treaties. A centrist politician with a reputation for sound judgment, he served as the provincial minister of agriculture from 1874 to 1878. He also served as president of the Winnipeg Game Club, his concern about starvation among Indian peoples engendering in him a special interest in saving bison.

In 1872, McKay and his business partner, Charles Alloway, went bison hunting in Saskatchewan with an annual hunting expedition of the Métis, a culture composed mainly of the descendants of local Indians and French Canadian trappers. McKay usually joined the annual hunt, as his mother was a Métis. The hunters traveled in distinctive red wagons and were highly skilled at bison hunting. McKay and Alloway were alarmed when the troop had to travel farther west than usual to find bison, and they discussed the need to protect the animals. The following spring, with the aid of their Métis allies, McKay and Alloway captured two heifer calves and one bull calf. McKay put the calves with milk cows on his farm at Deer Lodge and later fed them hay, as he would cattle. The following year, he and Alloway secured another bull and two heifer calves, but the bull soon died.

Despite the bull's death, the McKay-Alloway herd grew. In 1877, McKay sold five bison—four bulls and a heifer—to Colonel Samuel L. Bedson, warden of Manitoba's Stony Mountain Penitentiary. McKay fell ill in 1878, retired from politics, and died in 1879. At the estate sale, Bedson bought eight of the thirteen bison in the McKay-Alloway herd. By 1888, Bedson was holding eighty-three buffalo. In 1889 he sold fifty-eight of them to Charles "Buffalo" Jones, who ranched near Garden City, Kansas. Bedson also gave a few to Lord Strathcona, Sir Donald Smith, who in 1898 donated his herd of thirteen to Banff National Park, in the Canadian Rockies.

One of the most successful pioneers of bison preservation was Charles Goodnight. He came from a family that seemed to have an affinity for the frontier—his great-grandfather George Goodnight and great-uncle Michael Goodnight were killed by Indians in an era when Kentucky, where they had chosen to settle, was the Far West. One of George's sons, Peter, survived the Indian attack that killed his father and went on to have a son named Charles, who grew up in Kentucky. In 1825, when he was twenty, Charles married a girl of fifteen, Charlotte Collier. Three years later they moved to southern Illinois, where Charles Jr.—destined to be a famed bison rancher—was born on March 5, 1836. The birth occurred three days after American settlers declared Texas, then part of Mexico, an independent nation, triggering a war that lasted scarcely six weeks before the Mexican army left Texas, giving up the fight. Events in Texas—including a war between the United States and Mexico that resulted in Texas becoming the twenty-eighth state at the end of 1845—cast a long shadow that would soon fall over Charles Jr. and his family. In 1841, Charles's father died of pneumonia, leaving Charlotte and her four children destitute. With some alacrity and, no doubt, a passel of pragmatism, she married a farmer named Hiram Daugherty.

At that time, as Goodnight's biographer J. Evetts Haley put it,

> the entire nation was throbbing to the importance of Texas, the new republic to the southwest. The original colonizing schemes attracted national attention, and with the Texan War of Independence that interest grew and spread like wildfire before a prairie wind. . . . Everywhere talk of Texas flowed from the mouths of many men, and those who tore their livings from ungracious soil heard much of its fertility, its generous homestead laws, and its manifest advantages for energetic folk. Caught into the current of the migratory stream were Hiram Daugherty, his wife, and the

Goodnight children. Late in 1845, they loaded their household goods and farming tools into two covered wagons and set out for Texas.

The family crossed the Mississippi River at St. Louis, then cut across Missouri and Arkansas before traversing the Red River into Texas. They passed Dallas when the future metropolis was only a trading post. There, Charles Goodnight saw his first bison, a herd being cut down by hunters. Eventually his family made it to central Texas, rented a farm near Old Nashville, and settled in—briefly—because Charlotte, for what Charles later called "good reason," left her husband. Three months later she gave birth to her fifth child. Charles, eleven years old, went to work for a merchant, making four dollars a month. At about age twelve, he landed a job with a farmer who paid him twelve to fifteen dollars a month. His subsequent life included many odd jobs, from splitting logs to supervising slaves at twenty-five dollars a month. When he was seventeen, his mother married a preacher, whom Goodnight described as "extremely kind, and, in my estimation as nearly faultless as it is possible for a man to be."

The marriage provided a partner for Goodnight, too. He and the preacher's son, who was three years older than Charles, agreed to go into business together. The business took the form of managing 430 head of cattle for a rancher, with the two partners to get a quarter share of any increase in the herd. Recalled Goodnight: "As the end of the first year's branding resulted in only thirty-two calves for our share, and as the value was about three dollars per head, we figured out that we had made between us, not counting expenses, ninety-six dollars. It was a gloomy outlook at the time." But they stuck with their contract to the end, by which time their share totaled 4,000 head.

Then along came the Civil War, during which Confederates, Indians, and rustlers stole their cattle. Goodnight subsequently partnered with another aspiring cattleman, Oliver Loving, and they blazed a trail from Texas to Fort Sumner, New Mexico, where they sold cattle at such an unexpected profit—$6,000 in gold—that they went back to Texas, bought more cattle, and immediately moved them to New Mexico for sale. He stayed with the cattle business, amassing a fortune of $100,000 (today, arguably about $5 million). However, the Panic of 1873 struck, throwing the nation into a depression, and Goodnight watched his money ebb away. In 1876, he determined to start anew, moving his last remaining asset—1,800 head of cattle—to the then sparsely populated Texas Panhandle. In 1877, he partnered with a wealthy investor from the United Kingdom, John Adair, creating the Adair & Goodnight company with $372,000 of Adair's money and with Goodnight's expertise and management, for which he would get a one-third share. By 1888 they had 100,000 head of cattle. When the partnership ended, they were holding 63,000 head. Goodnight picked a site for his own ranch and built a large, two-story house.

Despite the disruption caused by the Panic, Goodnight at this time turned his attention to another issue. When Charles first entered his partnership with Adair, "buffalo hunting was still in full sway and there yet roamed over what in the past has been known as the 'staked plains,' vast herds of these noble animals, but the fall and winter of '77 and '78 closed out forever these great herds, and in the spring of '78 there were only a few scattering bunches left, and Mrs. Mary Goodnight suggested to her husband the advisability of preserving to Texas and the nation a few of the buffalo. Acting upon this wise suggestion, Mr. Goodnight hunted up a bunch and roped two calves, fortunately a male and female, and a few weeks after this Mr. Lee Dyer, a brother of Mrs. Goodnight, captured two more, also a male and female."

But Goodnight left out some dark details from this account. Laura V. Hamner, who interviewed Goodnight, commented in her 1935 book that "Western men were not squeamish about killing animals. That was part of their lives." When Goodnight was going with his men to look for bison, he had one purpose in mind: to kill off an entire bison herd that he felt was competing with his cattle for grass. He hired twenty-some additional hunters to go with him. Only Mary Goodnight's intervention saved some of the bison.

The remnant animals that he and his men roped were once part of a herd that he measured not in individuals but in miles—the herd, he said, "would probably average a hundred and twenty-five to a hundred and fifty miles long and twenty-five miles wide. The buffaloes in it were as thick as they could conveniently graze and left not a particle of grass behind them." He maintained his captive herd until his death in December 1929 at age ninety-three. His herd usually varied from 200 to 250 head. In the 1920s, he was still selling bison meat and hides. A single bison, slaughtered, would bring him $350, a hide an average of $100. He also provided bison for various facilities established to preserve the species, including Yellowstone and the Bronx Zoo.

When he died, the ranch passed into the hands of Joseph I. Staley, a Wichita Falls, Texas, oilman. In summer 1931, Staley, needing money to meet his mortgage on the ranch, announced he would allow the bison herd to be slaughtered by hunters whom he would charge a fee for shooting. Public outcry prevented the killing, and Staley turned over the ranch to mortgage holders, who auctioned off the bison, mostly to people in Oklahoma and Texas. However, a number of the bison eluded capture and sale and roamed the area in which Goodnight's ranch lay. In 1997, the ranch donated thirty-six bison to the State of Texas. Since the 1990s, some of the land there was purchased by the State and managed for bison by the Texas Parks and Wildlife Department. Today, descendants of the Goodnight herd number some 200 to 250 animals living on 12,000 acres at Caprock Canyons State Park, not far from the old Goodnight ranch. In 2002, tests showed that the herd was badly inbred, with the bulls nearly infertile. Since then, the herd has been supplemented with bulls from media-giant Ted Turner's Vermejo Park Ranch, in New Mexico, and is revitalized.

Goodnight was a historic figure, a trailblazer, a pioneer, a Texas ranger, a rancher, and an exponent of bison survival. Despite his accomplishments and his colorful career, he was rivaled by another frontier rancher, Charles "Buffalo" Jones, who took up the standard for bison protection even more ardently. His status among early bison preservationists can be measured from the dedication in *The Buffalo Harvest*, the autobiography of former market hunter Frank Mayer: "To the Memory of Charles (Buffalo) Jones because he was the only one among us who had sense enough to know that the buffalo could not stand up against the slaughter forever; because he with his own hands and single-handedly captured a few buffalo and saved the breed from extinction."

Jones was more effervescent than reserved Charles Goodnight, more clipper ship to Goodnight's barge. They were competitors in the bison world and had clashing personalities. "The expansive Jones, with his well-known tendency to stretch the blanket, was the type that thoroughly disgusted Goodnight with 'Western literature,' and put him on the prod worse than an old buffalo bull," wrote Goodnight's biographer, J. Evetts Haley. Haley quoted Goodnight's opinion: "Jones has been quite a hunter, and has been over a great deal of the Northwest. In that country they have great wind storms, known as 'chinook winds.' They are warm and harmless, but the Colonel seems to have got in one of those storms, and imbided [*sic*] immense quantities of hot air. It has been escaping from him ever since—mostly from the wrong end."

Born in Illinois in 1844, Charles Jesse Jones was the son of a farmer known in his younger years as an accomplished hunter of such game as deer, beaver, otter, and raccoons. "These were the real source of revenue, rather than the legitimate products of the roughly worked farms. The skins of the animals mentioned, and the flesh of the deer, particularly, were always in demand; and these were the principal support of the family while, for a few years, the land was being brought into subjection." His father was also an "earnest anti-slavery advocate" who served as a judge of elections when Stephen Douglas was a pro-slavery candidate for the US House. Jones's father "became politically involved in an altercation with the acknowledged pugilist of the neighborhood," and the two fighters ended up in court. Jones was defended by two attorneys, whom he paid ten dollars each. One of them was Abraham Lincoln, who became a family friend.

Small and wiry, Charles gave no evidence that he was prone to fisticuffs himself, but when about twelve he started to follow his father's footsteps in regard to commercializing wildlife. It began with a tree squirrel that he captured when the arboreal rodent took refuge in a hole in a burr oak after an extended chase up and down tree trunks and limbs. Jones tamed the creature, which became a pet named Dick that rode on his shoulder. During a visit to the town of Bloomington, about a dozen miles from the family farm, Jones sold the squirrel to a man who wanted it for his son. Jones had gone to town specifically to sell the squirrel, and the man gave him two dollars for the animal. "It almost took my breath," Jones said in his autobiography. "I had not hoped to receive to exceed [*sic*] fifty cents, and would have been proud of twenty-five. I had never had but one 'bit' (twelve and one-half cents) in all my life, and two dollars appeared like a colossal fortune to me. . . . From that time until this, I have never lost an opportunity in my power to capture every wild animal that runs on legs, as well as some that creep upon their bellies." He subsequently collected and sold for significant sums any animals he could capture, including rattlesnakes, which he defanged. "The capture of that little animal, Dick, molded the destiny of my whole life," he said in his autobiography. "It is the little things which govern the lives of the people of the world. The first money made by a child is never forgotten; he is sure to try the same method again and again."

Which, in Jones's mind, explained why, some thirty years later, he decided to start a herd of bison. By then he was living in Kansas and married to a descendant of the seventeenth-century nature writer Isaak Walton, a fitting match for a man who devoted many years to working with bison.

But first Jones hunted them, starting in the early 1870s. His first encounter with bison—which he described in his autobiography in some detail while leaving out salient facts, such as location and why he was there—was not what one might expect from a man who would claim to have killed thousands for market:

> The fact is, the first herd of buffalo I ever saw, was composed of about twenty old bulls. The gentleman who was with me, Mr. Shultz, first noticed them coming toward us, and we secreted ourselves in a shallow buffalo-wallow, having to lie very close to the ground to prevent their seeing us. Mr. Shultz was an experienced hunter, and both of us were possessed of good guns; but before the animals came within three hundred yards of where we were lying, I said to my partner in a whisper: "Let us compromise with the monsters; if they will let us alone, we'll let them go by." Mr. Shultz smiled as I trembled; I could not have hit a whole flock of barns two hundred feet away.

The bison came closer and closer as they grazed, and Jones could hear the grinding of their teeth on the tough prairie grasses and the puffs of their breath.

> They appeared to me hideous monsters. They resembled elephants, and as they moved toward us, the very earth appeared to shake. I paid no more attention to them; they were too near for comfort, and I shut my eyes, scarcely daring to breathe, when suddenly, like a clap of thunder, came the report of a gun, and I was nearly paralyzed. Mr. Shultz had fired at the leader of the herd. . . . When silence was again restored, I discovered that at least one buffalo couldn't scare me "worth a cent."

When Jones and his wife first moved to Kansas they lived in a sod house. But he was ambitious and soon made money selling bison hides—he told his biographer that "it was no uncommon thing for two men with a team to clear from thirty to fifty dollars a day," roughly worker's wages for an entire month. With his proceeds, he established a cattle ranch. In 1879, he and three other men founded Garden City, Kansas.

In 1886 he took a new approach to bison. At a time when conservationists like Theodore Roosevelt would still have potted a healthy bull bison if given the chance, Jones determined to search the plains for straggler herds and bring some calves into captivity in a breeding plan to help save the species. "I am positive it was the wickedness committed in killing so many, that impelled me to take measures for perpetuating the race which I had helped to almost destroy," he declared. He led an expedition to the Texas Panhandle and northeastern New Mexico in search of remnant bison herds. During a later search for calves, he found that the bison were widely scattered and hiding in deep canyons. "They instinctively know their doom is sealed. How different they appear from those of old!—the sluggish, drooping, lazy creatures they were. They now keep their sense of sight, smell, sound and feeling wrought up to such a tension that they are often gone long before we have discovered their presence, only their tracks remaining to betray their former haunts."

One morning they found a herd and swooped down on it. "They were terribly alarmed at our unexpected presence, perfectly frantic with fear, and began to stampede in every direction." Jones ordered his best roper to go after the calves. In another instant, the roper

> was rushing over the prairie toward them like the shadow of a rapidly moving cloud. Nearer and nearer he approached the frightened little brutes, which now, seeing they were pursued, strained every nerve to escape. Howard was swinging his lasso over his head, as is the custom, to give it the proper momentum, and I could almost hear it hiss, its velocity increasing as he gained on the soon-to-be captives. Gracefully it shot far out in a beautiful curve, and coiled around the neck of the calf in the lead, although it was hugging its excited mother's shaggy shoulders. It was a beautiful sight to the true hunter, and was enjoyed by us far beyond any utilitarian result it might possess.

On their first collecting expedition, Jones and his men succeeded in roping fourteen calves, ten of which survived the trip home on a diet of condensed milk. He caught more bison in 1888 and 1889. Also in 1888, he augmented his herd by paying $50,000 for eighty-eight of Samuel

Bedson's bison, some of them crossed with cattle. With that acquisition, his herd numbered about 150 animals. Always something of a showman, he trained calves to pull a wagon and occasionally drove into town in a carriage pulled by them.

During an expedition in 1889, Jones experimented with herding wild adult bison. He and his men drove twenty-two bison, a group composed of a bull and twenty-one cows, but the bull had been wounded—Jones didn't report how or where—and, on the second day of being driven, dropped out of the herd. Jones persisted in driving the remaining bison. Mr. Howard, the expert roper, reported at the end of the attempt that the men followed the bison day and night for forty-two days: "The buffalo became very thin and footsore, and seemed so lame they could scarcely walk, yet would not allow us to approach nearer than two hundred feet, when they would start off and run with as much alacrity as though nothing was the matter with them. Often we could trail them for miles by the blood left in their tracks." Eventually, all of the adults died, presumably from exhaustion, thirst, hunger—though Jones speculated that they "apparently" preferred "death to captivity. It appeared to me they had the power to abstain from breathing." This expedition arrived home with only seven calves to reward their toil.

Jones's dominion over bison was short-lived. In the early to mid-1890s he made a few unsuccessful business investments, including an attempt to establish a bison ranch near McCook, Nebraska, and was forced to sell his herd. Some went to a rancher on the West Coast, and others to Michel Pablo. The loss of Jones's herd did not keep him from advocating for bison protection. In 1896 and 1897, he visited Washington, DC, and lobbied the Secretary of the Interior as well as Presidents Grover Cleveland and William McKinley to provide more funding and protection for Yellowstone bison. He even offered to make arrangements to do the job personally, but he received no response.

In 1899, he published his autobiography and won national acclaim. In 1902, he was hired as Yellowstone National Park's game warden. That year he corralled in Yellowstone fifteen cows from the Pablo-Allard herd and three bulls he selected from Goodnight's holding. In 1904, he added another thirty-nine bison, including some of his own. Though his term as game warden marked the beginning of bison recovery, he was fired within three years after other staff rebelled against his strict no-swearing and no-drinking policies. After he publicly criticized the park administration, the Secretary of the Interior reinstated him as administrator of park wildlife, but other staff refused to work with him, and he resigned in September 1905. Regardless, he left his mark on the West as one of the key early bison conservationists.

With the exception of Pablo and Allard, these bison rescuers amassed their herds by capturing animals in the wild. Other private herds were owned by bison enthusiasts who bought them rather than caught them. Charles E. Conrad, a Montana businessman who invested in cattle, mining, timber, and banking, bought twenty-eight head of the Allard herd. By 1908, six years after Conrad's death, the herd was still on his property and numbered ninety-two animals, including eighteen calves. Similarly, Austin Corbin, a railroad magnate, in 1888 purchased six bull and six heifer calves from Buffalo Jones and used them to start a herd on his Blue Mountain Forest and Game Preserve at Newport, New Hampshire. He added more bison that year from Samuel Bedson and purchased ten more of Jones's bison in 1892 for $1,000 each. The preserve, also known as Corbin Park, covered more than 25,000 acres, including grasslands around the Croydon and Grantham mountains. The herd would vary in size from as many as 173 bison to as few as 60 before 1920 and would help to create herds in other areas, with donations to the National Zoo in Washington, DC, and to Van Cortlandt Park, which covered more than 1,100 acres in the northwest Bronx.

IN THE TWO YEARS AFTER BUFFALO JONES'S RESIGNATION FROM YELLOW-stone, the focus of bison advocates turned to the Wichita Forest Reserve in Oklahoma. In the wake of Loring's report, Hornaday and Roosevelt had gravitated toward it as an ideal place for bison reintroduction. The area was already closed to big-game hunting, except for the attempted extirpation of wolves, mountain lions, and coyotes (the first two would be wiped out), which was seen by wildlife managers at the time as a form of protection for animals such as deer and buffalo. Bison would be supplied by the Bronx Zoo, which held animals from the Goodnight and Jones herds, handpicked by Hornaday to ensure genetic diversity. Meanwhile, Baynes, the journalist and bison enthusiast, was touring the nation, giving speeches on behalf of bison and sometimes attracting attention by showing up at engagements driving a carriage pulled by two young bison he had painstakingly trained for months on end. With

Roosevelt's backing, the American Bison Society and the Boone and Crockett Club joined other groups in advancing the idea of turning the Wichita Forest Reserve into a wildlife preserve as well. When all forest reserves were renamed national forests on March 4, 1907, the future site of bison reintroduction became the Wichita National Forest and Game Preserve.

All the effort—the lobbying, the buffalo-calf roping, the founding of two zoos with national stature, the establishment of private bison herds, the creation of a new category of federally protected wild lands, federal funding to enclose 8,000 acres of the Wichita preserve with bison-proof steel fence— came to fruition in autumn 1907. Roosevelt had set aside nearly 61,000 acres in the Wichitas and closed it to all hunting and fishing. On October 11, seven bull bison and eight cows, riding in iron and wood crates in which they could lie down, rolled out of New York City. The animals rode in two separate cars as part of a passenger train rather than a freight train, presumably for a less jarring ride. American Express, Wells Fargo, and the New York Central rail line covered the cost of transport. During the weeklong trip, the bison traveled in the care of H. Raymond Mitchell, chief clerk of the New York Zoölogical Park, and Frank Rush, keeper of the Wichita bison range. The bison "snorted and bellowed their disgust for the proceedings through- out their journey," according to one newspaper reporter. The New York Zoological Society's official photographer, E. R. Sanborn, told a reporter in Oklahoma City that he, Mitchell, and Rush had been "bumped and jerked and hauled about until I am glad the trip is just about ended. It has been bad couplings, broken brake rods, bad track, and almost everything else to delay us." He added that "we were about frozen to death from riding in the car with the buffaloes where we had no fire."

Met by twelve teams of mules hitched to wagons for hauling the bison to the refuge, all the bison arrived alive and well on October 18 at Cache, Okla- homa. Thousands of people, including myriad Indians, the older of whom had hunted bison in the time of the great herds, swarmed around to see the animals unloaded. Among them was Quanah Parker, an influential member of the Comanche people. He had for years made war against white pioneers in Texas but surrendered in 1875 as the buffalo disappeared. The federal gov- ernment named him the overall leader of the Comanche people. By 1907, he was a friend of Theodore Roosevelt, who had kept a promise to restore the bison and, thus, the soul of Parker's people. Parker watched with tears in his eyes and helped to unload the animals when Forest Service staff transferred the crated buffalo to the mule-drawn wagons. They hauled the bison across a dozen miles of dirt road to the game preserve. All along the way, people were streaming toward the preserve from the countryside to witness the bison galloping into freedom. The arrival of buffalo at the Wichita preserve heralded the beginning of attempts to reverse the excesses of the past century.

During winter, the bison would be kept in four pens, each 100 feet wide and 200 long, with large sheds where the animals could seek cover from the cold. In spring they would be turned loose on the larger range, enclosed by the tall fence that would keep out predators. Their management would be administered by forester Frank Rush, whose experience with large hoofed animals was limited mostly to cattle.

The early conservationists, had they known more about the needs of large animals that roam vast spaces, would have recognized that one of the key factors that made bison reintroduction possible also would become a cause for concern and contention in the future. This factor was the very thing that towered over and encompassed the fifteen bison released at the Wichita preserve: the eight-foot-tall steel fence. Future conservationists would look at such barriers and ponder their meaning—were they for the benefit of bison or humans; when fenced, were bison, which evolved to range across wide grasslands and play a role in sustaining prairie ecosystems, truly bison, in the ecological sense, or merely corralled livestock? Moreover, locking the animals up in winter and feeding them was not only unnecessary—bison were adapted to life on plains and prairies—but could be harmful, as the individuals composing the herd might become less hardy as generations passed. These and other issues would be framed and examined by later conservationists.

But for the moment, all seemed well. A great advance had been made for bison recovery. The *Cleveland Enterprise* reported on October 25, 1907, that "no longer will the bristly necked beasts be the prey of the animals of the forest and plain, no longer will the red man take sport in their death, only in his dreams of the Happy Hunting Grounds; no longer will the white man ride the tops of the passenger coaches as the trains cross the plains, and slay the animals for the sport of seeing them fall. Protected by the government in the heart of the Wichita Mountains in southwestern Oklahoma, The Bos Americanus or bison, erroneously called buffalo, the African stag, is expected to thrive and again become numerous."

CHAPTER 4

AMERICAN BISON STEP OUT OF THE ER

In spring 1908, a Montana newspaper, the *Missoulian*, covered a subject that had unleashed a flood of ink in newspapers throughout the state and across the nation. A headline on page two of the June 15 edition declared:

BUFFALO RANGE NOW ASSURED FACT

The article began:

> *The Montana national bison range is now, to all intents and purposes, an accomplished fact. Congress has promptly and cheerfully entered into the plan of the American Bison society* [sic] *for joint action by the government and the society in the creation, on the Flathead Indian reservation, of a great national herd of pure-blood American bison, perpetually endowed with a range of 20 square miles of good grazing ground.*

A bill introduced in the US Senate sought to appropriate $30,000 for the purchase of prairie grazing land from the Flathead Indians and $10,000 for building a fence around the range. According to the *Missoulian*, "The plan that is now being triumphantly carried into effect was formulated by the president of the Bison society, Dr. W. T. Hornaday, who, at the proper moment, laid it before Senator Joseph M. Dixon of Montana." The paper highly lauded the role played by Dixon—a North Carolinian who had moved to Missoula in 1891, when he was in his midtwenties, and then became wealthy through business dealings and marital connections. Montanans might have suspected the newspaper's praise, since Dixon actually bought the *Missoulian* in 1900 to promote his political career, with mixed success. A progressive Republican, while running for reelection to the Senate in 1912 he also would serve as Theodore Roosevelt's campaign manager during TR's run that year for the White House. Neither would win. Dixon also would serve as a one-term Montana governor.

The site for the proposed bison preserve was chosen by a University of Montana professor, Morton J. Elrod, who was selected for the task by the American Bison Society. The location lay adjacent to the Northern Pacific Railroad's Ravalli Station, near the confluence of the Pend Oreille and Jocko Rivers, the very place from which portions of the Pablo bison would be shipped yearly to Canada. The proposed range fronted seven miles of the rail line, making it convenient for loading and unloading bison. "In ravines and water courses there is an abundance of water and sufficient timber to afford shelter for bison in the severest storms," reported the *Great Falls Tribune*. Elrod chose the site because it had already been used by the Pablo herd, "which has grown up on the Flathead Reservation from 30 animals to a total today of 638 head, not counting two or three hundred head previously sold," indicating that the land was excellent for buffalo.

The bison-range bill passed the Senate with blurring speed. President Roosevelt lobbied members of the House, where the bill breezed through as an amendment to an agricultural appropriation bill. On May 23, 1908, Roosevelt unhesitatingly signed the bill, creating the National Bison Range. It was the first congressional appropriation to buy land specifically for wildlife conservation, but the law resonated with conservationists on other levels, too. The northern plains, where the bison range would lie, carried important symbolic value—it was there that hunters wiped out the nation's last large herd. To top it off, restoring bison to the Flathead Reservation, where the Pablo-Allard herd had grazed, gave advocates a sense of restitution over the loss of those bison to Canada while letting Congress correct its wayward decision.

Buying the land was a matter of some urgency. It was slated to be stripped from the Indians in 1909 and made available for white settlement under the terms of a federal law enacted in 1904. Purchase of the land for the bison had to be handled swiftly, as it would no longer be available once "it is thrown open to settlement." This sort of taking of Indian land can be traced back to the Dawes Act of 1887. Also known as the General Allotment Act, the law was shepherded through the Senate by Massachusetts senator Henry Dawes, who favored plans designed to turn Indians into landowning farmers. The law allowed the heads of families to apply for allotments of 160 acres of farmland, more or less making them homesteaders on land that was once theirs. Single adult men could apply for 80 acres, and minors for 40. Those who wanted grazing land instead of farmland could request acreages twice that size. Four years after the law was enacted, any Indian who had failed to apply for a plot would have one selected for him by the federal government, to ensure that all reservation land was assigned. Under the terms of the allotment for the Flathead Reservation, after twenty-five years the land would belong to the allotee, who would then have US citizenship bestowed upon him. The hidden purpose of this hocus-pocus was not about citizenship or turning Indians into farmers, it was about the "surplus" land left over after the federal government assigned all the allotments. This "surplus," which might be thousands of acres greater in size than the allotted land, would be sold to settlers under the various homestead arrangements that had turned large parts of the West into a crazy quilt of patchwork holdings. These properties would prove too small and too arid to be turned into farms by anyone, let alone untrained Indian people.

Even key Indian-rights advocates actively supported the Dawes plan and its various later incarnations. Herbert Welsh, head of the Philadelphia-based Indian Rights Association, said that in terms of moving Indians toward civilization, the Dawes Act was the Magna Carta, Declaration of Independence, and Emancipation Proclamation all rolled into one. He dreamed of a time when allotments would replace tribal ownership with individual ownership and turn Indians into farmers, into white people, and solve the conundrum of a future for Indians. It didn't. Instead, it "instituted a kind of progressive poverty," according to historian T. H. Watkins. "By the 1920s tens of thousands of Indians were economically destitute and not only locked out of general American society but bereft of the cultural ties that had sustained them for generations, their ancient traditions weakened and in many cases broken altogether by the inexorable forces of bureaucracy and reform." By

1934, the amount of land owned by Indian people nationwide had fallen from 138 million acres to 47 million.

The federal government promptly bought land in the Flathead Indian Reservation's Mission Valley, forcing the Flatheads to sell it so it could be used for a bison preserve—something the Indians themselves would have done had they been given a free hand. With the question of land acquisition laid away, Hornaday went to work soliciting donations of a dollar on up from the American public for the purchase of bison. People from twenty-nine of the forty-six states contributed more than $10,526 during the one-year effort. Most of the donors, like the leaders of the early conservation movement, were from eastern states. Kansas, North Dakota, South Dakota, and Texas, recently littered with the desiccating carcasses of slaughtered bison, yielded "not one red cent."

Meanwhile, the building of twenty-three miles of fence around the bison range, a task administered by the US Forest Service, hastened at the pace of about a mile a day, along with the building of sheds and a house for the manager of the bison range. The Northern Pacific Railroad built a spur line into the range to ease the unloading of bison. The fence was completed on October 8, 1909, and William Hornaday inspected it personally, declaring that it was nearly as perfect as anyone could imagine.

By then, Hornaday had selected bison from the Conrad herd—fifteen bulls and twenty-two cows—paying $275 a head, a total of $10,175. The Conrads also donated their "finest" bull and cow, according to the *Bismarck (ND) Tribune,* and Charles Goodnight donated a bull, expanding the potential gene pool. The Corbin herd in the Blue Mountains of News Hampshire provided three more. Hornaday expected another dozen donated bison from other sources. The nucleus of thirty-seven American buffalo was shipped via the Northern Pacific Railroad to the unloading chutes near the Ravalli Station. From there, the bison were carried to the range by horse-drawn wagons and, on October 16, 1909, "given their liberty in their new home."

The *Anaconda (MT) Standard* had praised the effort the year before: "Five years ago it would have been impossible for any man or body of men to have succeeded in inducing congress [sic] to appropriate as large a sum as $40,000 for the preservation of any species of wild animals other than the fur seal. But the sentiment in favor of wisely conserving the resources of nature has lately aroused many men who previously had not paused to consider that subject." The cost of $40,000 for setting up the bison range was not exceeded by another wildlife preserve until 1923, when Congress appropriated $1.5 million for a refuge encompassing three hundred miles of river bottoms around the Upper Mississippi River.

Indeed, among some citizens there arose a spirit of excitement regarding the promise of bison reintroduction, as indicated by a newspaper in Kansas, a state that did not donate one red cent to the success of the new preserve:

> We hope these eleventh-hour efforts to save the American bison from complete extinction will be successful. From the countless thousands of buffaloes that only a generation ago covered the plains of the west, but a few hundred now remain. Such a wanton massacre as marks their bloody trail is unparalleled in American history, but, before it is too late, we hope to be saved from the disgrace of having completely destroyed another species of our native fauna.

The trend for reintroducing bison continued. The *Pierre (SD) Weekly Free Press* reported on August 24, 1911, that Wind Cave National Park, in the southeast corner of the Black Hills, had been selected by J. A. Loring of the American Bison Society as a bison preserve, combining 16.5 square miles from the park with about 4 square miles of surrounding land. That same day the paper also editorialized a slightly jaundiced view of the Bison Society's plan: "This is the working of sentiment, not an economic proposition, for the buffalo is not a factor in the food problem. He was made for wild men. Tame men prefer the South Dakota steer."

Wind Cave was located about twelve miles northwest of a hot-springs area that had served as a tourist attraction since the 1880s, featuring hotels and spas. The national park was named for its central feature, a cave composed of thousands of chambers and noted for the winds that sighed out of the entrance. Iowa representative John Lacey, who had initiated the law that protected Yellowstone National Park from poaching, introduced a bill into the House to make the South Dakota landmark a federal reserve. After the bill reached his desk, Theodore Roosevelt signed it on January 9, 1903. The American Bison Society, interested in a site for bison, suggested Wind Cave, and Roosevelt backed the idea. However, other sites took priority, and the society didn't send Loring, who had approved the Wichita

Mountains site, to inspect the Wind Cave area until 1911, two years after Roosevelt left the White House. Eventually, the new Wind Cave National Game Preserve was composed of 4,000 acres from the park, 6 from Harney National Forest, and 80 from private ranches.

As with the other bison ranges, Wind Cave hinged on the federal government providing funds for land, fences, and buildings—in this case $32,000—and on a donation of bison, to be arranged by the American Bison Society. On November 25, 1913, fourteen bison from the New York Zoological Society were on their way to South Dakota. The buffalo traveled in crates loaded on a passenger train of the New York Central railway, as had the animals sent to Oklahoma. Accompanying them were the zoological society's chief clerk, H. Raymond Mitchell, and Frank Rush, warden at the Wichita preserve, both of whom had tended to the Wichita bison during their journey west. The federal government's primary wildlife agency, the Bureau of Biological Survey, served as the administrator of the Wind Cave National Game Preserve.

The reintroduction proved a success. A report from the preserve for 1921 indicated the bison herd now stood at seventy-two animals. By 1923, bison were numerous enough at Wind Cave that about thirty had to be culled—removed from the herd—yearly to ensure that overabundance did not lead to habitat damage. Most were taken away live for breeding, restocking, or exhibition. In 1928, the *Argus-Leader* of Sioux Falls, South Dakota, published a short article that illustrated emphatically that the preserve was generating surplus bison. The University of North Dakota, the emblem of which was a bison, sponsored an annual Bison Day festival, and in October 1928, school officials asked for a buffalo from the Wind Cave preserve so they could barbecue it for the November fiesta. By the 1930s the preserve was providing bison to the Pine Ridge Lakota of southwestern South Dakota so the tribe could build its own herd.

Much the same could be said of the other three early centers of bison restoration and survival—Yellowstone, the Wichita Mountains, and the National Bison Range. A fifth early preserve—located in north-central Nebraska and today called the Fort Niobrara National Wildlife Refuge—started in 1912 with bison donated by a farmer from Friend, Nebraska, by the American Bison Society, and by Yellowstone National Park. All of these preserves still exist today, each supporting a few hundred to a few thousand bison. They offer visitors a chance to see fragments of a lost wilderness, preserved by early conservationists barely knowledgeable about the ecology of the bison—or of any other species—but determined that, against all odds, the bison would not vanish on their watch.

AT THE SAME TIME THAT BISON NUMBERS WERE BURGEONING THROUGH THE 1920s, '30s, '40s, and beyond, the early advocates of bison protection were passing away—Roosevelt and Buffalo Jones in 1919, Hornaday in 1937, George Bird Grinnell in 1938—as a cadre of next-generation professional biologists, rather than amateur naturalists, took center stage in the story of bison recovery. The administrative structure that made bison restoration possible—with government agencies as foundation blocks and science as the mortar that held them together—underwent momentous changes that would metamorphose the practice and politics of wildlife conservation during the next few decades. From these changes arose the four federal agencies that manage bison today—the National Park Service, the US Forest Service, the Bureau of Land Management, and the US Fish & Wildlife Service—along with various forms of state wildlife agencies that set policies based on state laws.

The oldest federal wildlife agency is the US Fish & Wildlife Service. Its roots can be traced to 1871, when Congress created the Commission on Fish and Fisheries, assigning it to determine whether fish taken commercially and sold for food were declining in lakes and coastal waters. A year later, the commission was opening fish hatcheries and raising fish to augment wild populations. This activity led the commission to active roles both in the protection of fish and shellfish and in a search for new commercial fishing areas. When it was transferred into the Department of Commerce and Labor in 1903, a certain sign of its commercial rather than strictly conservation role, the commission was renamed the Bureau of Fisheries. During President Franklin Roosevelt's second term in office, he sought to consolidate all wildlife agencies into the Department of the Interior, which is where the Bureau of Fisheries landed in 1939.

Meanwhile, back in 1885, Congress appropriated funds for a study by the Department of Agriculture on the impact of birds on crops, which led to the creation of the Division of Economic Ornithology and Mammalogy a year later. The division's study of how birds and mammals affected forests and farms led to surveys in the 1890s of plant and animal distribution across the nation, a sort of census of wildlife species. Hornaday's collection of small mammals during his 1880s bison hunt in Montana may have been a harbinger of the surveys. These studies led to the permutation of the agency into the Division of Biological Survey in 1896. It was elevated to bureau status in 1905, becoming the Bureau of Biological Survey.

Two years before the agency's promotion, President Theodore Roosevelt took an action that would greatly affect its subsequent history: at the behest of the American Ornithologists' Union, he named 3.5-acre Pelican Island, off the coast of Florida, as the first federal wildlife refuge. Roosevelt valued the site because its black mangrove thickets were used for nesting by egrets, herons, and other bird species being slaughtered for the fashion industry. Equally important, the thickets gave him the legal justification he needed to set aside the island under the 1891 Forest Reserve Act. Otherwise, he had no real legal authority for creating a national wildlife refuge. However, subsequent legislation gave him that authority, and he used it liberally, creating a total of fifty-one national wildlife refuges before leaving office in 1909. Today, the system he started includes 567 refuges. During the 1930s, refuges were established to protect ducks and geese, which were then declining from overhunting and from loss of habitat to drought and drainage. In 1956, Congress expanded the purpose of national refuges to include all wildlife.

By then, the refuges fell under the administration of the US Fish & Wildlife Service, created in 1940 by combining the Bureau of Biological Survey with the Bureau of Fisheries. Today, the Fish & Wildlife Service is the lead federal agency in wildlife management and protection. It is responsible for putting wildlife species on the federal threatened and endangered species list and for creating recovery plans for all listed species, except marine animals, which are handled by the National Marine Fisheries Service. The Fish & Wildlife Service also advises other agencies about threats to wildlife under the National Environmental Policy Act, which, as one of the nation's strongest wildlife-protection laws (and therefore much maligned by land developers) requires that no federally funded projects shall harm wildlife or habitat irreparably. The service conducts research and administers a state and federal cooperative education system with stations at land-grant colleges throughout the nation. As the administrator of the National Wildlife

Refuge System, the Fish & Wildlife Service manages refuge bison herds, such as those at the Wichita Mountains National Wildlife Refuge (classified as a refuge in 1936, the year it was transferred to the management of the Bureau of Biological Survey).

The National Park Service still plays a major role in bison protection and recovery, although the first national parks were not centers of wildlife conservation. The dozen parks that Congress created in the half century after Yellowstone were meant to protect not wildlife but scenery. With virtually all of them lying among western mountains, they were subject to harsh winters, making them less than prime, or even good, habitat for hoofed species and the predators that preyed on them. The advantage for Congress of making mountains into parks was that the land was economically insignificant and gave the railroads scenic destinations to which they could bring vacationers. Despite the rail industry's persistent attempts to cut Yellowstone National Park in two, the industry also lobbied Congress for more parks. Louis Hill, the head of the Great Northern Railroad, for example, pushed the idea for Glacier National Park through Congress and, when the park was created, promptly built a chain of lodges within it. Prevailing political winds shed so little regard on national parks that, for forty-four years after Yellowstone became the world's first national park, no specific agency was responsible for park management.

That began to change in 1914, when Franklin Lane—the Secretary of the Interior, whose responsibilities included the parks—met businessman Stephen Tyng Mather through a mutual friend. Mather, forty-seven years old, had become a wealthy entrepreneur through the development of a company that produced household cleansers—Twenty Mule Team Borax. He had visited many of the parks and climbed many western mountains. What he had seen made him openly critical of park management. His longtime associate, Horace Albright—who would work with Mather on behalf of national parks for fifteen years—said, "He was exuberant, warm, yet had an aura of authority about him. . . . He was like a wound spring. His reactions were sharp and unguarded."

He may have been sharp and unguarded, but apparently Lane liked him, for he asked him to take over park administration. At that time, each park was run as a separate unit, with little coordination among superintendents, some of whom were military officers. The annual budget for the nearly 5 million acres of parks was $20,000 (arguably about $600,000 today), and in Washington, DC, only two people worked full time for the parks. Nationwide, park staff numbered fewer than one hundred, most of them local people hired seasonally. Mather agreed to run the parks for a year and was sworn in on January 21, 1915. Lane had told Mather, when hiring him, "I'm not asking you to sit at a desk and run a department. I'm looking for a new kind of public official, one who will go out in the field and sell the public on conservation, then work with Congress to get laws passed to protect the national parks. The job calls for a man with vision." Lane got what he wanted. Mather immediately threw himself, and his money, into the parks, personally paying nearly half the salaries of upper-level staff, purchasing new land, and lobbying for a law that would create a park administrative agency and define the parks' purpose. In this endeavor he encountered fierce opposition from elected officials and industries that feared that parks would not allow logging of ancient trees, mining, livestock grazing, and other consumptive uses.

Despite such resistance, his efforts were rewarded. In August 1916, President Woodrow Wilson signed a bill creating the National Park Service. Although Congress did not fund the agency until the following April, the law did define the purpose of the national parks: "to conserve the scenery and the natural and historic objects and the wild life therein and to provide for the enjoyment of the same in such manner and by such means as will leave them unimpaired for the enjoyment of future generations." In May, Mather became the Park Service's first director, a position he held until illness forced him to retire in 1929. During his tenure, he focused on building a constituency for the parks in order to maintain congressional support. He prompted the development of concessions, such as gift shops, restaurants, and lodges, within the parks and promoted travel to and in the parks by automobile, which necessitated roadbuilding. Wildlife was given little thought.

When Mather retired in 1929, the parks were on the verge of change: biologist George Wright became the first National Park Service scientist. Descended from a wealthy family, he applied his personal fortune to funding a two-year survey of wildlife in all the parks—how could park ecology be managed if no one knew what species the parks contained? The status of park wildlife was changing rapidly. Wright wanted to establish a baseline to determine what wildlife was like during a more pristine time, information critical to knowing how wildlife should be protected. He also advocated reducing or ending predator control in national parks in an era when park staff were still laboring to wipe out wolves and cougars in Yellowstone and at the Grand Canyon, predators that park officials saw as a threat to elk and deer. Many wildlife managers and politicians even today have not caught up with Wright's thinking on predators. Alaska persists in slaughtering wolves, ostensibly to save moose and caribou, while Montana, Wisconsin, and Wyoming responded to removal of the wolf from the federal endangered species list by quickly opening wolf hunting at a level that jeopardizes the animal's survival in those states.

Wright put the National Park Service in the vanguard of a new movement in conservation: game management. Early conservation measures were focused on the protection of land, such as forests, and on the preservation of vanishing hunted species, or game. But by 1915, these two goals were converging, more so as game animals such as deer and waterfowl continued to decline through the 1920s and into the 1930s. Out of necessity, the field of wildlife management evolved during this period. Its history can be traced in the life of one man, Aldo Leopold, an Iowan who studied forestry at Yale and worked in several positions with the US Forest Service.

Though a forester, he was less interested in marketing timber than in the recovery of depleted game-animal populations in national forests. In June 1915, he assumed responsibility for recreation, public outreach, and coordination of a new fish and game program in the Forest Service's District 3 in Arizona and New Mexico, encompassing the Grand Canyon. He proved to be a master of compiling technical information and translating it into language that a popular audience could understand. Before the end of summer 1915, he had produced a game handbook for the edification of Forest Service staff. In it, he stated his central concern about wildlife:

> North America, in its natural state, possessed the richest fauna in the world. Its stock of game has been reduced 98%. Eleven species have been already exterminated, and twenty-five more are now candidates for oblivion. Nature was a million years, or more, in developing a species. . . . Man, with all his wisdom, has not evolved so much as a ground squirrel, a sparrow, or a clam.

Shortly after publication of the handbook, Leopold attended a speech presented by William Hornaday in Albuquerque, New Mexico, on October

13, 1915. By then Leopold was active in attempting to forge local hunters into game protection associations that would advocate for wildlife conservation. According to Leopold's biographer, Curt Meine:

> *Hornaday presented a fiery lecture, replete with lurid slides of slaughtered game, to the concerned sportsmen of Albuquerque. The sportsmen gave Hornaday an enthusiastic reception. Hornaday, in turn, encouraged them in their new organizing effort and backed up his words with several hundred dollars from his Protection Fund. Before leaving town, he gave Leopold a copy of his latest book,* Wild Life Conservation in Theory and Practice.
>
> *The sparks that emanated from Hornaday's orations ignited Leopold's own highly combustible convictions. On October 19, he led the organizational meeting and was elected secretary of the Albuquerque Game Protective Association.*

Leopold at this time was frenetically active making rapid tours of New Mexico, urging hunters to form protection associations and to lobby for game species. He also began publishing a newsletter, *The Pine Cone*, which spelled out the needs of wildlife and habitat and would become a critical educational tool for the game protection associations. In a letter to his Forest Service supervisor, written on Valentine's Day 1916, he made his professional goals and inclinations clear: "To speak plainly, I do not know whether I have twenty days or twenty years ahead of me. Whatever time I may have, I wish to accomplish something definite. Unless, however, I can settle down to one thing, I have small chance of such accomplishment. This 'one thing' for me is obviously game protection."

In 1928, Leopold left the Forest Service to conduct a nationwide survey of game species for the Sporting Arms and Ammunitions Manufacturers' Institute, composed of representatives of an industry that depended on healthy game populations for the sale of guns and ammo. Working on the surveys helped Leopold formulate ideas about what could be done to expand wildlife populations. By 1932, he was working on a book that would organize his ideas and, incidentally, play a key role in creating an entire field of wildlife conservation. Published in 1933, *Game Management* got straight to the point in its opening sentence: "Game management is the art of making land produce sustained annual crops of wild game for recreational use."

It is notable that the book was not called *Wildlife Management*. Leopold's emphasis was on hunted species. He referred to animals as crops, rather than prey, and indicated they should be available for *recreational* use, when he might more specifically have said *hunting*. Even today, practitioners of wildlife management speak of "harvesting" wildlife, as if animals were wheat or corn rather than flesh and blood killed for sport. Leopold's language, and the approach to wildlife management that he formulated, still affects much of today's hands-on wildlife conservation.

Leopold stressed that in the United States, wildlife was not the property of individual people, as it was in Europe, but was held and protected by the states and the federal government until taken into possession by individuals such as hunters. He contended that early conservation efforts focused on reducing the shooting of game species and that this approach was misguided: "The thought was that restriction of hunting could 'string out' the remnants of the virgin supply, and make them last a longer time. Hunting was thought of and written about as *something which must eventually disappear*, not as something which might be produced at will." Leopold promoted a different view, writing, "Both scientists and sportsmen now see that effective conservation requires, in addition to public sentiment and laws, a deliberate and purposeful manipulation of the environment—the same kind of manipulation as is employed in forestry." In 1933, Leopold's potential for influencing the course of wildlife conservation exploded in magnitude: he was named the nation's first professor of game management at the University of Wisconsin and was given a grant of $8,000 per year for five years to cover program expenses, including his salary. The publication of *Game Management* and his career at the university led to his being widely recognized as the father of game management.

Leopold helped pull the protection of game species into the modern world by putting it on a firm scientific basis, which led to later revelations about wildlife behavior and the importance of habitat. In the 1960s, more than a decade after Leopold's death, the development of radio telemetry, which allowed researchers to collar wild animals with transmitters and track their movements and use of habitat, unveiled many of the secrets of wildlife behavior. This equipment has become increasingly sophisticated with the development of satellite technology that allows the recording of animal wanderings and activities for weeks and sometimes months at a time, with microchip transmitters small enough to be attached to hummingbirds. Of particular importance, efforts to maintain or increase wildlife populations have moved beyond only game animals. Federal endangered species laws since 1966 have stretched protection to vanishing wildlife of all sorts, and nongame programs in some states have added to the protection of non-hunted, nonendangered species. Nevertheless, for the most part hunted species still dominate the interests of wildlife-management biologists. This continued emphasis on game species is driven by two federal laws—the Federal Aid in Wildlife Restoration Act of 1937, which placed excise taxes on hunting goods, with the money to go to game protection; and the Sport Fish Restoration Act of 1950, which does the same thing with fishing gear to provide funding for fishery management. Moreover, hunters and anglers are required to pay for licenses to hunt and fish, giving them powerful influence over wildlife-management programs, an advantage that nonhunters and nonanglers lack.

Leopold's views on wildlife management evolved during the course of his professional years. Early in his career, he advocated the killing, even the extermination, of wolves, cougars, and other predators in an effort to make the world safe for livestock and to protect deer, elk, and even bison from predators with which they had cohabited for hundreds of thousands of years. But by the time *Game Management* was published, he clearly was on a wavelength with George Wright's plan to roll back predator control in national parks.

Wright's wildlife survey compiled some of the first significant data on species such as bison, elk, and the rare trumpeter swan. He even succeeded in cutting back predator control in the parks. In 1933, Horace Albright, who became the Park Service's director in 1929 after Mather's retirement, created a wildlife division within the service and appointed Wright as its head. However, Wright died in an automobile accident in 1936. The service soon went back to predator control, and Albright persisted in following Mather's road map for park development.

A major change in this approach began in the 1960s, when the Park Service created an advisory board headed by Aldo Leopold's son Starker Leopold. The board produced a report in 1963 that called for the Park Service to maintain parks that featured natural habitat and wildlife—as opposed to historical sites, such as Ford's Theatre, site of the Lincoln assassination, in Washington, DC—in "a reasonable illusion of primitive America." This phrase was widely interpreted as meaning that parks such as Yellowstone must be kept in a pre-Columbian condition. For example, natural cycles, such as forest fires, would be allowed to play out as they would have around the time the *Nina*, the *Pinta*, and the *Santa Maria* set sail from Spain. This policy influenced park management into the 1980s, although, as management of Yellowstone bison and elk show, the policy was selectively applied, generating tremendous controversy (see chapter 9).

National wildlife refuges and national parks are, or can be, managed largely for the benefit of wildlife. For other federally administered lands, wildlife protection is a considerably lower, or at least less magnified, goal. This policy is true of the national forests, which can trace their origins to the Forest Reserve Act of 1891 (see chapter 1), which authorized US presidents to create federal forest reserves at their discretion during an era in which forests were being rapidly cut down, not unlike the cutting down of bison herds. Fear of a timber famine, including wood for heating as well as building, struck the nation. Nevertheless, some special interests, such as logging companies, opposed the new forest reserves and the restrictions that protected them.

Like the national parks, the forest reserves initially had no management guidelines spelled out in the legislation that authorized them. To fix this problem, Charles Sprague Sargent, a wealthy Bostonian and director of the Arnold Arboretum at Harvard, and John Muir, founder of the Sierra Club and author of many popular books on wild places and their protection, joined forces in 1894 to lobby Congress for creation of a commission to survey western lands and make recommendations for forest-reserve management. Congress acquiesced by budgeting $25,000 for the commission. The youngest member of the commission was Gifford Pinchot, a member of a wealthy New York City family who drew his ideas about forest management from experiences in Germany. There, forests were not forests so much as tree farms. Unlike Muir and Sargent, Pinchot wasn't as interested in preserving forests as he was in managing them for lumber. As for forests that had grown for centuries—in some cases for millennia—creating ancient ecosystems of intricately interacting species mutually dependent upon one another for survival, he was all for cutting them down, as old trees did not grow as fast as young ones and did not produce lumber rapidly. In his view they just stood there, taking up space and producing nothing.

Initially, Muir and Sargent's views predominated, but when western political interests reared up in protest of bans on livestock grazing, mining, and logging, Congress responded by passing the Forest Service Organic Administration Act in 1897, which ordered that forests be protected, be managed to protect rivers and streams, and also be a perpetual source of timber. The last goal tended to undermine the first two. In addition, the new McKinley administration put Pinchot in charge of studying the value and need for forest reserves created by outgoing president Grover Cleveland. Muir labeled this decision in language that Hornaday might have used at his most acerbic: "For a parallel to this in downright darkness and idiotic stupidity the records of civilization may be searched in vain."

Pinchot's commitment to logging sweetened his appeal to western forest-consumptive interests. President William McKinley subsequently named Pinchot to the directorship of the Department of Agriculture's Division of Forestry. In 1905, all forest reserves were put under his jurisdiction, and Pinchot, with Theodore Roosevelt's blessing, restructured the division into the US Forest Service, under which forest reserves were dubbed national forests. Pinchot made timber production the service's chief goal, and even today the national forests remain multiple-use lands where outdoor recreation and wildlife protection meet private livestock grazing, mining, and of course logging. Pinchot's dream for the forests has led to decades of battles for the protection of wildlife, such as the spotted owl in the Pacific Northwest, and of centuries-old trees in the Tongass National Forest, where logging companies persist in trying to open the eleven-million-acre site to the cutting of the largest surviving stand of ancient trees in the United States, and one of the largest in the world. As for bison, national forests surrounding Yellowstone National Park have for years served as slaughtering grounds for buffalo that leave the park to reach lower elevations during harsh, deadly winters (see chapter 9).

Similarly, bison on the public domain—federally administered lands that do not serve as national parks, forests, or wildlife refuges—are not a management priority. These lands are managed by the Bureau of Land Management, the largest federal land agency, with 244 million acres under its jurisdiction, compared to 85 million for National Park System units, 193 million acres in the National Forest System, and the more than 95 million acres of the National Wildlife Refuge System and wetland management districts administered by the US Fish & Wildlife Service. Bureau lands lie largely in the West, where they are heavily used for mining, grazing, and other consumptive purposes that can cause extensive harm by, for example, polluting air and water and degrading habitat. The bureau can trace its origins to the General Land Office, the original home for forest reserves, and to the Grazing Service, created in the 1930s to stop the abuse of public grazing lands by ranchers who put out more cattle than the grasslands could support. In 1946, the Truman administration, as part of its federal reorganization, combined these two agencies to form the Bureau of Land Management, which to this day is still wrestling with issues such as overgrazing. Cattle on bureau lands are often seen as competitive with bison, an issue that has put the bureau into the center of an ambitious, and controversial, bison restoration plan (see chapter 5).

The restoration and management of bison have become modernized in ways Hornaday and his cohort, or even Leopold and Wright, never could have imagined. Since 1994, Wind Cave staff have been implanting microchips behind each buffalo's right ear as a secondary means of identification, along with traditional metal ear tags. A scanner connected to a special computer program reads the microchips, so data can be automatically updated. The line between "wild" and "livestock" is increasingly blurred in an increasingly humanized world. Similar bison management is conducted on the National Bison Range and on the Wichita Mountains National Wildlife Refuge in Oklahoma, home to about 650 bison. Fort Niobrara National Wildlife Refuge today is home to 360 bison, a number maintained by natural losses and gains and by culling. Refuge staff also conduct an annual roundup during which calves are labeled with computer chips, data from which help park staff to maintain genetic diversity.

Despite the security of the bison as a species today, it survives only in minuscule numbers compared to 150 years ago. And it still remains at the center of management controversies and deficiencies. According to bison expert James A. Bailey, "Based on today's knowledge of genetics, ecology, natural selection and evolution, we know that restoration is far from finished. Worse, opportunities to restore plains bison on native range have diminished as more land has become more intensively used and developed.

We realize that we have been warehousing plains bison, awaiting a time when knowledge, public awareness and public support might prompt restoration with some truly wild herds of plains bison on large grassland reserves."

Because bison are big, potentially dangerous herding animals and, under natural conditions, are nomadic, following the scent of grasslands and watering sites, they pose challenging problems for conservationists bent on restoring them not to fenced pastures, as Hornaday did, but to a condition more nearly like their far-traveling patterns of the past. This complex problem of maintaining a species adapted to Pleistocene times in an era of human global domination is one that involves not only bison but also other herding, roaming species, including African and Asian elephants, giraffes, and wildebeest. What biologists and conservationists are learning from the bison may bring great strides in the advancement of protection for all nomadic herding animals. The conservation challenges facing modern biologists and wildlife-management agencies are imbued with such questions as whether the bison is still a wild species, or has it become livestock?

CHAPTER 5

PRIVATE HERDS: HOPES, ASPIRATIONS, ROADS TO RECOVERY

From the 1930s to the 1960s, bison numbers lingered nationwide at about 20,000 animals. In the '60s, the number of herds and of individual animals began to grow rapidly as interest in bison ranching caught on. In about 1970, commercial bison—those raised for meat and other products—began to exceed the number of conservation buffalo—those raised primarily to preserve the species under conditions as natural as the limits of habitat allow. In the United States today, still only about 20,000 bison belong to conservation herds. The rest of the nation's bison—some 183,780 of them, owned by 1,775 ranchers and farmers—belong to commercial herds, according to a 2017 US Department of Agriculture census.

Visit a grocery store that's part of a major chain, and you are likely to find bison meat for sale, much as it would have been 150 years ago in markets on the East Coast. Run an online search for bison ranches, and you should not be surprised if you turn up at least one near you, allowing you to buy meat directly from the source. To supply this market for meat, bison raisers slaughter about 70,000 bison every year, which is about half the number of cattle that the beef industry slaughters every *day*—around 125,000 animals, according to David Carter, a former executive director of the National Bison Association, an organization that represents bison producers' interests while maintaining strict standards for the trade. In other words, every workday, the beef industry kills almost two times as many animals as the bison industry does in a full year. The average US resident eats 50 pounds of beef yearly, compared to 0.08 pounds of bison, Carter says. Not all of that meat comes from US bison farms and ranches. The Canadian domesticated herd stands at about 100,000, almost all in western Canada, allowing for export of about 4.5 million pounds of meat yearly. According to the US Department of Agriculture nutritional database, bison meat has 87 percent less fat and 26 percent more iron than an equivalent cut of beef and seven times more vitamin B^{12} than chicken.

In the 1990s, which marked the beginning of modern bison agriculture, commercial herds were raised like cattle, Carter says. They were often dehorned, and ranchers attempted to breed them through artificial insemination. "As late as the early 2000s, we were stuffing them in feedlots," Carter says. "In the following years, we had to peel a lot of that back. We let the bison teach us."

One curse handed down from the early years, notably by Charles Goodnight and Buffalo Jones, was a yen among some ranchers to crossbreed bison with cattle. History showed that such efforts faced generally insurmountable difficulties and failures, including such common shortcomings as infertility among crossbred offspring and aborting. But the yen continued sporadically in the 1970s and into the 1980s with the production of curly-haired animals called beefalo. They have faded away, but the legacy of crossbreeding lingers on. "That's a huge frustration for bison ranchers," according to Carter. "People think we're crossbreeding the animals, but it's not true." Because attempts at crossbreeding have cropped up repeatedly over the years, "there are a lot of bison out there that have these legacy genetics," Carter says. The largest bison operations today test their bison for cattle genes and cull the animals that carry them (the complex question of bison genetics is explored in chapter 10). This elimination is good for the bison industry as well as for the bison. Buffalo without cattle genes do better than crossbred animals when subsisting on natural grass, which is low-quality forage. "With crossbreeding, you aren't getting the best of both animals," Carter says.

Though classified as livestock in many states, bison are no longer treated like cattle. They are no longer routinely dehorned. Bulls are not turned into steers. Artificial insemination and branding are no longer imposed on the animals. Although cattle are treated with growth hormones when being finished for the market, use of hormones on bison is banned by federal law. In fact, Carter says, many ranchers don't even provide feed because, as a native North American species, the bison can fend for itself on natural plants. However, buffalo can be treated with antibiotics if they fall ill, though this practice is rare, Carter says, because bison avoid attracting the attention of predators by hiding signs of illness: "If you see a sick animal, it's too late to do anything about it."

The bison's sturdy frame, its adaptation to natural grasslands, and its ability to withstand heat and arctic blasts give it distinct advantages over cattle. Bison do carry some disadvantages, though. Bison cows don't produce calves until three years old, but cattle calve at age two, giving cattle a head start in meat production. However, Carter says, bison cows are more productive in the long run, generally continuing to drop calves for up to twenty years, while beef cattle are worn down at age nine or ten.

One critical advantage offered by bison comes at calving time, when the young are born. On cattle ranches, the weeks of calving mark a demanding time, as cows must be checked every few hours, night and day, rain, sleet, or snow, to be sure they are not having trouble giving birth. Domestic beef cows give birth to calves that weigh 100 to 110 pounds. With an offspring that large, birthing can present potentially fatal problems. Bison calves are born at 40 to 45 pounds from April to June. The cows have no need for help. For bison growers, "calving season is the best time to go fishing," Carter jokes. If you hover around during calving, the cows become stressed. They prefer to be left alone and will go off from a herd with a couple other cows that help out. Carter once saw a female birthing when coyotes showed up; the other cows kept the coyotes away from the calf.

All in all, bison can take care of themselves, though they still have to be moved from pasture to pasture to prevent overgrazing, depending on the number of bison and the size of their pasture. Because of fences, they cannot roam freely in search of nutritional mineral needs, such as salt, and so may have to be supplemented. But ranchers prefer a hands-off approach. "We want to make sure we never breed those natural behaviors out of them," Carter says. Their wildness can present challenges, but it also makes them desirable for commercial herds. "Bison are a little bit harder to handle than cattle, but a whole lot easier to raise," Carter says.

Rob Ferguson, co-owner of the largest bison farm in Virginia but in many ways representative of independent bison operators, gives a different slant to the comment that bison are a little bit harder to handle. "They're dangerous animals," he says. When in a pasture with bison, he and others on his staff keep a close eye on them. "The bulls will chase you down during the rut, which runs from July to September," he says. A cow with a calf will chase you from all the way across a pasture, even if the calf is nowhere nearby. When in a bison pasture, Ferguson stays along the fence for quick exit or rides an ATV.

A native Californian, Ferguson attended Humboldt State University in Arcata, California, initially pursuing a degree in wildlife management before switching to a journalism major. He followed that course of study with a graduate degree in international trade before setting up a transportation company in the Washington, DC, area twenty-five years ago, working with federal agencies such as the US Department of Agriculture to hire ships and deliver commodities to other nations. He completed a two-year program at the University of Maryland in applied agriculture, a field that was in his family background: his grandfather owned a farm near San Diego on which Ferguson spent time when growing up. That nascent interest led him to establish a meat-production farm on 500 acres of rolling pastures and woodland outside Culpeper, Virginia, about seventy miles southwest of Washington. Eventually, his farming plans focused on bison. His goal was to become the major distributor of bison meat in the Washington metropolitan area. Now his Virginia Bison Company, headquartered at Cibola Farms, has a commercial reach that extends as far as Baltimore, and some of his bison products may make it as far as Delaware via wholesalers. The farm is open to the public every day of the year except Christmas.

He was introduced to bison in California while at Humboldt State, where for barbecues he bought bison meat from a local dealer. Raising bison combined his early inclination for wildlife management with his interest in entrepreneurship. He didn't want to get into industrial agriculture, he says, and was pleased that technology is not a big part of raising bison. For example, because bison can't be artificially inseminated, breeding has to be done naturally—one bull to ten cows. "I didn't want modern technology to get in the way of my agricultural endeavors," he says.

Ferguson and his business partner, Mike Sipes, buy calves and yearlings from nearby states, including Ohio and Pennsylvania, and from distant locations, such as Florida and ranches out West, transporting the animals to Virginia either in their own trailer or by hiring trucking companies that specialize in moving livestock. The National Bison Association posts bison sales online from private ranchers, from sites such as Wind Cave National Park, and from reserves owned by The Nature Conservancy. The Cibola operation raises calves for two or three years before processing. Ferguson also breeds calves from his adult bison.

In one major way, the Virginia Bison Company is not typical of the bulk of bison operations, Ferguson says. Bison ranches tend to be concentrated in the West, where herds are kept on large pastures that allow expansive movement. East Coast ranches usually operate on a smaller scale. He has put up fences to break his land into forty pastures. Such small pastures are unique to the East, Ferguson says, where abundant rain produces a rich plant growth that makes small pastures highly productive. He says he needs around one acre per one thousand pounds of bison, while in Wyoming a rancher would need about 40 acres per one thousand pounds. He rotates bison from pasture to pasture every two days to prevent overgrazing. He has only sixty adult bison out of generally three hundred head on the farm at any given time.

Mike Sipes works with staff on day-to-day bison activities, such as pasture moves, but Rob pitches in when moving a herd. Their farm, like many modern operations, uses low-stress techniques in moving bison, which are reluctant to be herded like cattle. "We taught our bison to follow rather than be pushed from behind," Ferguson says. Initially, he and Sipes used grain in a bucket to get the bison to follow them, rattling the grain and associating the sound with a special call. The bison learned to go in the wanted direction when they heard that call. New bison subsequently followed the trained herd and adopted the same pattern. "We have an ATV in front of them," he says. "They respond to the call and will rush forward. You need to be on an ATV to get out of the way as they stampede toward you. We never chase them."

Keeping stress low is important, as stress can debilitate a bison just as it can a human. The trick is to avoid practices that weaken the animals. Ferguson agrees with Carter that once bison show signs of illness, "these animals are going to die, there's nothing you can do." The challenge of ensuring bison health is compounded by a lack of veterinarians knowledgeable about the bottom line of bison vital signs. In the East, Ferguson says, you have to look hard to find a veterinarian who "knows anything about bison. It's different in the West." He says he has found a veterinarian in Virginia who was originally from the West, knows bison, and, at the time of this writing, was hiring an intern who also is from the West. As bison become more popular, knowledge about them is growing. In the late 1990s, Ferguson points out, the State of Virginia didn't see bison ranching as an agricultural business. "That's changed big-time over the last twenty years," he says.

Fortunately for bison raisers, Ferguson says, medical aid is rarely required. For example, he has lost only one cow during calving in twenty-five years. But more research is needed for raising healthy bison, he says. Under natural conditions, bison can find necessary foods and minerals on their own. "They learn the land. But now they are fenced." The small pastures characteristic of the East can be a problem for natural behavior. "In the West, with 40,000-acre pastures—those animals get to move around." In the East, bison diets must be supplemented with minerals. However, very little science-based research is being done on bison nutritional balancing and parasite management, which are vitally important or, Ferguson says, "bison can go down."

Meanwhile, the market for bison meat is going up. In the late 1990s people didn't know you could eat bison. "They thought bison were an endangered species and never saw it in grocery stores," Ferguson says. When he entered the bison business, Cibola staff visited thirteen farmers' markets per week to sell meat. "Once demand increased nationally, we were able to sort of evolve our marketing," he says. Now he sells 75 to 80 percent of the Virginia Bison Company's meat to a wholesaler in Baltimore who supplies a grocery chain as well as restaurants and food clubs. The farm also sells bison leather and wallets online. Bison leather, he says, is twice as soft as cow leather and three times more durable. He sells fifty to eighty jawbones per month on eBay and Etsy. There is a demand for horn sheaths, but he usually doesn't sell them, generally keeping them with the skulls, which are more valuable when the sheaths cover the bony horn cores. He says that demand for his raw dog-food mix is exceeding his supply of one thousand pounds per month. He also sells hooves and dog chews as well as a lot of bones for broth stock.

Although the emphasis of commercial herds is clearly the sale of bison products, the industry also seeks to aid in bison conservation. "We walk a delicate balance—we are raising the animals for meat, but don't want to domesticate them," David Carter says. "Mother Nature did a really, really good job developing the animal, so we don't want to change it." A few years ago, he wrote in a blog on the National Bison Association website, "Policy debates often brought the conservation community into direct conflict with commercial bison producers." Now, however, the association has partnered with such groups as the Wildlife Conservation Society, the International Union for the Conservation of Nature, and the InterTribal Buffalo Council. The association recently participated in a successful four-year effort to persuade Congress to name the bison as the national mammal, a goal that became reality when President Barack Obama signed the National Bison Legacy Act into law on May 9, 2016. Carter is listed as one of the authors of the seminal paper "The Ecological Future of the North American Bison," and the bison association has created a code of ethics that stresses sound business and bison-raising behaviors, including a pledge that members "never engage in deliberate cross-breeding of bison with another species." The association offers a North American Bison Registry that requires DNA sampling to ensure that registered animals are free of cattle genes. Recently, the association launched a conservation management plan that rewards producers "for continuous improvement in the management of the land, animals and people in their operation."

The association also is sponsoring Bison 1 Million, an initiative to build North America's bison population to one million animals by 2027, the total to be based on all types of herds: commercial, conservation, and tribal. To which, Carter says, must be added a fourth partner, the consumer. "The consumer gives the incitement for our producers to restore those herds," he says. Elements of the initiative are designed to support bison ranching, but it also calls for "incentives for expansion of tribal/First Nation community herds for tribal and commercial markets" and "restoration of bison in federal and state parks that were part of the historic bison habitat."

RESTORATION OF BISON ON GOVERNMENT LANDS AND ON LANDS OWNED by nonprofit conservation groups is the domain of conservation herds.

Managers try to have as little manipulative contact with the animals as possible and seek to maintain bison genetic purity. Bison preserves usually are open to the public for activities such as hiking, camping, fishing, and hunting.

An explosion of bison restoration efforts during the past twenty years began when an evaluation of grassland sites in the Great Plains—conducted around 2000 by The Nature Conservancy and the World Wildlife Fund, two of the world's largest conservation groups—led to creation of The Prairie Foundation in 2001, an ambitious restoration plan now called American Prairie. This initiative seeks to create some 3 million acres of protected prairie in north-central Montana, including both privately owned and government-administered lands, and to populate the reserve with ten thousand free-ranging bison.

The early 2000s continued to prove beneficial to bison. The Wildlife Conservation Society (WCS, formerly the New York Zoological Society) revived the American Bison Society in 2005, the 100th anniversary of the original group's founding. That same year, under the auspices of the American Bison Society, WCS began collecting data for science-based bison restoration, conducting an assessment of the nation's bison habitat and potential habitat, which they completed in 2006. WCS then convened experts on bison and biology to produce a plan, or standards, for the ecological recovery of bison across North America, from Mexico to Canada and Alaska. At a meeting that involved tribes, bison producers, conservation groups, and other interested parties, a group of biologists and bison managers of various sorts created the Vermejo Statement, which defines the mission of bison restoration. The statement was named after the site where the meeting was held, a New Mexico bison ranch owned by Ted Turner—the inventor of 24/7 TV news programming, via his founding of CNN, and one of the world's leading conservationists. The Vermejo Statement declares:

> Over the next century, the ecological recovery of the North American bison will occur when multiple large herds move freely across extensive landscapes within all major habitats of their historic range, interacting in ecologically significant ways with the fullest possible set of other native species, and inspiring, sustaining and connecting human cultures.

This mission would be achieved by such measures as maintaining herds that meet the criteria for ecological recovery; managing herds for the long-term maintenance of health, genetic diversity, and species integrity; restoring native ecosystems; providing conservation incentives for bison producers, managers, and other stakeholders; and cooperating across international borders. According to bison biologists Glenn Plumb and Keith Aune, thanks to the meeting at Turner's Vermejo Park Ranch, "a new forward-thinking vision for the future of American bison was introduced into the North American conservation dialogue."

The vision's goals are ambitious, but the authors of the Vermejo Statement are grounded in reality. In a related paper, "The Ecological Future of the North American Bison," they wrote, "No one believes there will be 'multiple large herds, moving across extensive landscapes in all major habitat types across the historical range' within the next 10 years. Nevertheless, it is possible this might happen within 100 years." The magnitude of that goal is huge. The historical range covered an estimated 3.7 million square miles of North America in the year 1500, which biologists use as a baseline for bison distribution. The western part of that range, which is the main focus of bison recovery today, encompassed 3 million square miles. Bison occupy less than 1 percent of it today.

Concurrent with these efforts, the International Union for the Conservation of Nature in 2005 created its North American Bison Specialist Group, composed of seventy bison experts who in 2010 completed an assessment of bison status and management needs, followed in 2017 by a status update. The specialist group "provides a lasting resource of experts to help inform management of existing wild bison and restoration of new herds," according to Aune and Plumb, who are former leaders of the group.

Subsequent to these advances in bison restoration, the Department of the Interior in 2008 established its own Bison Working Group to ensure that all Interior agencies—which include the US Fish & Wildlife Service, the Bureau of Land Management, and the National Park Service—would coordinate their bison programs. Two years later, the department published a report on current and future opportunities to reintroduce bison to federally administered lands. In 2015—as it approached the centennial year of its founding—the Park Service laid out plans to expand several of its bison herds and to inaugurate plans to create new herds.

In 2019 and 2020, Interior Department officials pushed for more work regarding management of all department herds as metaherds, among which animals would be moved around and mixed to avoid inbreeding and to enhance genetic diversity (for more details on this problem, see chapter 10). In 2020, the department revamped its 2008 Bison Conservation Initiative, designed to improve and coordinate bison management. The new initiative, for the first time, set up principles and actions for departmental bison recovery, according to Paul Santavy, a biologist with years of experience managing federal wildlife refuges. The department subsequently began drafting a metapopulation plan, with transfers of bison among refuges, parks, and tribal herds.

States have taken a newly enlightened approach to bison management as well. Alaska reintroduced wood bison to the central part of the state in 2015, the first wood bison restoration in the United States. A year later, Montana officials announced a plan that allows bison freer access to land surrounding Yellowstone National Park, a measure that Aune and Plumb characterized as "the most significant expansion of the range of wild bison from Yellowstone National Park since their protection in 1872."

While wildlife enthusiasts in general, and bison aficionados in particular, might think that states and local residents would readily endorse the establishment of bison conservation preserves—given the bison's ability to attract tourists and their dollars—trying to establish a bison preserve is often fraught with difficulty, including opposition from local residents who see any new entity as a rejection of their agricultural heritage and as a threat to their culture. In ranch country, paradigm shifts in land use, removal of fences, and replacement of cattle are often responded to as threats to a way of life that has for decades existed in isolation from outside influences. This opposition is nothing new. It has been around since the beginning of bison restoration.

THE YEAR IS 1900: BUFFALO JONES HAS OFFERED TO ESTABLISH A NATIONAL bison herd in New Mexico and is "willing to bear all the expense of this experiment and asks no government aid." His plan requires an act of Congress to allow the restoration of bison on the public domain. The plan is enthusiastically endorsed by Iowa representative John Lacey, who tells the US House of Representatives, "Out of the 600,000,000 acres remaining of the public lands it is proposed by this bill to set apart a tract of 20,000 acres; not free of charge, as the sheep and cattle men now use the land, but subject to a nominal rental of one cent an acre, and also two buffalo in kind which are to be delivered to the Government each year, for the use of the public parks."

Without delay, ranchers and sheepmen oppose the plan, so the bill is revised to ask for fewer acres. Lacey writes, "The committee in reporting back this bill have cut the amount down to such dimensions that we believe the bill would meet the approval of even these interested parties. The addition of this herd of buffalo, instead of being an injury to New Mexico, will be of positive advantage, because it adds an additional industry, or, rather, restores one which has been destroyed. The lease is a temporary one, and runs but for twenty years. If it is found that the animals sufficiently increase under this arrangement the lease could be renewed, otherwise there would be no harm done in terminating it."

Despite Lacey's advocacy, the measure fails, stalling the first bison restoration project by seven years. Local opposition to such projects survives today, and indeed local opposition is often the only opposition.

ONE CONSERVATION GROUP THAT HAS HAD SIGNIFICANT SUCCESS IN BISON restoration is The Nature Conservancy, one of the largest conservation groups in the world. It claims one million members and an annual budget in excess of $1 billion. The conservancy works with species and habitats all over the planet. One project focuses on "putting bison back on the prairie, restoring its ecological role on select preserves in the Great Plains." It began in the 1980s with the release of eighteen bison on the Samuel H. Ordway Jr. Memorial Preserve, some 7,800 acres of prairie that comprises the conservancy's largest preserve in South Dakota. The herd now numbers about three hundred animals. The conservancy today has 5,500 bison grazing on the 130,000 acres encompassed by the twelve grassland preserves it has established in North Dakota, South Dakota, Nebraska, Iowa, Illinois, Indiana, Colorado, Kansas, Missouri, and Oklahoma.

Many of the conservancy herds started with bison from Wind Cave National Park, which can maintain no more than five hundred buffalo. This number is about half the minimum needed to protect a herd's genetic diversity. The conservancy has been working with the Park Service to establish satellite herds on conservancy land and thus to exceed the one thousand head needed for genetic integrity. The conservancy tests its herds periodically in an effort to ensure that the animals carry no cattle genes.

Conservancy biologists believe that the bison are good for the group's pastures. According to Mary Miller, manager of the Ordway preserve, "They graze all year, even in winter, and focus on grasses, allowing wildflowers to thrive. The result is a varied grassland that is good for more kinds of butterflies, pollinating insects and grassland-nesting birds. Biodiversity is enhanced."

"Prairies need disturbance, like the disturbance created by fires and by bison," says Eric Rosenquist, manager of the conservancy's Cross Ranch Preserve in North Dakota. "Both prevent the build-up of a litter layer beneath the grass that can shelter invasive, non-native species. Bison graze the grasses that contribute to the litter and also create open areas in their wallows or by trampling the ground that become good locations for the seeds of new prairie plants to germinate."

The largest of the conservancy's bison reserves is the Joseph H. Williams Tallgrass Prairie Preserve in Oklahoma. At 39,650 acres, it is also the world's largest protected tallgrass prairie, an ecosystem that once ran from Texas to Minnesota, crossing fourteen states. About 96 percent of the tallgrass prairie has been destroyed by development. Open to the public, the preserve is home to three hundred bird species and eighty mammal species. Each year, the conservancy rounds up the buffalo and checks data from numbered electronic ear tags that provide information such as gender, age, weight, and other factors. The preserve then sells enough bison each year to keep the herd below 2,500. The number removed is based loosely on the number of calves born in a given year, which can hover around a high of 500 or 600 animals. In 2020, the conservancy sold 306 bison, with bulls sold at six or seven years old, when they become more aggressive, and cows at age ten to twelve, when they are "less physically fit for withstanding the rigors of roundup," even though they will produce calves into their twenties. In this regard, the conservancy preserves lean a bit toward the commercial approach to herd management, an approach that bison expert James Bailey has suggested could be harmful in the long term:

Mate selection, with the dominance of large agile bulls, has been another major selective force in bison. In wild bison herds, most breeding is accomplished by bulls that are 8 or more years old. Dominant bulls have proven their abilities to survive, to resist debilitating diseases, to forage effectively and to digest forages efficiently in order to outcompete other bulls. Years of natural selection are represented in each dominant breeding bull. In many managed plains bison herds, this selection is lost as most bulls are culled at an early age based on human decisions, and bull competition is largely eliminated by maintaining a herd sex ratio of 1 bull per 10 or more cows.

Arguably the most ambitious attempt to restore bison and keep them as close to wild as possible was initiated in 2004. According to its mission statement, American Prairie (formerly the American Prairie Reserve) seeks "to create the largest nature reserve in the contiguous United States, a refuge for people and wildlife preserved forever as part of America's heritage." A biological assessment determined at the outset that this reserve should include about 3.2 million acres—one and a half times the size of Yellowstone National Park—if it is to serve as a complete ecosystem capable of sustaining grasslands and corridors for native wildlife species, from prairie dogs to coyotes, eagles to bison.

The key to that amassing of natural habitat is the combining of private and public lands, including land purchased and owned by the reserve and land leased from private and government sources. American Prairie has acquired more than 400,000 acres of grassland, including nearly 110,000 acres owned by the organization and more than 315,000 acres of federal- and state-administered land that the organization leases. Some of the holdings lie adjacent to Montana's 1.1-million-acre Charles M. Russell National Wildlife Refuge, administered by the US Fish & Wildlife Service and historically part of the bison's range.

American Prairie wants to help put bison on the Russell refuge, but the plan has been blocked by local opposition, at least for now. American Prairie seeks to cooperate with the Bureau of Land Management on 375,000 acres in the Upper Missouri River Breaks National Monument, a bureau-administered area that would have been familiar to William T. Hornaday from his 1886 bison hunt. With the help of donors, American Prairie staff are patiently, slowly, and resolutely buying parcels of land that fill the gaps between these large sweeps of grassland, building toward the goal of 3.2 million acres. The group's acquisitions have resulted in the retirement of nearly 65,000 acres of cattle-grazing leases within the Russell refuge, allowing the Fish & Wildlife Service to begin restoration of areas damaged by overgrazing, making them more suitable for wildlife. (See chapter 10 for more information on the Charles M. Russell refuge.)

American Prairie installed its first bison in 2005, marking the first time since the 1880s that bison had inhabited the newly acquired land. But bison are not the sole beneficiaries of restoration. Working with state and federal agencies, the reserve staff are helping with the protection and recovery of other species, such as the swift fox, bald and golden eagles, mule deer, black-footed ferret, and prairie chicken. They partner with nearby ranchers to increase tolerance for wildlife, reducing the slaughter of coyotes and even of declining species still being systematically destroyed by federal control agents, such as the prairie dog. The reserve also is restoring habitat it owns, removing or relocating fences and providing corridors that allow wildlife such as deer, pronghorn, and cougars as well as bison to move from one area to another, as they did before the land development that began in the 1880s. Stream restoration is helping fish populations.

American Prairie also is helping local economies, bringing in more than $40 million since 2002, including wages paid to forty-nine full- and part-time local staff, equipment and land purchases, and tourism. The group pays full property taxes, more than $80,000 yearly, rejecting exemptions. The organization also gives cash bonuses to ranchers who complete an American Prairie wildlife program started in 2013. It is a financial benefit to ranchers who raise cattle with wildlife-friendly practices, allow predators on their land, and help provide wildlife travel corridors to sites such as the Greater Yellowstone Ecosystem, which includes land that surrounds the park. The reserve is even open to hunting, including the pursuit of bison. "Human hunters can help to keep certain wildlife species populations within the ecological carrying capacity of an ecosystem, especially in the absence of other keystone carnivores," declares the American Prairie website.

Although the reserve offers manifold benefits to the local and regional community, it initially faced the usual opposition, with ranchers protesting that replacing cattle with bison was an insult to a culture more than one hundred years old, as was the moving of fence lines and various changes in management emphasis—all in all, arguments that would have been familiar to John Lacey and Buffalo Jones. Even years after American Prairie was launched, a request by the reserve staff in 2021 to move some fences and make changes in bison and cattle grazing on a Bureau of Land Management site, which was quickly approved by the bureau, galvanized local opposition and resulted in an extension of the period for public comment on the plan. In the end, the plan went through, but local opposition persists.

American Prairie continues to pursue its main goals for bison restoration—high genetic diversity, a herd free of all cattle genes, and a species that fulfills its keystone ecological role in plains and prairies by engaging in natural behaviors. To ensure that the animals live and interact naturally, reserve staff use minimal intervention with the bison, allowing weak animals to die and strong ones to survive and breed. Staff contend that bison "have adapted and evolved according to the forces of natural selection over thousands of years and we want to ensure that they will continue to do so into the future."

TED TURNER STANDS OUT AS A BISON RANCHER WHO IS COMBINING BOTH commercial and conservation aspects into his operation, in a very big way. Turner told one of his biographers years ago that he believed that governments and the marketplace are the only entities powerful enough to engender change at a systemic level, such as saving an ecosystem or a broad range of habitats, but he also felt that private landowners can initiate change faster, given their relative freedom from political and funding constraints. Turner's avowed goal is to "manage the land in an economically sustainable and ecologically sensitive manner while promoting conservation of native species and habitats." Financially self-sufficient, Turner can indeed move quickly in striving to achieve his conservation goals.

In 1987, he bought his first ranch near Montana's headwaters of the Missouri River. Two years later, he laid out $21 million in cash for another Montana ranch, the Flying D, which covers nearly 114,000 acres between the Madison and Gallatin Rivers. With intentions of removing interior fences and releasing bison to roam freely within the ranch, Turner soon had his hired hands restoring pastures and hayfields. In 1990, he bought one hundred bison from the National Bison Range—linking himself to the legacy of Hornaday and

Roosevelt—and turned them loose on the Flying D. He told a biographer, "I was so excited. Part of me couldn't believe it was happening. I had goose bumps." Today, Turner owns more bison than any human or organization on the planet—about 45,000 of them, according to Mark Kossler, vice president of ranch operations for Turner Enterprises. Turner has bison roaming on fourteen ranches in five states—Kansas, Montana, Nebraska, New Mexico, and South Dakota. He's the second-largest private US landowner, with his 2 million acres in the United States and Argentina exceeded only by telecommunications executive John C. Malone's 2.2 million acres. Of Turner's holdings, "1,857,050 acres have bison associated with the land management," Kossler says. On the Flying D alone he has about 4,500 bison, roughly 1,000 more than you will typically find in Yellowstone National Park.

Turner has managed his bison as a blend of commercial and conservation herds. For example, the bison on the Flying D graze year-round. They are never fed hay. This approach protects the integrity of the grasslands, leaving forage for other wild grazers that inhabit the area, such as the 2,000 or so elk that drift across the Flying D from other habitats.

Conservation herds are managed first for maintaining genetic purity and broad genetic diversity, Kossler says, "as the genetics involved are both unique and important to bison conservation." Four herds on Turner ranches have never had a positive test for cattle mitochondrial DNA. Turner ranch managers minimize their selection of breeding individuals in these herds, allowing natural selection to take precedence while keeping a high bull-to-cow ratio, which keeps genetic diversity very broad.

Turner allows predators such as cougars, wolves, and bears on his ranches, as well as prairie dog towns and endangered black-footed ferrets, which are weasel-like animals that prey on burrowing animals. "Bison are a keystone species in North America, in that when they are on the landscape, they will create habitat 'niches' for other species through their biomass life cycle, grazing, traveling, and wallowing," Kossler says. "Also, they are a very hardy species and will live in harmony with predators and with predation pressure better than traditional livestock." Turner owns a ranch in Montana that is inhabited by a full complement of the native species that were present prior to European settlement. "Apex predators such as gray wolves and grizzly bears live on the ranch and interact with the bison herd," Kossler says. "This stands out as a capstone accomplishment of our conservation efforts."

Turner's commercial herds, on the other hand, are managed for pounds of red meat production first, with some attention to identifying and selecting individuals that show no cattle mitochondrial DNA. "There will be some selection pressure for production traits that allow these bison to excel in their environment, consistently producing year after year," Kossler says. Although his ranches are managed to maintain complete prairie ecosystems, Turner keeps a wary eye on the ranches' costs and profits, maintaining a positive balance on economic profit, ecological benefits, and benefits for the quality of life of local and regional people. Even with the aid of rising prices and demand for bison meat, twenty years passed from the start of his bison operations before the ranches turned a profit, with the help of his chain of Ted's Montana Grill restaurants, where bison dishes from meatloaf to steaks are mainstays. About 40 percent of the bison served comes from Turner ranches.

About 95 percent of Ted Turner's bison end up going to slaughter, Kossler says. The exceptions are very old cows, in their late teens to early twenties, that come in pregnant in the fall and are retained in the herd, but will succumb to natural causes in the next growth cycle. "Some of the conservation herds that are still growing will have a higher number of older animals in them that may die of natural causes compared to the production herds," Kossler says.

Even someone of Turner's stature—or perhaps because of it—drew the ire of local ranchers who resented his changes in fences, his allegiance to bison, his removal of cattle, and his attitude that he, like other ranchers, has a right to do what he wants on his land if he is harming no one else. During the early days at the Flying D, someone shot and killed one of his bison. Wrath, or at least a quiet level of rancor, still bubbles in the background in some of his ranch areas.

"Rural communities see bison restoration as economic and cultural threats, along with disease," says a biologist who is familiar with the ecological, economic, and political clashes between bison and humans and who wishes to remain anonymous. "There is a slew of reasons for opposition. All roll off of economic and cultural reasons, including property damage if bison get on their land and eat the ranchers' resources." Also, there is a danger factor—bison can be aggressive.

These cultural concerns are as real and as important as the economic fears, or even more so. "A lot of these folks are very serious about their lifestyle, and in small communities they are dependent on the land," the biologist adds. "They are also leery of land use for wildlife. They see agriculture and ranching as the only proper use for the land." In the view of many, perhaps most, ranchers, wildlife conservation should be a part of ranching, but they object to having the public's wildlife on their land. They may open their land to the public and to hunting, but they also believe that if habitat has any use for livestock, it should be used for livestock.

The opposition to bison can be "stepped up" because of the culture wars of the day, according to the biologist. Ted Turner moves in, taxes and property values go up, and the area becomes more attractive to commodity buyers. Now ranchers aren't competing with ranchers for land. They're up against people with very deep pockets. "It's all super complex," the source says. "It's almost not understandable." Ranchers on the ground recall how their parents and grandparents lived, and they see how things have changed in how they are living now, plus their kids are leaving. They pick on Turner, or on the American Prairie reserve, or on the Russell wildlife refuge as the enemy, as the source of change. "It's the threat of the unknown."

Changes in wildlife numbers also affect how ranchers see efforts to restore native species. Wildlife populations in the northern Great Plains largely collapsed in the 1870s and '80s, so by 1900 there was almost nothing left. Ranchers can recall letters written and stories told by their grandparents regarding how scarce wildlife was a few decades ago. Their ancestors in the 1930s helped to restore pronghorn and in the 1950s to restore elk. Today's ranchers look at these populations and say, according to the biologist, "Now there's all this wildlife around here, why do you want more? It's never enough with you people." Nevertheless, it's "super rare to get any rancher who says, 'Kill off wildlife.' Wildlife is part of their heritage," the source explains. "But they have a different perspective. They don't hate wildlife. They hate things that cause problems for them."

Despite the challenges, Ted Turner has found ways to win over ranchers and other local residents suspicious of his motives and actions. According to Kossler, Turner's intention from the beginning of his western land ownership was to be a good neighbor and to be part of the communities in which his properties lie. "Since 1986, Ted has consistently done both," Kossler contends. "Having good relations with our neighboring ranches is a function of treating others 'right' and helping neighbors when we can. This centers on ranch management and staff—who are often from the local community—being part of the community and striving to have positive relations with our neighbors. Over time, this has largely been successful." Turner has launched a Turner Community Youth Development Initiative in each of the communities where he owns property, providing significant funding for community youth education and for projects that help foster healthy growth and development of young people. This activity involves participation from the local ranch staff, the Turner Foundation, and Turner family members in many cases. It has been a vibrant program that has funded community-led youth programs. "Ted's ranches are consistent contributors to the local fire departments and support the local 4-H and Future Farmers of America programs in their communities," Kossler says.

Turner's operation clearly marries the commercial herd with the conservation herd. He shows what someone with financial muscle and conservation motives can accomplish when guided by an ethic for the planet. In "The Ecological Future of the North American Bison," a panel of authors composed of bison experts complained, "We live in a time of minimal expectations for nature, not maximal, inhabiting a planet more modified by human activity than ever before. . . . It seems odd that in nearly every other arena of human endeavor 21st century societies are generally looking forward to more—improved well-being, enriched spiritual lives, greater wealth and power—whereas most nature conservation efforts continue to be ad hoc, small scale, and short term; that is, there is less rather than more. When it comes to species conservation, especially for species as iconic and important as the bison, we can do better." Turner seems to offer the promise that, with proper examples and ambitions, society will do better, if only eventually. Meanwhile, Turner has arranged his conservation interests in a way that will ensure that his programs persist even without him.

A growing addition to commercial and conservation herds is represented by tribal herds. These herds center on the aspirations of American Indian peoples whose ancestors hunted bison as a staple of their diet as little as 150 years ago. The long-forgotten, ancient ancestors of today's Europeans, Russians, and Siberians also knew the vital uses to which bison could be put. Practically any human culture native to the Northern Hemisphere—however urban or urbane today—can trace its roots to the lost craft of bison hunting as it was done tens of thousands of years ago. The tribal herds are being created by peoples who have not lost the memories of those ancient days.

CHAPTER 6

TRIBES: FINDING HOME

Bison and humans have coexisted for a very long time in North America. Archaeologists have found thirteen-thousand-year-old stone spear points among bison bones in New Mexico. The bison served as a staple for many Indigenous cultures throughout North America, from what is today Canada into Mexico, and from the East Coast through to the Rocky Mountains. Bison provided not only food but also building materials, such as hides for tepees and watercraft. Native peoples used carved bones and horns for eating utensils, hides for clothing, stomachs as pots in which meat could be boiled, and sinew for bowstrings and ropes. They boiled hooves to make glue, burned dung as fuel, and used toe bones like dice. The relationship with bison formed the basis of many Plains Indian spiritual beliefs, with skulls used in religious ceremonies.

For example, among the Lakota, Tatanka, the buffalo god, was a powerful spirit that helped hunters and hardworking women. The spirit of the buffalo was believed to stay with the skull until the horns dissolved into the earth, which is why bison skulls were used in many Lakota religious ceremonies. In James Walker's book *Lakota Belief and Ritual*, he wrote, "The Spirit of *Tatanka* is pleased to see the skull of a buffalo. The spirit of *Tatanka* cares for the family. It cares for the young man or the young woman who should live together. It cares for the woman who lives with a man. It cares for little children. It cares for the hunters. It cares for the growing things (vegetation). It cares for everything that has young." Those who dreamed of bison might gain superior skills as hunters or as shamans. Those so blessed might wear a red circle in the middle of their chests as a sign that they had had a vision and a communication from the buffalo god.

Hornaday put it nicely: "If any animal was ever designed by the hand of nature for the express purpose of supplying, at one stroke, nearly all the wants of an entire race, surely the buffalo was intended for the Indian."

But the bison meant significantly more to Plains Indians than a source of vital commodities. The bison was an essential part of their identities as individuals and as tribes. Bison hunting defined the culture of the plains people. They strived all their lives, starting in childhood, to perfect the skills needed to obtain and use bison. Luther Standing Bear, a Lakota born around 1868—who later entered the federal school for Indians in Carlisle, Pennsylvania, designed to mold Indians into laborers and farmers—left clues in his autobiography about the skills needed to master bison hunting in the nineteenth century. He was only eight years old when he plunged for the first time into a stampeding herd of bison, one of the most important trials of his life—his earliest buffalo hunt:

> Soon I was mixed up in the dust and could see nothing ahead of me. All I could hear was the roar and rattle of the hoofs of the buffalo as they thundered along. My pony shied this way and that, and I had to hold on for dear life. For a time I did not even try to pull an arrow from my quiver, as I had all I could do to take care of myself. I knew if my pony went down and one of those big animals stepped on me, it would be my last day on earth. I then realized how helpless I was there in all that dust and confusion, with those ponderous buffalo all around me. The sound of their hoofs was frightening. My pony ran like the wind, while I just clung to her mane; but presently we came out of the dust. . . . When I looked at those big animals and thought of trying to kill one of them, I realized how small I was. I was really afraid of them. Then I thought about what my stepmother had said about bringing her a kidney and a skin, and the feeling that I was a man, after all, came back to me; so I turned my pony toward the bunch which was running north. There was no dust now, and I knew where I was going.

The horse, too, received an education, because the Great Plains buffalo culture was also a horse culture in its later years. "We trained our pony to walk or run right up to anything we wanted him to," recalled Standing Bear. "We picked out a good-size bush, shrub, or trunk of a tree. Our pony was trained to run up as close as he could to the object without dodging. Our pony must learn to go wherever he was told. Even if there was shooting, yelling, and great noise and much confusion, a well-trained pony would go anywhere he was told to go by his rider."

Standing Bear was describing a nineteenth-century hunt. Horses were then relatively new among the Indian peoples, brought from Europe initially by the Spanish in the early 1500s. The men who hunted with Standing Bear would have possessed firearms, both rifle and pistol, for shooting bison, another European product introduced by the Spanish as well as the English and French. Prior to the arrival of horses, Indians hunted on foot, sometimes cloaking themselves with wolf skins and stalking bison alone or in small groups and taking them down with arrows or lances. Hunters also engaged in communal hunts, in which tribal members worked together, and sometimes in cooperation with the wolves that perpetually trailed bison herds, slowly directing herds toward cliffs, and then stampeding the buffalo over the edge.

The advent of horse and firearm changed the plains cultures, allowing the people to hunt more efficiently. Unlike young Standing Bear, "usually an Indian on horseback preferred the lance to the arrow. His method was to run alongside his victim and jab a long-bladed lance into it just back of the ribs. One jab would never bring down a heavy buffalo, so he kept right after it, jab, jab, jab, until the poor critter toppled from loss of blood and cuts to his vital organs."

Bison in the millions made the Plains Indians strong, allowing them to fight white encroachment on their territory long after resistance had ended in the eastern United States and the South and along the West Coast. Bison meant freedom for the Plains Indians. But dependence on the bison made the Plains Indians vulnerable. Destruction of the buffalo played an important role in subduing the tribes between the Rockies and the Mississippi. Frank Mayer, an 1870s buffalo hunter, said that a high-ranking officer in the plains service told him: "Mayer, there's no two ways about it: either the buffalo or the Indian must go. Only when the Indian becomes absolutely dependent on us for his every need, will we be able to handle him. He's too independent with the buffalo. But if we kill the buffalo we conquer the Indian. It seems a more humane thing to kill the buffalo than the Indian, so the buffalo must go."

Officials at the highest levels of government agreed with this sentiment. "I would not seriously regret the total disappearance of the buffalo from our western plains, in its effect upon the Indians," declared US Interior Secretary Columbus Delano in 1871. "I would regard it rather as a means of hastening their sense of dependence upon the products of the soil and their own labors"—as if hunting massive, horned beasts, killing them, and butchering them was not labor and didn't take years of training for a participant to be adept at it.

The military backed this approach. General William Tecumseh Sherman—who had commanded the northern army's march across Georgia to the sea, wiping out everything in its path, using total war to force the Confederate states into submission—was not about to balk at wiping out a species. He wrote to General Philip Sheridan—a former Civil War officer credited with coining the phrase "The only good Indian is a dead Indian"—that they should "invite all the sportsmen of England and America this fall for a Great Buffalo Hunt and make a grand sweep of them all."

Sheridan carried on the concept of bison destruction as a tactic of war. When the Texas legislature in 1875 prepared to enact a law protecting bison, Sheridan told a joint assembly of the state's house and senate that rather than being blocked from killing bison, market hunters should be supported. "They are destroying the Indian's commissary, and it is a well-known fact that an army losing its base of supplies is placed at a great disadvantage," he said. "Send [the hunters] powder and lead, if you will; for the sake of lasting peace, let them kill, skin and sell until the buffaloes are exterminated. Then your prairies can be covered with speckled cattle and the festive cowboy."

According to Mayer, the military did aid buffalo hunters, or "runners," as the hunters called themselves. "Don't understand that any official action was taken in Washington and directives sent out to kill all the buff on the plains," he wrote in *The Buffalo Harvest*. "Nothing like that happened. What did happen was that army officers in charge of plains operations encouraged the slaughter of buffalo in every possible way. Part of this encouragement was of a practical nature that we runners appreciated. It consisted of ammunition, free ammunition, all you could use, all you wanted, more than you needed. All you had to do to get it was apply at any frontier army post and say you were short of ammunition, and plenty would be given you. I received thousands of rounds this way."

One decade and it was over. Colonel Richard Dodge, in 1882: "Ten years ago the Plains Indians had an ample supply of food. . . . Now everything is gone, and they are reduced to the condition of paupers, without food, shelter, clothing, or any of those necessaries of life which came from the buffalo."

Mayer, in his autobiography, wrote what could well have been a funeral oration for the species that had dominated the Great Plains at the start of one decade and all but disappeared at the start of the next: "The buffalo served his mission, fulfilled his destiny in the history of the Indian, by furnishing him everything he needed—food, clothing, a home, traditions, even a theology. But the buffalo didn't fit in so well with the white man's encroaching civilization—he didn't fit in at all, in fact. He could not be controlled or domesticated. He couldn't be corralled behind wire fences. He was a misfit. So he had to go."

Contemporary commentators attributed the end of Indian resistance to the runners. In his autobiography, "Buffalo" Jones declared,

> The great generals and those in authority in the United States have been credited with subduing the red warriors of the Plains, but such is not the case. The buffalo-hunters conquered the whole Indian race—not by unerring aim at the red devils themselves, while perchance they encircled the camp, or in combat when they often met; but simply by slaying the buffalo, and thereby cutting off their source of supplies. As soon as the red man was compelled to beg or starve, then his proud heart broke, and he pled for mercy at the feet of the paleface; while as long as the buffalo lasted he was richer than a millionaire, defied and baffled the greatest generals and the most formidable armies of the United States and Canada, but at last was compelled to bow to the inevitable buffalo-hunter of no pretensions.

Emanuel Dubbs, an associate of Goodnight's, agreed: "All the danger and hardships suffered by the scouts and soldiers in that milk and water system had no permanent effect in settling the Indian question and a permanent peace. Not until the bravest of all pioneers, the buffalo hunters, disposed of the buffalo forever, and which prevented the Indians obtaining sustenance, when they cut loose from their reservations, was the Indian question settled, and their depredations stopped. Not only that, but a grand fertile country was opened up for settlement."

Red Cloud, a warrior chief among the Lakota people, expressed a more despairing view of the endless slaughter when he gave a speech in 1903 as he stepped down from formal leadership:

> *My sun is set. My day is done. Darkness is stealing over me. Before I lie down to rise no more, I will speak to my people.*
>
> *Hear me, my friends, for it is not the time for me to tell you a lie. The Great Spirit made us, the Indians, and gave us this land we live in. He gave us the buffalo, the antelope, and the deer for food and clothing. We moved on our hunting grounds from the Minnesota to the Platte and from the Mississippi to the great mountains. No one put bounds about us. We were free as the winds and like the eagle, heard no man's commands. . . .*
>
> *The white man came and took our lands from us. They put [us] in bounds and made laws for us. We were not asked what laws would suit us. But the white men made the laws to suit themselves and they compel us to obey them. This is not good for an Indian. . . .*
>
> *Now where the buffalo ranged there are wires on posts that mark the land where the white man labors and sweats to get food from the earth; and in the place of the buffalo there are cattle that must be cared for to keep them alive; and where the Lakota could ride as he wished from the rising to the setting of the sun for days and days on his own lands, now he must go on roads made by the white man; and when he crosses the bounds the white man has set about us, the white man says to us Indians, "You must not be on the lands that are not on the road."*

He summed it up in a single phrase: "The white man has taken our territory and destroyed our game so we must eat the white man's food or die."

After the great destruction of the bison, tribes tended to lose contact with the species that had sustained them for so long. Not until the 1970s did tribes begin trying to revive their age-old link with bison by acquiring their own herds, beginning with the Crow Indians putting bison from Theodore Roosevelt National Park in North Dakota on their reservation in southeastern Montana, on the border with Wyoming. Within twenty years, about twenty-five tribes were herding some 3,600 bison on reservation lands.

The tribes tend to seek bison restoration, in part, as a means and an incentive for cultural renewal, a rising up of an epic past when Indian and bison dominated the West. A new movement in tribal bison restoration began in 1992, when western tribes that had met the year before reconvened to form the InterTribal Bison Cooperative (ITBC; the cooperative was reorganized in 2009 as the InterTribal Buffalo Council). Prior to the creation of the ITBC, tribal bison efforts did not feature cooperation across a broad region. Tribes worked alone, and many lacked expertise in bison management. The ITBC brought a defined purpose to tribal bison initiatives, pledging to "act as a facilitator in coordinating education and training programs, developing marketing strategies, coordinating the transfer of surplus buffalo from national parks to tribal lands, and providing technical assistance to its membership in developing sound management plans that will help each tribal herd become a successful and self-sufficient operation." It is a non-profit organization with a mission, designed to restore bison "to the Indian nations in a manner that is compatible with their spiritual and cultural beliefs and practices." Member tribes choose representatives for the board of directors, and the organization is run by an executive council.

Working with government and private grants and with private donations, the ITBC features four departments—development, for fundraising and publicity; tribal business management, which offers business training and business plans; a quarterly newsletter under publications and cultural education; and technical services, which does research on bison disease, manages congressional funding, and provides assistance and advice on bison care and management as well as other activities.

Under ITBC guidelines, most tribes handle their bison as little as possible, preserving the wild nature of the animals. The council also seeks to work with other local stakeholders, such as cattle ranchers, and to ensure genetic diversity in the herds. A key goal is the distribution of bison meat, which is seen as a healthy source of nutrition for combating diabetes and heart disease, which are major challenges on many reservations. For example, the Cheyenne River Lakota in South Dakota seek to manage their herd in a way that allows every member of the tribe to have at least one meal daily of bison meat.

The ITBC was an immediate success. During its first decade, the number of bison under Indian management went from 1,500 to more than 9,000, and reservation bison pasture increased by 100,000 acres. Today, at least seventy-six Native American tribes from nineteen states are members of the ITBC and run some 20,000 bison on 1 million acres of Indian land.

Tribes also united into regional groups cooperating on bison restoration. In 2008, the Blackfeet of north-central Montana, near Glacier National Park, joined with the Wildlife Conservation Society in visiting other tribes in the region, including those living on the Flathead (Confederated Salish and Kootenai Tribes), Fort Peck, and Fort Belknap Reservations, with visions of cooperating to restore bison and protect their habitat on some 6 million acres of reservation land in the Great Plains. These meetings were called the Elder Dialogues because the discussion of bison restoration began among the elders of the Blackfoot Confederacy. Some involved more than one hundred people, others as few as ten, and they led eleven tribal bands, including the Assiniboine, Gros Ventre, and Lakota, to attend a treaty-planning meeting on June 25 and 26, 2014. Was it coincidence that June 25 marks the date on which Lieutenant Colonel George Custer made a terrible miscalculation at the Little Bighorn? In any event, after this meeting, eight tribal governments sent representatives to the Northern Buffalo Treaty Convention to sign a pact for bison restoration on September 23, 2014, at a site on the Blackfeet Buffalo Pasture near Browning, Montana. The tribal councils for the signing tribes then ratified the treaty, which created tribal alliances for bison restoration, cultural revival, youth education, research, and economic development. Within two years, the treaty was signed by Canadian tribes in Alberta and Saskatchewan.

National parks and refuges cooperate in programs designed to place bison under tribal control. For example, Wind Cave National Park staff have allotted an average of roughly thirty live bison yearly to various tribes since 1987. In 1994, park officials began collaborating on bison management with the InterTribal Bison Cooperative. The US government also allows Salish, Pend d'Oreille, and Kootenai people to hunt a small number of bison on federally administered land each year. Nevertheless, securing bison remains a political challenge for the tribes. For example, at Fort Peck, the Assiniboine reservation, some local ranchers, including Indian ranchers, have opposed releasing the animals for fear of disease transmission to cattle.

Although tribal herds are proliferating across the nation, though primarily in the West, no two herds are alike, says Cristina Mormorunni, director of the conservation advocacy group Indigenous Led, which seeks to grow a buffalo restoration movement under Native American leadership. She is also founder and principal of the conservation-strategy consulting group

TERRAMAR. Formerly director of the Wildlife Conservation Society's Rocky Mountain Program, she has spent twenty-five years working in wildlife conservation, including bison restoration and tribal efforts. "There are tons and tons of variability" in the way each tribe manages its herd, she says. Some tribes speak about economics, others culture. Some tribal governments allow sport hunting of bison by nontribal people, with fees in the thousands of dollars to shoot a trophy bull, while others do not allow outside hunters.

THE CHIPPEWA CREE PEOPLE OF THE ROCKY BOY'S RESERVATION—AT A sprawling 125,000 acres still the smallest of the seven reservations in Montana—are in the process of starting a tribal herd as of this writing in winter 2021. The reservation serves as home to about 6,500 enrolled members of the Chippewa Cree people. Their effort to bring back bison to the reservation, which lies in north-central Montana about ninety miles north of Great Falls, began "a couple years ago," Jason Belcourt, the tribal sustainability coordinator, says. The Chippewa want to restore their relationship with bison and have produced a five-year plan for managing up to thirty head. "We're hoping to grow bison to the point where they can be a real food source for our people," Belcourt says. They want a herd that will sustain a kill of twenty bison yearly, enough to provide food for the people and local stores. The Chippewa, Belcourt says, want to "stand on our own two feet." One way to do so is to rectify the loss of the bison that occurred when Europeans came to North America, which the Chippewa call Turtle Island. "It was really tough when our white brothers came over here and decimated the herds," he explains. "It was the first sin that we did to Turtle Island. A keystone species was taken out. What did we do to the plant life, birds, and other creatures? We created a huge sin against nature. And then we wonder, Why do we have problems like global warming?"

The people of the Rocky Boy's Reservation shared their land with a bison herd in the 1990s but lacked the funds to maintain it and had to give up the animals. In the new effort, which has relied heavily on Belcourt's dedication and perseverance to achieve success, participants formed a board of directors that asked the tribal council—the leadership of the reservation—for permission to purchase bison and for a donation of 1,200 acres of reservation land as a bison reserve. The council gave them the land and the money. The herd directors acquired six bison from American Prairie and five other buffalo offered to them by the Salish-Kootenai. As natural bison habitat, the reservation can provide the herd with the minerals, water, and forage needed for survival. The ITBC, with which Belcourt is affiliated, also helped Rocky Boy's start its bison program. "They are a blessed organization," Belcourt says.

In the eyes of the Chippewa, bison represent food security. "We can't be a healthy people if we don't have our culture," Belcourt says. "The bison reminds us of our language, our culture, of who we are." He points out that the reservation, including its younger members, suffers from a burden of methedrine addiction and a high suicide rate. "We aren't whole because we don't know who we are," Belcourt says. Before European contact, and for two or three centuries afterward, the Chippewa recognized themselves as hunters who—with muscle, lance, and bravery—provided for the needs of their people. Even today, the bison is part of their spiritual life. "One of our biggest ceremonies is the sun dance," Belcourt says. Bison skulls are used as part of the altar. "How can our ceremonies be here and be blessed if we don't have our own landscape?" he asks.

The buffalo also bolster more material needs. Bison meat, Belcourt says, is "definitely healthier" than beef. The Chippewa Cree have a "food sovereignty" program that includes anyone selling food on the reservation and that seeks to ensure that all reservation food is locally sourced. "We are really serious about trying to eat what we grow and grow what we eat," Belcourt says.

The biggest challenge to bison restoration is the agricultural industry, he says. "Cattlemen don't want bison back. How do we flip that table and make a place for bison?" He points out that some ranchers do raise "green cattle"— livestock operations that encompass the needs of wildlife. For example, they use fences with openings large enough for elk and deer to pass through but not cattle, and they use "slick" top and bottom wires, wires without barbs that put wildlife at less risk of injury. "These guys are welcoming prairie dogs," he says, sounding almost incredulous at the idea that cattle raisers would attempt to protect a species that competes with livestock for grassland. "The buffalo need heroes," he adds.

A key issue is how bison advocates can change the cultural mindset of those who feel grasslands are meant for cattle. "Baby steps might be the way,"

Belcourt says, rather than expecting to make leaps or even wide strides. "Get bison on Charles M. Russell National Wildlife Refuge, on every national wildlife refuge, on all unoccupied lands." Currently, if a bison herd wanders beyond fences, "it's going to be destroyed. We've got to rethink land use." The native people that were here lived in balance with nature, he says, but the US government gave them small reservations. Indigenous people, he believes, should sit on every board that oversees land use. "We have not recognized the voice that was here for thousands and thousands of years. Why isn't the native voice heard on federal national parks?"

The tribes, says a biologist long familiar with the bison conundrum but who wants to remain unattributed, "have done a spectacular job setting up herds on tribal lands across the Great Plains." He agrees that bison herds administered by agencies in the Department of the Interior should be managed more like free-roaming herds, rather than treated as captive populations. A refuge as large as the Russell could host bigger herds on large swaths of grassland that allow the animals to be "reconnected ecologically to their environment." He underscores the divisiveness of the bison issue, however, saying that you can find both overwhelming support and overwhelming opposition to putting bison back on the landscape anywhere in Montana. "Bison are the last large ungulates missing from the landscape," he says. The staff of wildlife refuges like the Russell need to discuss whether there is a path to "put bison back" on vacated habitat where they once grazed, bred, and supported the Indian peoples' bison culture. Officials need to figure out what the path forward will be. The Montana state wildlife agency recently stepped away from bison restoration, with officials saying they won't do anything with buffalo for ten years. This withdrawal leaves Interior Department authorities and tribal people to explore next steps without the critical involvement of the agencies that serve the state where so much tribal bison restoration is being pursued.

With bison restoration, Mormorunni says, "there absolutely is opposition and conflict." She cites, for example, ranchers' fear that bison will spread disease to cattle despite a lack of data that such a risk exists anywhere. "But the real conflict is about identity," she says. Ranchers see land being converted, kids leaving. They think Native Americans, conservation interests, and "New West" immigrants are coming for their land. "Conservation is fraught with conflict," she says. Part of the odium is centered on the mere act of bringing in bison to lands used for cattle grazing for decades. "We are rewilding species we don't really live with any more, and further, there are no doubt race and equity issues at play." She adds that bison advocates need to understand the whys and the wherefores of the opposition. "How do you transform it is the crux," she says. "People want to see buffalo again. How do we deal with conflict?" She acknowledges that conflicts over bison restoration also exist within communities, including within tribes. Buffalo advocates haven't even begun to "unpack the layers of conflict," she says. If we want to be part of the solution, "we have to look at the culture behind the issues. At that point, facts get lost. It's not an argument that is won through ration and data." She believes we need to meet people where they are and work collectively to transform conflict if we are to achieve success and conserve the lands and cultures that sustain human communities for the foreseeable future.

Belcourt puts the situation in less sweeping terms: "The cattlemen are so powerful. I've never been political. I don't like politics." But, he says, legislators are for sale. "Why don't the bison buy some?"

As with other Indian nations, the Chippewa Cree worry about the loss of the Old Ways, of tribal traditions and even of the tribal voice. "If we don't do something drastic," Belcourt says, "we're going to lose our language." Although traditions are being transferred to youth through sweat lodge rituals and the sun dance ceremony, this moment in history, when only sixty Cree speakers remain, is perilous for those committed to saving tribal culture. "We're going to have to do some drastic things to save our culture and save the bison," he says, adding, "We're like the buffalo. The only buffalo saved were at Yellowstone. The only Indians were on reservations. When buffalo come home and flourish, our Indian people will flourish."

FAR TO THE SOUTH OF MONTANA, IN THE NORTHEAST CORNER OF OKLA-homa, a slightly older bison restoration program is taking hold. It began in 2016 when the Osage Nation bought Ted Turner's 43,000-acre Bluestem Ranch for $74 million. The purchase was part of an Osage plan to reacquire reservation land they had lost as a result of the 1904 reallotment act, which left them holding only 4 percent of the 1.5 million acres the reservation had previously covered. The purchase of Bluestem not only restores bison to the tribe but also helps restore their landscape.

The Turner ranch, which lies near Pawhuska, Oklahoma, was used for bison and livestock, and some stray bison remained there after the Osage bought it. Around two hundred bison now roam on 3,000 acres of the ranch, according to Jason George, business development specialist for the Osage Nation Department of Natural Resources. Because bison had been there for some years under Turner ownership, the Osage didn't experience the antipathy that bison restoration often generates. Their restoration plan also is linked to the early history of bison recovery, as the US Fish & Wildlife Service has been providing the Osage herd with animals from the Wichita Mountains National Wildlife Refuge, George says. "We are working on getting bison from the Bronx Zoo and around thirty-five head from Colorado State University's herd," he says.

The bison are managed as a conservation herd, says Galen Crum, former chairman of the Osage Ranch Board and now a board consultant. "Animals are currently only removed for management purposes and then used mainly for tribal, cultural, and consumption-opportunity purposes." Because the animals roam freely, visitors driving by the pastures may see them on the open range. "We are working on building a recreational/educational area out at the ranch that will have classrooms and meeting space, as well as arbors for family outings and picnics around a large pond," George says. "Some of our bison will be pastured on smaller acreage close to this area, which will hopefully allow them to be seen more often." The Osage Nation has plans for using the bison as tribal food, though the herd is new enough that a program for producing bison meat is still in the planning stage. "We are in the conservation mode right now, and we will move into providing food for tribal members eventually," George says.

The greatest management effort is probably focused on the bulls, because they can be challenging to handle and contain. "The biggest and strongest bulls will run the other bulls off," Galen Crum explained in an article in the *Osage News*. "Those loner bulls who get run off are called bachelor bulls." The bachelors suffer a sort of selective fate: "We'll send bachelor bulls to the butcher because they tend to get into mischief," Crum added. Moreover, bulls are not allowed to fully mature, in much the same way that bulls are managed on The Nature Conservancy reserves. "Fully mature bulls will become a nuisance and like to get out of the pastures and roam the roads, where they can become a major hazard to traffic," George says.

The Osage Nation includes about twenty-four thousand registered members. The nation has long had financial resources that other tribes lack, thanks to oil discovered on Osage land in the 1920s. The money flowing in has diminished, but members still receive royalty checks. Moreover, the Osage have exclusive legal authority over their land. This status is likely one reason that the Osage did not face opposition to their bison plans. "I don't really remember too much issue with setting up our bison at the ranch," George says. "Since we have both cattle and bison, I don't think many people had a problem with them, plus what we do on our own land isn't up for dispute by anyone outside the tribe."

What is the ultimate, long-term goal for the Osage people regarding bison? "I think the goals of the Osage Nation and the goals of the ITBC are very closely aligned," George says. "Not only are we looking to preserve cultural and spiritual relationships with the bison, we are also looking at their restoration as an ecological benefit as well. The impact that they can have on the land is wide-ranging, and we are looking to collaborate with colleges and organizations such as the Wildlife Conservation Society to test and monitor these benefits."

WORKING ON BISON IS ONE OF THE WILDLIFE CONSERVATION SOCIETY'S longest-standing projects, Mormorunni says. She served as the regional director of the society's Rocky Mountain Program beginning in 2018 but left in early 2022 to direct Indigenous Led. She has worked since 2018 with the four nations of the Blackfoot Confederacy, among other Indian nations. The idea of free-roaming buffalo herds across the Confederacy is not new, Mormorunni says. The society has been working with the Confederacy for more than a decade, beginning when the Blackfeet Nation started building a conservation bison herd around 2011. Mormorunni looked at what the society does in terms of science, partnerships, and other activities. Studying the Blackfoot effort—the Iinnii Initiative—to bring back bison, she wanted to go "deeper and wider," developing a strategy to restore the species to the vast scale it once had "by building a bigger tent for the ecological and cultural restoration of bison at a continental level."

The Blackfeet Nation abuts Glacier National Park to the east and Canada to the north. Covering 3,000 square miles, the reservation is twice the size of Glacier National Park. The Blackfeet Nation has 16,500 enrolled members, headquartered at Browning, Montana. They were the originators of the Elder Dialogues. The Blackfeet Nation is part of the Blackfoot Confederacy, composed of tribes culturally related to the Blackfeet—the Siksika First Nation, the Piikani First Nation, or Piegans, and the Kainai First Nation, or Blood; these three hail from southern Alberta in Canada.

The Blackfeet have no specific population goal for bison. The current plan for the bison is to let them roam openly on Blackfeet land, but realistically, fences will be needed for the time being, Mormorunni says. The reservation is next to Glacier, and bison might wander into the park, but eventually they will hit a fence. The Blackfeet Nation also owns a separate, economic herd.

In 2009, the four tribes of the Blackfoot Confederacy created the Iinnii Initiative—*iinnii* is Blackfoot for bison and is pronounced *ee-nee*—to return free-roaming bison to their traditional homelands. The main goals of the initiative are to restore buffalo, conserve traditional lands, protect Blackfoot culture, and create a home to which buffalo can return.

The Iinnii Initiative also seeks to engage tribal youth with bison. This connection is critical to the tribe, as it is to other Indian nations. "The Blackfeet people believe that when the ancient buffalo return to their homeland, so too will the Blackfeet language and culture," according to the Blackfeet Nation website. The Iinnii Initiative, Mormorunni says, is centered in connecting youth to buffalo culture and also to horse culture. Doing so can be accomplished by creating a link between youths and elders, by sharing Blackfoot knowledge, stories, and ceremony, and by engaging in scientific research on bison and the prairie ecosystem.

The challenge for the Blackfeet and their allies, and for anyone attempting to restore bison, Mormorunni says, is achieving wild, free-roaming herds at the scale required by ecology or culture (a question investigated more extensively in chapter 10). How we wrestle with it, she says, is at the crux of our crisis—in biodiversity, in politics, in culture. "We've lost our way. We no longer remember what it is to live with buffalo as a relative; we no longer remember or know what it is to live in reciprocal relationship with the natural world. The impact of our current worldview on nature and human well-being is evidenced in every aspect of our lives, which is why the idea of imagining living with 30 million bison again is so compelling, as it would need a paradigm shift" in how we manage land. "We really need to rethink our relationship to the world," she says. It's a philosophical question—are we really satisfied where we are? Because given the current state of the world, with species loss, habitat destruction, and climate change, if we don't alter our behavior and our status on the globe, "it's really game over," she says.

Meanwhile, the Blackfoot Confederacy is moving forward with their program for bison restoration. In June, the Blackfeet Nation holds a community buffalo celebration—Iinnii Days. In addition to strategy sessions, celebrations, and storytelling, the community engages in a cultural harvest of buffalo. Youth are taught how to field dress a bison and how to use every part. "It's huge" in its cultural impact, Mormorunni says. Tribal culture goes hand in hand with the bison, coupling the learning of the Blackfoot cultural practice and language with using bison. "Language holds the memory," she says.

The Blackfeet Nation is also playing hardball in the political arena. In recent years they led a challenge to federal plans to allow drilling for oil in the Badger–Two Medicine area, a mountainous zone sacred to the Blackfeet. Legal action with Blackfeet participation resulted in cancellation of the last oil and gas leases in Badger–Two Medicine. Now the Blackfeet Nation can consider restoring bison to this area.

History does seem to be turning back on itself, entering a period of restoration for bison and for Native American cultures. One development symbolizes this transition: Recently the Confederated Salish and Kootenai Tribes brought to the Flathead Reservation, their home in Montana, eighty bison from Canada's Elk Island National Park in Alberta. These animals are descended from the Pablo-Allard herd that, to William Hornaday's intense disappointment, was shipped to Canada during the first two decades of the twentieth century. Not only are the bison coming home from Elk Island, but in another sweeping change the federal government is turning over the National Bison Range to the Salish-Kootenai. These animals include descendants of the Conrad herd of North Dakota, the Corbin herd of New Hampshire, and the Goodnight herd of Texas (see chapter 3).

Indian people also are a critical part of the bison story north of the Medicine Line, as tribal people call the border with Canada. In the late nineteenth century, when the US military was charged with implementing the sweep of Manifest Destiny across the continent, and tribes were devastated by the loss of the buffalo, Sitting Bull—whose name, Tatanka Iyotanka, carried

the meaning not of sitting but of immovable resolve—refused to surrender. In the late 1870s, not long after he witnessed the battle that destroyed
George Custer, Sitting Bull crossed the Medicine Line into the Grand-
mother's Country (in reference to Queen Victoria), hoping to find bison
for the sustenance of his band of Lakota, the Hunkpapa. But the bison had
been wiped out north of the border, too, and, finally, his people starving,
Sitting Bull became the last of the Lakota to turn in his rifle to the US Army
and surrender to reservation life. History seemed to have come to an end
for the Plains Indian bison hunters and for the bison themselves. But as in
the United States, so too in Canada and Mexico bison recovery has become
the aim of federal and local governments, turning a page for a new chapter
on bison survival.

CHAPTER 7

LOST HERDS:
MEXICO AND CANADA

The late 1970s: Rumors of a free-roaming bison herd that ranges across the US-Mexico border leads Raul Valdez, a wildlife-management professor at New Mexico State University, to phone his friend and former student Andrew Sandoval to see if he would be interested in joining a bison roundup. Sandoval is completing a master's degree in wildlife management at Colorado State University, where he has been studying desert bighorn sheep, a slowly vanishing species. He has learned to drug them with a dart gun so he can fit them with electronic collars for tracking. Valdez wants to enlist Sandoval's skills to capture some of the bison.

The plan was initiated by a former student of Valdez's, Jose "Pepe" Treviño, who has studied pronghorn in Mexico and has recently become the first director of a newly created state wildlife department in Chihuahua, Mexico. He wants to capture some of the bison that are roaming the border and take them farther south.

The border area lies on the periphery of bison range. Buffalo have not been recorded there for so long that some biologists doubt that they ever lived there. But here, emerging from the shadows of history, is a small herd, defying scientific knowledge. People living in the area of course know about the animals. The US rancher on whose land the bison sometimes graze, for example, considers them "an inconvenience," Sandoval says, and would be pleased to see the last of them. To the wildlife biologists, the herd is an opportunity to restore to northern Mexico a species long thought lost.

The opening scene of the ensuing drama is the area of New Mexico called the Bootheel—a chunk of land that extends from the United States into Mexico. The would-be bison capturers, including Sandoval, plunge southward from Antelope Wells in a caravan of two 1.5-ton flatbed trucks with wooden frames to contain the bison. Sandoval looks at the wooden barriers and doubts they will stand up to the assault of a freedom-loving buffalo. A third vehicle also is on the trail, a Volkswagen Thing, a sort of VW version of a Jeep or Land Rover that is enjoying brief popularity in the 1970s. The drivers, biologists, and vehicles press on into Mexico, launching an exploit reminiscent of the bison captures of Charles Goodnight and Buffalo Jones a century before but forgetting, perhaps, the difficulties that Goodnight and Jones experienced in herding bison—the animals' rebellion, their tendency to die en route.

About ten miles south of Antelope Wells the hunting party finds the bison moving across an open grassland punctuated with clumps of desert brush. The land is level but riven with gullies. Sandoval, Pepe, and a driver get into the VW Thing. Sandoval is armed with a dart gun from which he will shoot double-barbed darts that can hold 60 cc of xylazine, a drug used to sedate mammals, including pets and livestock. The drug was provided by the Chihuahua wildlife agency, but unfortunately xylazine cannot immobilize animals unless combined with an analgesic such as etorphine, a drug unavailable in Chihuahua at that time. The biologists decided to work with what they had. "So off we went, hi-ho Silver, after the buffalo," Sandoval, now a consultant for a global corporation in Mexico and a manager of his family ranch in New Mexico, recalls today.

They target yearling animals, assuming that the flatbed trucks cannot hold full-grown bison. Sandoval's aim is true, but the bison aren't cooperating. Some have two or three darts in them. They may slow down, but none fall. "So we reconvened and scratched our heads," Sandoval recalls. "What do we do?"

Pepe says he'll go to the nearest ranch house and talk to the vaqueros. He returns with about five of them. The plan: rope the sedated yearlings.

Sadly, no one knows how easily a bison dies when roped around the neck. The first one lassoed dies within a minute. After that loss, the vaqueros take more care and succeed in bringing down six live yearlings, scattered over a square mile of prairie. The biologists go to work, hobbling the bison with ropes and blindfolding them. The other members of the herd run out of sight, somewhere beyond the horizon.

The next problem is how to load the bison onto the trucks, the beds of which are four feet off the ground. Pepe asks the vaqueros if they have lumber. They do. So the team rigs a ramp with two-inch boards, mounts a pulley at the front end of the bed, runs a rope to the legs of the bison, and uses horses for pulling each bison up into the trucks. The hobbles aren't removed during transport, for fear that the bison, once liberated, will destroy the trucks. Sandoval also worries that the bison might aspirate and die, but they don't. Instead, they are released about two hours south of where they were captured, in the vicinity of Janos in the state of Chihuahua.

After that, these bison, too, disappear into the past. Pepe later tells Sandoval that two more of the yearlings died after release. Of the three survivors, Sandoval knows nothing.

THE BISON OF NORTHERN MEXICO WERE A MYSTERY THROUGHOUT MUCH OF the twentieth century, animals lost to the knowledge of even trained biologists. In 1987, nearly ten years after the bison roundup, Gerardo Ceballos, a wildlife-management professor at the Institute of Ecology at the National Autonomous University of Mexico in Mexico City, went into Chihuahua in northeastern Mexico to survey a colony of black-tailed prairie dogs that covered some 150,000 acres of arid grassland. The town was a relic from the 1800s, from a time before prairie dogs had been nearly wiped out by poisons and habitat loss. It was the largest remaining prairie dog town on the continent, an artifact that could inspire the dreams and imaginations of people who knew that at one time, in the western territories of the United States, a massive prairie dog metropolis might run 250 miles long and 100 wide, with 400 million of the plump ground squirrels running among the mounds of earth that marked the entrances to their burrows. With the help of bison, these animals can create an ecosystem all their own. The process begins when bison (or even cattle) graze an area close to the ground, eliminating tall grass (see chapter 9 for details on this foraging approach). Prairie dogs cannot function in tall grass, but when the grass is trimmed, they can move in. "But of course, because of the burrowing activities of the prairie dogs, the plants have a higher nutritional value within the edges of the prairie dog towns—the newest parts of the towns—and this attracts herbivores, including bison," says biologist Rurik List. Towns also provide habitat for weasel-like black-footed ferrets, which feed primarily on prairie dogs; for rattlesnakes; for burrowing owls, barely larger than sparrows and nesting in the burrows; and for badgers, coyotes, wolves, pronghorn, deer—all part of the prairie dog world.

One could say that Ceballos discovered the continent's largest prairie dog town, because he brought it to the attention of other scientists, although local residents were familiar with it. They also spoke of something else, something larger, something of historic proportions—a herd of bison that grazed both sides of the nearby border. Hearing rumors of the herd, Ceballos traveled to the Berendo Ranch, which was alleged bison habitat. An hour after he got there, he saw them. "It was like being transported back 100 years in time," he told a reporter for *Wildlife Conservation* magazine. "Huge colonies of prairie dogs, bison, a few pronghorn antelope. It was a lost world. This is the kind of discovery that a biologist dreams about and very rarely makes."

A decade later, in 1998, Rurik List, now a professor at Gerardo Ceballos's lab at the National Autonomous University of Mexico's Institute of Ecology, visited Chihuahua to study prairie dogs for his PhD. Ceballos had told him about the bison, and he learned from members of the Border Patrol that they still saw the animals every now and then. List flew over the area in an airplane and spotted the Janos-Hidalgo herd, named after the Mexican municipality of Janos, which borders New Mexico's Hidalgo County. This transborder expanse marks where they roamed. "The question came to mind, What the hell are those bison doing here?" List says. "Where did they come from?"

List, Ceballos, and other colleagues delved into those questions, looking at archaeological materials and historical records dating back to the Spanish conquistadors. They found evidence of bison in northern Mexico going back centuries. They probably vanished there, as they did in so many places, at the end of the nineteenth century. One telling historical record dates to the end of bison survival in the region. General Lew Wallace, a veteran of the US Civil War who would gain lasting fame after he wrote the novel *Ben-Hur* in 1880, went to Mexico in 1866 as a secret envoy to the Juaristas—a political faction that wanted to restore Benito Juárez to the presidency of Mexico, from which he had been ousted by the French. Wallace's mission would prove successful in 1867, when Juárez returned to power. While en route from Monterrey to Chihuahua City for secret meetings, Wallace stopped off in the grasslands surrounding the town of Parras, about sixty miles west of Saltillo in the southern part of the state of Coahuila, to hunt bison with local ranchers and his traveling companion, an army colonel. They located a herd. When Wallace asked a ranchero how many were in the herd, he replied, "Caramba, señor. We cannot kill them all before night." Kill them all. So now we know what happened to Mexico's bison, if not on that day, soon.

Wallace chased down a bison cow. As a right-handed man riding on the left side of the buffalo, he found that he could not properly aim his Winchester rifle. He braced the weapon across his saddle and drew his pistol—"a Smith & Wesson, the best of revolvers then, yet not near as good as now; for that I was in place. Forward again, and closer in—closer—now, fire! The bullet lodged in the shoulder. Again, and in the heart; hurrah! My horse shied; the rifle fell to the ground; I barely escaped tumbling after; the victim moaned, staggered, stumbled, fell."

Wallace's account of the hunt can be found in a book called *Mexican Game Trails: Americans Afield in Old Mexico, 1866–1940*. The editors noted that "the bison were extirpated from Mexico shortly after Wallace's encounter with them, and almost nothing is known about the size and extent of those southern herds. Indeed, some mammalogists have questioned whether bison even occurred south of the Rio Grande."

List, Ceballos, and biologists from institutions in the United States, including Montana State University and the Turner Endangered Species Fund, established that bison had been "an integral part of southwestern grasslands." Archaeological remains dated back as far as 1,300 years. The earliest historical report they found for northeastern Mexico dated to the seventeenth century, written by Franciscan friars who found bison in the Monterrey Valley. A report from northwestern Mexico placed bison there as early as 1565. Several reports from the nineteenth century indicated their presence in northeastern Mexico into at least the second half of the 1800s.

The question remained: Where the hell did the Janos herd come from? The researchers wrote, "Apparently bison were extirpated from Coahuila toward the second half of the 19th century, but whether they persisted that long in the Janos-Casas Grandes region in Chihuahua is less clear. We think it most likely that bison disappeared from the Janos region after 1820 and that the present herd is derived from reintroduced animals." After sorting through various reports on the origin of the bison, the researchers concluded that the animals likely came originally from the Grand Canyon Cattle Company in Arizona in 1924, starting with a dozen bison calves shipped to the company's affiliated ranch in Mexico. In 1941, fifteen bison from the Wichita Mountains National Wildlife Refuge in Oklahoma—descendants of the first bison reintroduced into the wild (see chapter 3)—were released into the Janos herd, with eighteen more in 1945. In 1949, fifteen bison, yearlings and two-year-olds, from the House Rock Ranch in northern Arizona were turned over to Fort Huachuca, Arizona, and sent to Mexico in the mid-1950s. These animals included bison descended from members of the Buffalo Jones herd.

The researchers' work attracted the attention of the International Union for the Conservation of Nature (IUCN), which invited List and Ceballos to be part of the IUCN's North American Bison Specialist Group, a coalition of biologists focused on bison research and restoration. The researchers ran surveys of Janos-Hidalgo. The bison herd there is one of only five truly free-ranging herds in North America, List says. They roam with no limits or constraints, unlike at Yellowstone National Park, where bison often are shot or sent to slaughter if they leave the park (see chapter 9).

Work with Mexico's bison soon bore fruit for wildlife conservation. On November 28, 2009, twenty-three bison from Wind Cave National Park in South Dakota, after two weeks in quarantine, were released into the short-grass prairie of Janos. Several days later, on December 8, a presidential decree established the bison habitat as the Janos Biosphere Reserve—the first federally protected area in Mexico designed to preserve native grassland. The reserve encompasses 1.2 million acres, including 543,000 acres of imperiled grassland.

Mexico's protected lands, including the biosphere reserve, are not owned by the national government. The story of the nation's complex system of land ownership and administration begins with the 1910 Mexican Revolution, which was predicated on demands made by landless peasants for property. The revolution was followed by agrarian reform. The government expropriated land from large private owners and gave the land to peasants to form communal holdings called *ejidos*. The supply of land ran out before the demand for it did, so in the 1930s the government of President Lázaro Cárdenas allocated remote federal lands to the ejidos, "leading to the settlement and exploitation of the Mexican frontier," List reported in an article he cowrote with ornithologist Patricia Manzano-Fischer. "Today, no federal land is large enough to figure in the conservation of Mexican wildlands. Indeed, the settlement of these areas has had far-reaching impacts on natural systems—further exacerbated by regulations that required the clearing of native vegetation and continuous exploitation of the cleared land."

In Mexico, 11.7 percent of protected land lies in national parks that were established on ejido, private, and Indigenous lands without compensation for the owners. "These landowners retained title to their property but restrictions on use were imposed, resulting in less available area for people to make a living, and often leading to lingering resentment," wrote List and Manzano-Fischer. Owners responded by ignoring the restrictions, which were poorly enforced, and engaging in illegal logging, hunting, and other resource destruction. "The result is a loss of biodiversity to such an extent that sometimes national parks are more degraded than adjacent non-protected areas," they noted. Grizzly bears, gray wolves, and the imperial woodpecker became extinct in the region and, ultimately, in Mexico. Today, List says, the once-sprawling prairie dog community, a victim of habitat loss to ranching and of prolonged drought, is down to only 12,000 acres, a shadow of itself and yet—sad commentary on prairie dog status—probably still one of the largest prairie dog communities on the continent.

In the 1970s, the concept of biosphere reserves brought a change in how the land was administered. Under the older system, parks were created to protect attractive landscapes. Under the new plan, land managers selected areas based on ecosystem representation. Strict restrictions on owner activities were replaced with support of sustainable development in ways designed to achieve both conservation and economic goals, wrote List and Manzano-Fischer, "the idea being that unless people are included in conservation efforts, protecting these areas for the long term is impossible." By the early 2000s, Mexico was creating biosphere reserves chosen for their biological significance. The reserves soon outnumbered national parks, tallying nearly 70 percent of protected areas in Mexico. The land remains in private ownership, List explains, and the owners still must practice certain restrictions on what they can do with the land, but their economic interests are also taken into consideration. "Their activities have to be compatible with conservation, so no new settlements, no paved roads," he says. About thirteen thousand people live in the Janos reserve area, Ceballos says.

The Janos's status as a biosphere reserve is spurring wildlife restoration. About fifty gray wolves roam the reserve, part of a reintroduction program. Ceballos is hoping to reintroduce grizzly bears and elk. And bison are doing well. Mexico now has thirty-three bison herds, List says, though thirty-one of those are commercial herds. Only two herds, each a distinct population, serve as conservation herds, roaming free on thousands of grassland acres. None of these populations are genetically pure, a recent study discovered, making the implications of this genetic challenge a subject of ongoing concern among bison specialists, List says. More studies are needed to determine the full genetic status of the Janos herds. The 23 bison from Wind Cave, released in 2009, now number 300. Total bison—commercial and conservation—in Mexico, List says, is about 1,500 animals. Commercial herds are scattered across northern Mexico and into central Mexico, and not all are in original bison range.

The bison thrive in Mexico despite being locked out of their range in the United States by private fences and by the US border wall. A New Mexico rancher used a helicopter to drive bison from his ranch across the border into Mexico and fenced them out. In New Mexico, bison are categorized as livestock, and ranchers are taxed for bison on their land as if the animals were cattle. Ranchers also have to pay for expenses that "their" bison incur if they destroy property. In Mexico, the bison is a protected species.

Ceballos says that his negotiations with Mexican ranchers involve both confrontation and concession, though he says that the ranchers generally don't oppose bison on their land. He thinks local support for bison would increase if bison-hunting permits could be sold, bringing in about $5,000 each. He also thinks that working with ranchers will create agreements that will provide room for 1,000 more bison. Ranchers, he contends, are less of a problem than the border wall. Since the Trump presidency, he says, biologists have made no progress in transborder protection of bison and other wildlife that used to range back and forth across the border. Studies show that the border wall cuts across the ranges of 1,506 native terrestrial and freshwater species, including 1,077 animal species and 429 plant species. Although the IUCN has listed sixty-two of these species as vulnerable, endangered, or critically endangered, the US Congress, during the Trump administration, passed a law that waived any regulations that might slow construction of the border wall, including the Endangered Species Act and the National Environmental Policy Act, which requires studies of the environmental impacts of any projects funded by the federal government. The wall is essentially fragmenting wildlife habitat along its entire length, currently several hundred miles. "It's an environmental disaster," Ceballos, one of the authors of the paper cited here, says.

Rurik List sees three major issues as key challenges to bison restoration in Mexico. The first is a disease caused by *Mycoplasma bovis*, a bacterium common among cattle but harmless to them. The disease is deadly to bison, however, infecting the lungs and causing the animals to cough as they slowly suffocate and waste away. According to the *New York Times* in March 2022, it was first documented in bison in 2013, but little is known about how it is spread and what can be done about it. There is no cure and no vaccination against it, List says. The US Department of Agriculture has labeled it an emerging bison disease that could kill an estimated 25 percent of each infected herd. No one knows how many herds across the continent are infected. One veterinarian reported twenty-two diseased herds in South Dakota in 2022. The Tallgrass Prairie National Preserve, in Kansas, lost twenty-two bison—close to 25 percent of its herd—but the disease has not been reported in other bison herds managed by the National Park Service. Like List, bison ranchers in the United States and Mexico are worried about the threat the disease poses.

Another of List's key concerns is limited to Mexico. He contends that the legal status of bison in Mexico as a protected species confuses the issue of how bison can be used, making the process of persuading ranchers to raise bison more of a challenge. It is not clear whether ranchers can allow hunting of bison on their land or can sell them for meat. Bison advocates, such as Ceballos and List, would like to restore bison on their original range. This goal is in the planning stage. At present, List says, they are focused on trying to persuade owners "to take out cattle and replace them with bison." Doing so would be good for grassland restoration, he says, but it is possible only if owners have certainty about the uses of bison.

He also is concerned that in the area of Mexico suitable for bison recovery, only wealthy landowners will be able to cooperate. Mexico, he says, no longer has huge expanses of land where bison can roam as they did in old times. Success for bison requires the participation of many landowners if bison are to have the room they need. Bison advocates are trying to get owners to take down fences, "but we are not anywhere near" achieving this goal, List says.

THE BISON OF MEXICO AND THE UNITED STATES SOUTH OF THE BORDER WITH Canada are plains bison. Natives of prairie regions but also highly adaptable, the plains bison lived all across the continent, from northern Mexico into western Canada, where they rarely ventured north beyond central Alberta and Saskatchewan. In Canada they were wiped out, just as they were in the United States and Mexico, hunted for hides and meat markets. When the last of the large bison herds was demolished in Montana in 1883, hunters persuaded themselves that the animals were not extinct but had gone north. But no. "Eighteen eighty-three was the last year of buffalo," wrote historian Martin Garretson. "Many have been the stories told by old hunters that year, a vast herd numbering between fifty and eighty thousand buffalo crossing the Yellowstone to Fort Keogh going north over the British Line and never returning. The fact is, very few if any escaped the cordon of hide hunters that lined the Missouri River, but were all killed before they could cross." Plains bison disappeared from the Canadian range by 1879, four years before the last large herd was wiped out in the US territories.

The history of US and Canadian bison intersects at the point where destruction of bison was yielding to recovery. It begins with a familiar herd, the Pablo-Allard bison, but is told with a slightly different twist by residents of the Flathead Reservation in Montana (see chapter 3 for a different version of the following origin story). As the history of the plains bison was coming to a close in Canada in the 1870s, a Pend d'Oreille man in Montana, Atatitsa (Peregrine Falcon Robe), suggested to the council of tribal leaders that they locate a bison herd, separate out a herd of calves, and drive them over the mountains to the Flathead Reservation. This idea was radical in Pend d'Oreille terms, because the tribal bison culture taught that capturing bison was ethically wrong. But times were changing, the dwindling of bison was causing intertribal conflict—something had to be done to address the current crisis.

After three days of discussion about the proposal, the council could not reach consensus on what to do, as their rules of government required. Atatitsa withdrew his request. However, a few years later, as the bison herds bottomed out, the council gave Atatitsa's son, Latatitsa (Little Peregrine Robe) permission to round up bison calves. He did, and he herded them over the mountains. What number he started with is not recorded, but he reached the Flathead Reservation with about half a dozen calves. He raised them on land around his mother's home on the Flathead River, and the six became thirteen. One day, when Latatitsa was away from home for a time, his stepfather, Samwel—a.k.a. Walking Coyote—sold the bison to Michel Pablo and Charles Allard, which is where this rendition of the story about Walking Coyote begins to converge with the version related in chapter 3. Walking Coyote eventually paid off Latatitsa for the bison, but the animals were now the property of Pablo and Allard, who, in 1893, added to those animals another twenty-six bison, allegedly purebred, from Buffalo Jones. The herd led a productive life on the grasslands of the Flathead Reservation, growing to hundreds.

As related in chapter 3, Allard died, and Pablo took possession of his own share of the herd. When, in 1904, the US Congress passed a law that would break up the Flathead Reservation in Montana, subdividing the land with fences, the reservation was home to the largest plains bison herd in the world, the more than six hundred animals owned by Michel Pablo. He recognized that he was going to lose his bison pasture and offered to sell the animals to the US government, which said, "Nope." So he offered the entire herd to Canada, where the government, with some lobbying by wildlife advocates, agreed to buy the animals. William Hornaday, a devoted US bison advocate and director of the Bronx Zoo, had been eager for the United States to buy them and must have been pale with distress when he wrote about Canada's purchase in the *Annual Report of the American Bison Society, 1905–1907*:

> *The Canadian Bison Herd.—The most important event of 1907 in the life history of the American Bison was the action of the Canadian Government in purchasing the entire Pablo-Allard herd of* six hundred and twenty-eight *animals, and transporting* 398 *of them to Elk Island Park, Canada. . . . The Canadian Government deserves to be sincerely congratulated upon its wisdom, its foresight and its*

*genuine enterprise in providing $157,000 for the purchase of the Pablo herd, in
addition to the cost of transporting the animals, and fencing Elk Island Park.*

But it must have been with relief that he added: "The friends of the Bison
may indeed be thankful that the great northwestern herd is not to be scattered to the ends of the earth, and finally disappear in the unstable hands
of private individuals." The shipment of the Pablo herd to Canada, which
transferred a few score bison at a time, took about five years to complete. In
all, Canada purchased 708 Pablo buffalo.

The bison arrived by rail at Elk Island National Park, which lies about
twenty-five miles east of Edmonton, Alberta, and was fenced to protect the
last free-ranging elk population of the prairies. The lieutenant governor and
his wife were on hand to see and photograph the unloading of 190 bison on
June 3, 1907. At that time, bison lived in only one Canadian park, Rocky
Mountains Park, which was Canada's first national park. When the Pablo
bison were being unloaded, Rocky Mountains, renamed Banff in 1930, covered 4,900 square miles, a figure cut nearly in half by subsequent legislation.
Its sixty-some bison were confined in a paddock and not permitted to roam
wild, but these animals allowed the park to boast that it was home to Canada's largest bison herd. Clearly, that claim would now transfer to Elk Island,
which encompassed only 11 square miles (it was later expanded to today's 75
square miles). The intent was to let the bison roam the entire park. Given
the park's small size, a boxcar of bison from the first Pablo shipment was
sent to Rocky Mountains in exchange for seven bulls to enhance the Pablo
herd with new genes.

In October 1907, a second shipment arrived at Elk Island, bringing the
total number of bison to 377 and crowding the tiny park. The solution was
already under way: the government had established a new reserve—Buffalo
National Park—near Wainwright, Alberta, specifically for the Pablo bison.
The new park was not fenced and ready for buffalo until November 1909,
when all but forty-five bison were removed by railroad from Elk Park. Subsequent shipments of Pablo bison were sent directly to Buffalo National
Park. Two years later, Canada reported to the American Bison Society that
the nation now possessed 1,006 bison, with 27 held at Rocky Mountains in
a paddock, 61 at Elk Island, and 918 at Buffalo. Canada began distributing
bison to various parks in former bison range. In the 1911 annual report of

the American Bison Society, Canadian officials reported, "It is observed with satisfaction in Canada that the efforts . . . to preserve this, the most conspicuous and characteristic game animal of pioneer days on the western plains, are being followed with appreciative interest, not only by her own citizens, but by many in the neighboring Republic." By 1915, Buffalo National Park alone was home to 2,000 bison. Four years later, the Buffalo, Rocky Mountains, and Elk Island populations tallied 4,033. At that time, Yellowstone's herd was still fewer than 200. Since that time, buffalo from Elk Island have been used to populate areas ranging from western to eastern Canada, and from parks in the United States to reserves in Europe.

In Canada, agricultural development overwhelmed the bison's prairie habitat more than a century ago. As in the United States, agriculture poses a stalwart obstacle to bison recovery. "The biggest hurdle today is the protectionist attitude of cattle ranchers," says Wes Olson, who grew up in the foothills of western Alberta and served thirty-two years as a national park warden, including many years at Elk Island, where about 60 percent of his time was dedicated to bison management and research. Recently, he and his wife, photographer Johane Janelle, produced a book on bison ecology. Ranchers, Olson says, don't want to see bison expanding onto provincial lands.

He explains that after the Dust Bowl period in the 1930s, Canada sought to restore farmland under the Prairie Farm Rehabilitation Act, which created huge tracts of land for the use of farmers and ranchers. The government closed the tracts in 2020, but retained ownership of the land. Cattle growers can still use the land, but they now have to hire their own cowboys and maintain infrastructure. The community pastures range from 50,000 to 70,000 acres and would be prime plains bison habitat, Olson says, but ranchers resist sharing these lands with bison mainly because many ranchers own more cattle than they can keep on their own land. Olson compares it to federal grazing allotments in the United States on land administered by the Bureau of Land Management and the US Forest Service: ranchers there, too, don't want to give up the public land that they lease because without it, most big ranchers could not maintain their herds. "It all goes back to habitat," Olson says. "Without that, ranchers are doomed." He maintains that bison restoration is dependent on finding ways for cooperation between individuals with a stake in bison recovery and government agencies that administer public lands, agriculture, and wildlife conservation.

Another source of doom hangs over bison, whether in Canada, the United States, or Mexico. After the US Civil War, the livestock industry experienced a burst of growth that attracted investors from the East and from Europe, who expected to get rich from raising cattle. Ranching expanded from Texas into the central and northern plains, with Texans bringing upward of 10 million cattle and a million horses northward. In Canada, western grasslands became cattle range, and bison not only were squeezed out but also became the victims of lethal cattle diseases, such as tuberculosis and brucellosis. These diseases infected thousands of plains bison at Buffalo National Park. When the park was turned into Canadian Forces Base Wainwright, in the 1940s, the nearly seven thousand bison living in the former park had to go. Where they went marked a major management error that threatened the survival of another lost bison herd.

TWO CANADIAN WILDLIFE BIOLOGISTS IN 1959 FLEW OVER THE REMOTE northwestern region of Wood Buffalo National Park, which covers 11,070,321 acres of boreal forest, nearly five times the size of Yellowstone National Park, making it the largest national park in North America. Straddling the border of Alberta and the Northwest Territories, it is larger than Switzerland. From the plane, the biologists scanned the land below—dark stands of evergreen forests broken by stretches of meadows and wetlands—and saw moving across the meadows large animals that shouldn't be there: a herd of purebred wood bison whose existence until then was unknown, at least to science.

The wood bison is bulkier than the plains bison, with a less rounded, more squarish hump. The heaviest of them might outweigh the heaviest plains bison by a couple hundred pounds, putting a large wood bison at slightly more than a ton. They lack the shaggy forequarters of plains bison, their hair a more uniform length over the entire body. Some biologists believe they are a subspecies, or breed, of bison separate from the plains buffalo. Others think the wood bison's large size is an example of Bergmann's rule at work, an ecological tenet that says that at the cold, northern extreme of their range, individuals of a given species will be larger than their southern kin, because a larger body allows a warm-blooded animal like a mammal to do a more efficient job of staying warm. The argument about the wood bison's taxonomic status remains unsettled, but in any event, it certainly looks like a different animal than the plains bison. The two animals also display some behavioral differences, and, left to their own preferences, they live in different habitats and under different environmental conditions. Most noticeably, the highest part of the hump rises up forward of the front legs in the wood bison, while in the plains bison the highest part of the hump is over the forelegs.

The wood bison had plenty of opportunity to obey Bergmann's rule, as it ranged through large portions of northern Alberta, British Columbia, and Saskatchewan, throughout Yukon, into southern and central Alaska, and across a large portion of the Northwest Territories, all to the north of the plains bison's northernmost reach. This area lies in the heart of Canada's vast sweep of boreal forests, dominated by spruce trees and other evergreens. J. Dewey Soper, a Canadian zoologist and Arctic explorer who became the Canadian Wildlife Service's chief federal wildlife officer for Alberta, Northwest Territories, and Yukon in 1948, estimated that wood bison in the early 1800s numbered about 168,000 animals, a minute number compared to the vast number of plains bison. Uncontrolled hunting, changes in habitat, and severe winters drove down the bison's population to fewer than 250 animals by 1896, in Soper's estimation. In a move reminiscent of Yellowstone's takeover by the military, the Royal North-West Mounted Police in 1897 took charge of protecting wood bison in their northern range. The Canadian government designated the wood buffalo's central range, surrounding the Peace and Slave Rivers, as Wood Buffalo National Park, designed to protect the buffalo and its habitat. Under the protection of six full-time bison rangers after 1911, wood bison numbered upward of 1,500 to 2,000 animals in 1922.

Meanwhile, there were problems to the south, where the herd of plains bison at Buffalo National Park was also growing rapidly—to 2,000 animals by 1916 and still growing, expanding more rapidly than the park could accommodate. Solution: between 1925 and 1928 the federal government moved 6,673 plains bison by train from Buffalo National Park to the small village of Waterways, near present-day Fort McMurray, and then by barge down the Athabasca and Peace Rivers to the eastern edge of Wood Buffalo National Park and released them there. The bison were mostly young animals, selected by managers "under the assumption they would be less likely to harbor the diseases than older adults," Olson says. The shipment included 4,826 yearlings, 1,515 two-year-olds, and 332 three-year-olds, most of them in poor physical condition, Olson says, "due to the overgrazed grassland ranges they left behind." People who helped unload them reported that about half died en route or shortly after they were released into a boreal forest—not their typical habitat—shortly before the onset of winter. Lurking in the forest: a thriving wolf population, Olson says.

This solution to one problem unleashed another: The plains bison introduced deadly diseases—brucellosis and bovine tuberculosis—to the previously uninfected wood bison. The plains bison also bred with wood bison. A count in 1934 revealed that the park was home to 12,000 bison, "in part due to the introduction of Plains Bison that mixed and interbred with the resident Wood Bison." Because the animals from Buffalo National Park were young, those that survived the first winter would not have been able to compete for mates with mature wood bison bulls. The few plains bison bulls that survived five to seven winters to get to breeding age would have been scarce, so most of the hybridization was due to wood bison bulls mixing with plains cows. Today, Olson says, Wood Bison National Park is home to three distinct groups. Those closest to the original release site show some plains bison traits, those in the west carry no plains genes, and those in between display varying characteristics of mixed genetics.

By the 1950s, Canadian wildlife officials concluded that the wood bison was extinct, swamped out of existence by plains bison. However, a bison expert at the University of Alberta in Edmonton hypothesized that some pure-blooded wood bison might survive in the remote, all-but-inaccessible northwest corner of Wood Buffalo National Park. He was right. The Canadian Wildlife Service biologists in the plane spotted what proved to be a herd of two hundred pure-blooded, disease-free, wood bison.

In 1963, 168 of these bison found themselves being released into a newly established bison park in the Northwest Territories—the Mackenzie Bison Sanctuary, which lies northwest of Great Slave Lake. The government released another twenty-three wood bison into Elk Island National Park. When officials discovered that some of the buffalo were infected, the animals were destroyed, leaving eleven disease-free calves. The Elk Island population and other local populations (those in, for example, sites designated as sanctuaries rather than national parks) are descended from these eleven animals, which were hand-reared at Elk Island in the 1960s.

Today, wood bison survive in nine free-ranging, disease-free local populations. Three other free-ranging herds are infected with livestock diseases. Elk Island is still home to a conservation herd of about three hundred wood bison. As many as seven hundred live in perhaps as many as sixty commercial herds and are not part of federal recovery plans. Two local populations, the Wentzel Lake population and the Slave River Lowlands population, are close enough to Wood Bison National Park that they are sometimes referred to in toto as the Greater Wood Buffalo National Park metapopulation. These groups interbreed. Two other local populations—Wabasca Lake to the west of the park and Ronald Lake to the south—do not appear to interact with the metapopulation and remain disease-free.

Though diseased, the metapopulation is biologically important because it is one of the best sources of genetic diversity among wood bison. Canadian officials recognized the importance of these animals in a government management document, *Recovery Strategy for the Wood Bison* (Bison bison athabascae) *in Canada*, which declares, "All local populations within and around Wood Buffalo National Park (including Wabasca and Ronald Lake) represent the only location worldwide where Wood Bison have continually persisted or naturally colonized. All other extant populations derive from Wood Buffalo National Park by human-mediated translocation either directly or via Elk Island National Park."

The Canadian government has outlined several goals for bison recovery, including disease control to prevent infections transferring from bison to cattle and to commercial bison herds; reducing threats to bison habitat, such as land development and mining; reducing traffic accidents with bison, which often travel and rest along roads; and increasing public awareness and acceptance of wood bison, "including acknowledging and augmenting social, cultural, ecological, and economic relationships among Wood Bison and Indigenous peoples and local communities." A key recovery goal calls for maintaining at least 90 percent of wood bison genetic diversity for the next two hundred years. This goal, under current planning, seeks to establish individual bison populations of at least one thousand animals. Achieving such herd size will require suitable habitat corridors connecting existing local populations of free-ranging, disease-free animals. Other threats include hybridization; fire and fire suppression, which can affect plant growth; dams and other water projects; natural factors such as droughts and floods; and agricultural development and ranching, though wood bison are not as exposed to agricultural threats as plains bison are.

Unregulated hunting has been singled out as a major threat to wood bison. No hunting is allowed within national parks, except in some parks at the northern extreme of bison range, where Indigenous people are allowed to hunt. There, hunting is used to control the population size of at least two local populations, but the hunting is strictly regulated. In some areas, the government has established bison-free zones, or control areas, as perimeters around parks, such as Ronald Lake, so that any bison that appear between that site and Wood Bison National Park can be shot to prevent the spread of disease to the disease-free Ronald Lake population. "Virtually every bison that sets foot outside the park is fair game for anyone to shoot," Olson says. He adds that this approach, nevertheless, has no impact on the Wood Buffalo National Park metapopulation, because the area is so remote, and in winter almost impossible to reach, that hunting is insignificant.

The only real threat from shooting is unregulated hunting. Regulated hunting may even benefit bison management by improving public acceptance of bison, a key need for bison recovery. According to one government document, initial local opposition to bison management in southwest Yukon under the 1998 wood bison–management plan "may have decreased somewhat with the initiation of bison hunting. Bison have become an increasingly valued resource and tolerance for them has increased somewhat over time."

The reintroduction of wood bison into former habitat led the federal government to work cooperatively with Indigenous, or First Nations, people. As in the United States, the First Nations of the prairies and boreal forests have a long cultural interest in bison. As early as 1857, the Plains Cree initiated a council with the goal of forbidding Europeans to kill bison on tribal hunting territory. The plan failed, as did an effort in the 1870s by a Cree chief to persuade the Canadian government to protect bison. Instead, the Indians were destroyed culturally, as in the United States, by loss of land and wildlife and by attempts to school them into being farmers and ranchers. But in the 1980s, on the heels of changes in US Indian policies that started in the 1970s, Canadian relations with First Nations began to evolve, too. The Canadian government adopted three agreements to co-manage wildlife with First Nations peoples and brought them in as official decision makers, a major step—at that time in the United States, tribal peoples were only consulted. In 1986, the Canada and Alberta Fort Chipewyan Cree Band Settlement delegated to Cree living east of Wood Buffalo National Park the right to join federal agencies in making management decisions. In 1988, the Comprehensive Land Claim Agreement in Principle also made First Nations people living north of the park into bison co-managers. A 1987 law allowed the Dene Band to resume hunting bison for food, in the way of their ancient culture, and to guide carefully restricted trophy hunters in the Mackenzie Bison Sanctuary.

Throughout the 1980s and into the 1990s, provincial governments also worked with First Nations on projects that resulted in Wes Olson, in 1984, moving thirty wood bison from Elk Island to the Hay Lake and Zama Lake area, west of Wood Buffalo National Park. One of several local herds started with First Nations input, the Hay-Zama herd now numbers around five hundred animals, Olson says. Indigenous people are free to hunt these bison for food and also wood bison in another local population in the Northwest Territories.

The First Nations played an instrumental role in stopping a federal bison-management decision that might have been as disastrous as the introduction of thousands of diseased plains bison into Wood Buffalo National Park in the 1920s had been. The controversy began in 1990 when Agriculture Canada officials proposed making the park and its environs disease-free, though not so much for the bison as for the protection of domestic cattle. To achieve this goal, Agriculture Canada adopted a plan to kill all wild bison in the area of the park and replace them with disease-free bison from other populations. The agency labeled the park's wood bison as genetically impure transmitters of disease, even though no more than a third of the bison carried tuberculosis or brucellosis. Local Indigenous people erupted in opposition, suggesting that "discrimination against bison resembled racism," reported Ken Zontek in his insightful book *Buffalo Nation: American Indian Efforts to Restore the Bison*. He continued:

> *They warily viewed the attempt to manipulate resources in the park as a step toward much further development in logging or agriculture. Additionally, they noted that agreements existed with the government regarding the Native influence in effectuating wildlife policy and that these proceedings would violate their rights to wildlife*

stewardship. Ultimately, the confrontation occurred over different visions of the landscape. First Nations sought an environment relatively free of manipulation, with bison maintaining their own autonomy. Agriculture and development interests sought a heavily manipulated landscape.

In the end, the decision was turned over to the new Northern Buffalo Management Board, formed in 1991 and composed of nine community members, five representatives of government agencies, and three representatives of nongovernmental groups. Indigenous people were among the community members, and one Indigenous person co-chaired the board. In March 1993, the board presented its report calling for studies of the bison and the park prior to any culling decision being made. In April 1995, the minister of Canadian heritage launched a five-year Bison Research and Containment Program. The Research Advisory Committee, which includes four First Nations people in its eight-person membership, serves as a scientific advisor to Parks Canada, which in turn administers Canada's national parks. The committee solicited research proposals in July 1996 as part of the research and containment program and eventually backed a management board proposal that would establish the no-bison zone, mentioned earlier, that runs south of the Mackenzie Bison Sanctuary and west of Wood Buffalo National Park. The proposal for a no-bison zone as a means to control disease was accepted by government officials, and the wood bison herd was saved from slaughter. First Nations, through their active participation on official commissions and boards, heavily influenced the outcome of the proposed wood bison slaughter.

Except for Saskatchewan and British Columbia, which officially recognize bison as wildlife, all other provinces designate them as livestock. The federal Committee on the Status of Endangered Wildlife in Canada more than a decade ago declared bison endangered, but the species has been given no protection under Canada's Species at Risk Act. Today, Canada provides habitat for some 125,000 bison, according to Wes Olson. About 20,000 of them are wild, and about 11,000 of those are wood bison. As in the United States, the bulk of the animals are in commercial herds. Though the numbers may seem relatively small, they are great enough that wood bison from Canada have been released in Alaska to reintroduce the subspecies to habitat from which it vanished about two hundred years ago, probably due to a series of severe winters in the late 1700s and early 1800s, Olson says. In April 2022, about forty bison from Elk Island National Park were shipped to Alaska, where a wood bison restoration program that was started in 2015 now includes more than one hundred animals. Finding suitable habitat, particularly for the plains bison, remains a major challenge to restoring bison everywhere, along with encouraging genetic diversity. However, the challenges faced by Canadian, Mexican, and US bison advocates might be envied by bison managers in Europe, where conservationists are endeavoring to restore the species in a heavily developed region that offers only shattered fragments of bison habitat and many opportunities for conflicts with landowners.

CHAPTER 8

THE WAY OF THE WISENT

In August 1915, as the First World War enters its second year, the German Army seizes western Poland's Bialowieza (pronounced Bee-ah-wo-vee-edge-oh) Forest, the last remnant of the great, dark forests that once cloaked northeastern Europe. As artillery resounds across shattered landscapes, the forest and its glades shelter one of the last two wild populations of European bison, called wisent in Germany.

German soldiers start to hunt the animals immediately. Only about six hundred wisent survive at the time of the invasion. By the end of September, the soldiers have killed at least two hundred of them for sport, meat, hides, and horns. After a German scientist warns that the wisent is nearly extinct, military officers issue orders against hunting in the forest, but poaching continues.

In February 1919, the Polish army reoccupies the woodland. The following April, the remains of a poached wisent cow turn up in the forest, the decaying finish of what had been the last free-living herd of lowland European bison. The only remaining wild wisent survive in the Russian Caucasus, a mountainous area between the Caspian and Black Seas, but they do not last much longer. In 1927, poachers kill these last wild representatives of a species that had figured prominently in the lives and diets of Stone Age peoples and that had been often commemorated in cave art dating back more than 40,000 years in Spain and France, indicating how far-flung the wisent's range once was.

UNLIKE THE CATASTROPHIC AND RAPID COLLAPSE OF NORTH AMERICAN BISON, the European bison ebbed away slowly. In ancient Rome, writers chronicled the dwindling of bison in the Mediterranean region as early as the third century AD. The species continued to decline as human populations expanded, converting wildlife habitat into agricultural lands. Early in the medieval era, wisent still roamed the forests of eastern Europe but in lower and lower numbers as hunters killed the animals for their hides and horns, the latter used as drinking cups. In 1538, King Sigismund II of Poland made bison poaching in Bialowieza Forest a capital crime. Three years later, he declared the forest a hunting reserve, a status that Russian tsars, once they took control of the area, continued almost into the nineteenth century.

Tsar Paul I—the son of Catherine the Great, he was sometimes called the Mad Tsar—ended wildlife protection in the forest and revived hunting there in the late eighteenth century, when the wild bison population numbered no greater than five hundred animals. Hunting reduced the herd to fewer than two hundred within fifteen years. In 1801, Tsar Alexander I declared the forest once again a wildlife reserve and hired peasants as game wardens, with the result that in fewer than thirty years the forest was home to about seven hundred bison. However, a peasant uprising in 1830, which involved all but two of five hundred game wardens, brought bison protection to an end. Thirty years later, Tsar Alexander II reestablished conservation regulations. In the years ahead, the tsars stocked the forest with deer, moose, and other game species that they hunted, along with bison. In this way, despite setbacks, the European bison survived in the wild until the 1920s.

AT VARIOUS TIMES IN THE PAST, THE WISENT RANGED IN EUROPE FROM WHAT is now France in the west to the Ural Mountains in the east, and from Bulgaria north to southern Sweden. Its distribution was often subject to local declines and extinctions. For example, the expansion of forests from 12,000 to 8,000 years ago changed grazing lands into habitat that was less suitable for large herbivores. Bison disappeared from most of Europe from 9,500 to 7,000 years ago but subsequently returned, presumably from pockets of habitat in the east. However, since the sixteenth century, the wisent has held on only where protected.

Now the last surviving species of wild European cattle, the wisent is Europe's largest land animal, with bulls often standing more than six feet tall at the hump and weighing about a ton. Adult European bison are not as shaggy as American bison and are typically taller because they have longer legs. To an American observer, Euro bison look something like buffalo in high heels. However, those coltish legs rush them along at speeds up to forty miles per hour.

Only one European bison species survives today, the lowland bison, which exists in two breeding lines: pure lowland and lowland crossed with Caucasian bison. Its closest surviving relative is the American bison. The American and European versions are so closely related that they can inter-breed and produce fertile offspring, but given their distinctively different physical appearances and widely separated ranges, they are generally treated as two different species.

Until recently, biologists thought the wisent was a creature of forest habitats. New research suggests that Euro bison prefer a checkerboard of grassland and forest habitat but were pushed into forests by farmers as sur-rounding lands were turned into agricultural fields. "Of the free-ranging populations of European bison reintroduced into forest habitats, more than half have expanded their range into open grassland," according to the con-servation group Rewilding Europe.

European bison vary their diet with the seasons. As blossoms and leaves bloom in spring, bison become browsers that favor young trees and shrubs, particularly willow, hornbeam, and aspen. In summer, they show an affinity mostly for the shoots and young leaves of grasses but also feed on shrubs, a combination of grazing and browsing. In winter, the herds seek refuge from snow and wind in forests, stripping bark from trees such as hornbeam, ash, and willow. They also eat shoots, branches, and seeds, including that favorite of wildlife around the world, the acorn. To survive, they need an abundant supply of varied foods. In the course of twenty-four hours, a wisent calf no more than a year old can eat nearly nineteen pounds of fresh food, while an adult can pack in forty-three to sixty-three pounds. The animals are not picky—they forage on more than two hundred different plant species.

Stripping away tree bark can kill trees, creating open areas within for-ests, which both helps to prevent the spread of fires across broad landscapes and provides diverse habitat for other animal species. In effect, Euro-pean bison create the forest glades in which they prefer to graze. Like the

American buffalo, the wisent wallows in grassy areas, creating patches of soil that increase plant diversity by encouraging the growth of species that favor bare earth. The wallows also attract bees, wasps, lizards, and other animals. Wisent produce massive amounts of dung that enrich the soil and spread ingested plant seeds, sustaining local biodiversity and providing forage for pollinators. Bison particularly benefit dung beetles, insects that are good indicators of biodiversity. Dung beetles aerate soil by digging, and they process dung into nutrients accessible to plants. At least thirty-five of the one hundred native dung beetle species studied at five locations in Germany, Poland, and Belarus, including six species that are on the International Union for the Conservation of Nature's (IUCN) Red List of Threatened Species, occur in bison dung. For some animals, bison themselves offer a smorgasbord of delights—birds, as well as squirrels, collect the shed winter hair of wisent for nesting material, and magpies pick ticks and other parasites directly off the bison. In all, Euro bison provide ecological benefits to nearly six hundred invertebrate and vertebrate animals.

In some areas, wildlife managers feed free-ranging bison during winter at special feeding stations, partly to sustain the animals through winter and partly to keep them from leaving protected areas and going into places that invite conflicts with landowners. These feeding stations attract the bison, creating herds composed of calves, cows, males, and females aged two to three, and occasional adult bulls. Such mixed herds generally number fifteen to twenty individuals that stay together until the first grasses and herbs appear at the start of spring. The winter herds soon recongregate into groups averaging a dozen bison and composed of cows with calves and subadult males and females. These groups generally are led by a cow.

Some 60 percent of mature bulls become either solitary or form groups of two to three, joining larger groups only during the rutting season, from August to October. Captive bulls usually begin to mature sexually in the second year of life, while free-ranging bulls on large reserves begin sexual maturity at the age of three. The latter generally do not breed until seven to twelve years old, when they are fully developed physically. European bison are fairly docile animals and are not typically aggressive toward one another. When they do conflict, they often avoid physical contact. Instead, they intimidate opponents through displays of aggression, such as sparring with and breaking young trees and pawing the ground with their forehooves.

During the mating season, however, bulls can become highly aggressive, with some fights leading to death.

When bulls are in rut, the presence of a female in heat can stimulate the bulls into fights that are brief but intense, though lower-ranking bulls tend to avoid fights with higher-ranking bulls. Once a bull encounters a female willing to mate, he will isolate her from the herd and remain with her for two to three days.

Wisent cows usually become sexually mature at age three and produce their first calves in their fourth year. Free-roaming females produce one calf every other year and can breed until the end of life, generally around twenty to twenty-four years old. The average cow may produce nine calves in a lifetime.

Calves are born 254 to 277 days after mating, putting most births in May or June, though up to 30 percent can occur as late as October. A cow about to give birth separates from the herd and goes to a secluded place. Cows defend their calves, which weigh about fifty to sixty pounds at birth, against any danger. Within a few days, cow and calf rejoin the herd. Calves suckle for at least a year.

RESTORATION OF EUROPEAN BISON THROUGH CAPTIVE BREEDING AND REIN-troduction to former habitat was proposed in 1923 by Polish zoologist J. Sztolcman at the 1st International Congress of Nature Protection in Paris, according to Rewilding Europe's *Bison Rewilding Plan, 2014–2024*. That year also saw the formation of the International Society for the Protection of the European Bison (Internationale Gesellschaft zur Erhaltung des Wisents) in Frankfurt am Main, Germany. The society's mission included restoration of European bison through captive breeding and reintroduction to large stands of forest.

The threats of inbreeding and of past crossbreeding were particular concerns of the society. As in the United States, programs to crossbreed surviving bison with close relatives had reduced the genetic integrity of the remaining European animals. Various zoos had crossed wisent with American bison and cattle. To sort out the genetic status of surviving wisent, the society created a studbook, the European Bison Pedigree Book—the first register of all living European bison, initially including hybrids, and the first for a wild species of any kind. Eventually, application of the book led to a ban on breeding hybrids with pure-blooded European bison. After World War II, the pedigree book was maintained in Poland by the State Council of Nature Protection. Since 1993, staff at Poland's Bialowieza National Park have published the registry, tallying all living bison and perpetuating an important source of data on the numbers of European bison in different locations.

In 1924, a year after Sztolcman made his proposal, only fifty-four European bison survived, all in only a few European zoological gardens. Of the fifty-four, twenty-nine were males and twenty-five were females. All of them were the off-spring of a breeding stock of twenty-three bison. However, research showed that eleven of the twenty-three ancestral wisent and their offspring were not genetically pure, so they were excluded from the pedigree book. All of today's European bison are descended from the twelve remaining founder animals, according to bison expert Wanda Olech. This severe breeding bottleneck has greatly reduced genetic diversity in today's wisent, raising the dangerous specter of inbreeding. "In the wild bison in Poland there are considerable problems with a viral disease that affects the male reproductive organ," forest director Johannes Röhl, chairman of the board of the Wisent-Welt Wittgenstein Association, told reporter Brigitte Osterath. "And other diseases can be traced back to an inbreeding depression." But in 1920s Europe, as in the United States in the late 1800s, bison advocates who wanted to save the wisent had no alternative to depending entirely on the depleted breeding stock.

Today more than two hundred European breeding centers, about sixty of which participate in the European Endangered Species Programme under the aegis of the European Association of Zoos and Aquaria, are helping to maintain genetic diversity through careful selection and distribution of breeding animals. The larger bison breeding centers are united under the European Bison Conservation Center, which helps to coordinate breed-ing. Only wisent from breeding centers registered in the pedigree book are eligible for restoration programs. Each bison is registered by name and identification number, and the book includes date and birthplace for each registered bison, along with the names and ID numbers of parents and information on the transport of the animals among different centers.

Saving a vanishing species of wild cattle was considered worthy of all this effort even a century ago, when ecological roles were poorly understood. The importance of bison survival is even clearer now. "For biodiversity, it is very important," says Florian Sicks, senior curator and deputy zoological director of the Tierpark Berlin (a part of the Berlin Zoological Garden). "The wisent has a definite impact on its environment. Through grazing, it opens up forested areas and keeps them open. Its dung attracts certain kinds of insects and fungi. The sand pits in which it wallows have their own biodiversity. Pollen gets caught in the fur of the bison and is carried away. The wisent makes itself noticeable in many positive ways. In addition, there's a subjective perception, a special feeling, that it would be a shame if it were allowed to disappear. Then the world would be one complex and fascinating animal poorer."

One of the groups seeking to save wisent is Rewilding Europe, founded in 2011 with the express goal, as its name implies and its website states, of making Europe a wilder place, "with much more space for wildlife, wilderness and natural processes, by bringing back a variety of wildlife for all to enjoy and exploring new ways for people to earn a fair living from the wild." Wisent recovery is of special importance to the group. "There is no species that better symbolises the state of nature conservation in Europe than the European bison," wrote Frans Schepers, then the managing director of Rewilding Europe, in a foreword to the *Bison Rewilding Plan*. "Nearly extinct in the last century, it was rescued by passionate conservationists from the last animals in captivity, and although it is now benefiting from a growing environmental awareness, the European bison is still not out of danger and remains virtually unknown to the general public." The group seeks to integrate bison recovery within the social and economic matrix of areas where bison are reintroduced. Local economies, Rewilding Europe maintains, can benefit from wisent recovery.

In cooperation with World Wide Fund for Nature–Romania, Rewilding Europe has been introducing bison into the Tarcu Mountains, in Romania's Southern Carpathians, since 2014. With more than eighty bison released in the area, the group is working to build local support. The European Safari Company organizes ecotourism trips into the area, such as tracking wisent in snow on snowshoes. Rewilding Europe also has helped introduce bison into the Rhodope Mountains of Bulgaria, beginning with seven free-roaming bison in 2019—the first there since the Middle Ages. The reintroduced bison all came from the European Wildlife Bank, which provides large herbivores for restoration to natural European habitat. By 2020, the bank had more than 130 bison plus more than 70 placed in the Southern Carpathians and Rhodope Mountains. That year, one of the cows gave birth, the first wisent born in the area since medieval times. "We are thrilled by the new addition," says Hristo Hristov, a member of the Rhodope rewilding team. "This calf was born in one of the wildest parts of the reserve and has been following the herd ever since. This young bison is a symbol of hope for a wilder and more biodiverse Rhodope Mountains. This is why we have named her Nadezhda [meaning 'hope' in Bulgarian]."

DESPITE ITS DIRE BEGINNINGS, WITH THE FATE OF AN ENTIRE SPECIES DEPEND-ing on so few animals, wisent recovery has given biologists and bison enthusi-asts cause for optimism if reintroduction programs stay on track. "I won't say the wisent is out of danger, but it is on a good path," Florian Sicks says. "I don't see it that critically. After all, for us the wisent is *the* zoological success story. Extinct in the wild, and just a few decades later well on the way to recovery. For us, those involved in recovery, it's the poster child of wildlife recovery."

The modern era of wisent reintroductions to native European habitat began in 1952 in Poland's Bialowieza Forest. Prior to that time, bison con-servation focused primarily on maintaining the animals in zoos, wildlife parks, and special bison breeding centers. By about 1960, the program in Poland's Bialowieza Forest had created a free-ranging population. Subse-quent projects helped to establish the wisent in the part of the Bialowieza Forest that lies in Belarus. Bison also were introduced in Lithuania and Ukraine. Attempts to create free-ranging herds in the Caucasus of Russia and Azerbaijan at that time failed, however—undermined by a lack of pro-tection that allowed poaching to extirpate the reintroduced animals.

Poland has long been a leader in wisent conservation. In 1963, biologists released bison in a wooded region near the border with Ukraine, starting with eleven bulls and eight females from Polish breeding centers. In the 1970s, another ninety-eight animals were released into the area, with further releases in the 1980s. Some of these bison formed small groups and shifted their range to the north, while others remained in a herd in the release area. Because all of the bison in both herds originated in Polish breeding centers, program managers sought the advice of genetics expert Wanda Olech, a biologist with the Department of Genetics and Animal Protection at the Institute of Ani-mal Sciences, a part of the Warsaw University of Life Sciences. She helped select bison from breeding herds in Sweden, Denmark, the Czech Republic,

Ireland, and Germany. This herd and a half dozen others in Poland have since grown steadily, some numbering more than one hundred wisent.

Bison in Bialoweiza park are fed in winter. "They have been fed starting in the eighteenth century," Olech says. "So every year they are fed, not because of the poor time in winter—because they can find a lot in the agriculture fields—but the feeding is used to keep them in the forest area, to prevent them from walking to agriculture and coming into conflicts." Feeding—mainly hay, hay silage, and beets—starts before winter, so the animals will establish an early pattern of eating at feeding stations. "The feeding starts in September, the beginning of October, because at that time they are starting to move," Olech says. "Usually, in the forest, the vegetation has stopped [growing], so they cannot find enough food, and they are starting to move. To keep them in the park, it is important to give them some food in October, to tell them, 'We will give you something.'"

From one perspective, bison restoration in Bialowieza has been highly successful. But the fallout of that success is, ironically, too many bison. "They already reached the maximum carrying capacity in the Bialowieza Forest a few years ago," Olech says. "This is why some of them are going out. The problem is that more animals should be going out." The herd remains in the same area year after year even as it grows in size and density through breeding. "Maybe there will be consequences of this, maybe not," Olech says. "I hope not, but in other populations we have had them." One consequence, she says, is the occurrence of diseases that can spread rapidly among a crowded herd. A dense population can also damage habitat, eating more vegetation than the forest can sustain. Olech hopes that as the herd grows, it will fracture into two groups, one of which will leave the area, moving into surrounding forest.

German conservationists began launching wisent reintroduction projects in the early 2000s. The first of these was established in the Döberitzer Heide, a 12,500-acre former Soviet military training area near Berlin that includes a fenced "wilderness zone" of 4,600 acres inhabited by red deer, Eurasian wild horses (Przewalski's horses), and the European bison that were released in 2010. Within three years the bison population increased from eleven to forty-six individuals, although surveys are difficult to conduct because of explosives still in the area.

Another project, launched in 2005 in Niedersachsen, a state in northwest Germany on the North Sea, collapsed within three years because of conflicts with a landowner. For a while this failure stood in marked contrast to a restoration project initiated in the Rothaar Mountains, which Rewilding Europe cited as "a good example of a carefully managed reintroduction, lessons from which could be used to inform further reintroductions." The mountains are located in North Rhine-Westphalia, a state in western Germany near the Netherlands and one of the most densely populated areas of Europe—nearly 1,400 human inhabitants per square mile. The reintroduction in the low mountains was started in 2003 by a private forest owner allied with the conservation group Taurus Naturentwicklung. The goal: establish a free-living herd of around twenty-five animals in a 10,625-acre area. The project drew support from a regional politician and local mayor who viewed bison recovery as good for the area's economy after a drop in winter tourism. The reintroduction's success depended heavily on early engagement with nearby communities, including a comprehensive feasibility study in 2005 to 2006 and several public hearings. One study served as a foundation for a communications strategy designed to encourage confidence in the project and to overcome negative attitudes held, for example, by farmers and foresters. As a consequence of the feasibility study, the Federal Agency for Nature Conservation and the state Ministry of Environment of North Rhine-Westphalia promoted and financed the project.

Bison arrived in 2010 and lived in an enclosure of fewer than 5 acres for six months before release into a 220-acre pasture. Project managers conducted a study on how the bison reacted to hikers, dogs, and other encounters, offering advice to local residents and assuring them that bison are typically not aggressive (something you can't say of American bison). Eight bison finally made it into the wild in 2013, the first free-ranging bison in Germany since roughly four hundred years ago. Soon, two calves were born. A local farmer was made into a bison ranger, and the animals were carefully monitored. Total cost of the project from 2003 to 2013: an estimated 1.5 million euros.

Nevertheless, neither the significance nor success of the North Rhine-Westphalia project could save it. After years of conflicts with foresters who sued over the loss of trees to the wisent, Wisent-Welt-Wittgenstein, the organization that was managing the free-roaming animals, was ordered by the Hamm Higher Regional Court in 2022 to take measures that would ensure that the bison would not harm trees. A spokesman for the organization,

Michael Emmrich, said that taking such measures was beyond Wisent-Welt-Wittgenstein's means and terminated its bison-management contract with the local government.

The twenty-five bison formerly handled by Wisent-Welt (Wisent-World) are the only free-roaming wisent in Western Europe. Now that Wisent-Welt-Wittgenstein has withdrawn from management of these bison, the animals are ownerless, and authorities are scrambling to decide what to do with them. As protected animals, they cannot be shot. However, they were not the only bison managed by Wisent-Welt-Wittgenstein. The organization also shelters eleven corralled bison in an exhibit called Wisent-Wildnis (Wisent-Wilderness). "The enclosure bison—we use them as ambassadors for the free-roaming herd," Kaja Heising, scientific coordination for Wisent-Welt, says. Visitors were welcome to hike in the Welt area and to look for free-roaming bison, but of course the first lesson learned is that free-roaming bison are not waiting around to be looked at. "We have this enclosure [Wisent-Wildnis] because we need a place to educate people and assuage their fears," Heising says. "The European bison are not well known. In Germany, many people believe that the bison is an American species."

Some 35,000 people a year came to see Wisent-Wildnis and Western Europe's only free-roaming bison herd at Wisent-Welt. "This is important," Heising says. "Western Europe is very densely populated. This is why Eastern European countries took the initiative in bison reintroductions. We want to see whether it is possible to share this environment [Western Europe] with the European bison. During its absence in Western Europe, we changed its environment. You have the higher [human] population density and land use, but still the bison are doing great here."

The success of Wisent-Welt, even given its uncertain destiny right now, makes it a potential model for other European nations. Wisent-Wildnis is already helping other nations with bison restoration: Five wisent born at Wisent-Welt were transferred to Romania for reintroduction there as part of a project started in 2014.

Wisent-Welt-Wittgenstein puts an emphasis on educating the next generation of conservationists, offering events for kindergarten and school groups at the Wisent-Wildnis enclosure. "This is the generation you want to focus on," Heising says. Children are more open to bison than some adults, for whom Wisent-Welt-Wittgenstein also offers educational programs. One of the reasons that people have conflicts with bison, Heising says, "is that people aren't used to these animals. Compare with acceptance to other animals, such as red deer and wild boar. They are being accepted. People are used to them. But people are not used to European bison, because they have only been roaming free for a few years. This is what we, or I personally, want to focus on. With acceptance, the conflicts will decrease."

Wanda Olech, however, remains skeptical about bison survival in Germany. She says she cannot envision large herds in Germany, because parcels of remaining habitat are limited in size. In Germany, she says, "I cannot imagine hundreds [of bison], because I know about the large problems with hundreds. Even in the western part of Poland they have problems with damage in agriculture, damage in forests—this kind of thing. Hundreds? For me there is no future, because the people will take everything into their hands and start to poach, for example." Establishing bison in Germany, she says, will depend on creating small herds with genetic diversity preserved by the movement of bulls among the herds.

Olech outlined how this approach would help to mitigate the effects of small herds living in small areas of habitat. Bison conservationists "are trying to create many metapopulations, small groups of European bison," she says. "In a typical European environment, it is impossible to make a huge group of European bison in one place." Larger herds tend to roam away from reintroduction sites and to conflict with local farmers. In Bialowieza Forest in 2020, for example, about a third of the park's four hundred to five hundred bison "went out of Bialowieza Forest and spent time in the agricultural area," Olech says. "In some places [the bison] make problems, in other places they were not making problems—it depends on the kind of agriculture." To avoid such conflicts, and to accommodate the limited wildlife habitat available in Europe, Olech says, "we are creating smaller groups." Individual bull bison will move on their own among such herds, helping to improve genetic diversity. "You have subpopulations—smaller populations—connected, so the distance between them is not very long for walking bulls," she says. "Bulls can walk many kilometers." Bulls from Poland already have shown up in Belarus, Ukraine, and Germany.

An example of the wandering power of bison comes from a population in West Pomerania, a mostly flat plain that lies along the Baltic Sea in northwest Poland and is home to some 330 wisent. "They grow in number and distribution and move westward," says Nina Gandl, project officer for bison and moose at WWF-Germany and part of LosBonasus-Crossing!, a European Union Interreg-funded transboundary project between Germany and Poland, designed to support bison recovery. "The closest small herd is located only thirty kilometers [about twenty miles] from the German border," Gandl says. "Especially wandering bulls are regularly spotted even closer to the border. One or more animals could thus move to Germany at any time."

Bison are considered game animals under German hunting law but are subject to no hunting season. Under the European Flora-Fauna-Habitat Directive and under national legislation, bison are strictly protected from poaching. Nevertheless, a bull that drifted out of Poland in 2017—originating probably in Poland's Ujscie Warty National Park, which lies on the border with Germany—was shot within hours of being spotted in Germany near the town of Lebus, about sixty miles east of Berlin. It was probably the first wisent sighted in Germany in centuries. However, local officials issued a permit to kill the animal, which they considered a threat to public safety. WWF-Germany immediately filed a criminal complaint against the officials. "Giving permission to shoot a strongly protected animal without a clear potential threat is a criminal offence," Christoph Heinrich, chief conservation officer of WWF-Germany and a member of its executive board, said in a statement reported in local media. "After more than 250 years a wild bison had been spotted again in Germany and all the authorities could think to do is shoot it." The public prosecutor did not press charges against the officials, however, although the Ministry of Justice in Brandenburg did call it an illegal action, which, Gandl says, is an important public statement. "Not much has changed since then," she adds. "Authorities need to prepare a management plan for bison, and financial, personal, and technical capacity needs to be built to adequately manage and protect bison in the transboundary area. LosBonasus-Crossing! is working on solutions and seeking contact with decision makers to prepare for a likely movement of bison from Poland to Germany."

LosBonasus-Crossing!, Gandl says, "is designed to initiate transboundary wildlife management of bison and moose [also called elk in Europe] between Germany and Poland in order to find sustainable solutions for coexistence between humans and both species." Sponsored by the European Union's Interreg program, the project, initiated in 2019, is implemented by five partners—the Leibniz Centre for Agricultural Landscape Research, WWF-Germany, Humboldt University of Berlin, the Polish city Miroslawiec, and the West Pomeranian Nature Society. The consortium also plans to work on the ground. "We are mainly working on management recommendations for both species, bison and moose, as well as a concept for a task force which shall reduce and prevent human-wildlife conflicts," Gandl says. "Such a task force already exists in western Poland, run by our project partners the West Pomeranian Nature Society. We have planned different formats to include stakeholders in the development of these recommendations and concepts, so that they are practicable for all relevant stakeholders and thus sustainable." These management options are supported by evidence generated by the research activities within the project. Among others, a habitat analysis for bison and moose is carried out to predict both habitat suitability and connectivity across the study area. In addition, the project tracks several bison herds in western Poland through GPS collars and explores citizen-science approaches such as smartphone applications to monitor sightings of bison and moose.

Another central component of the project comprises awareness-raising and environmental information to foster the acceptance for both species among the public. The project develops creative information material about the two species—a brochure about their biology, behavior, habitat, and food habits; a short documentary film about the project and the return of bison and moose from Poland to Germany; a teaching unit for younger schoolkids; an online education module for adults; and a mobile exhibition about European bison and moose.

THE CAUCASUS, A MOUNTAINOUS REGION BETWEEN THE BLACK AND CASPIAN Seas and the area where Europe and Asia meet, lies within the historical range of a wisent subspecies, the Caucasian bison. A keystone mammal of the mountain broadleaf forests for centuries, the Caucasian bison was a subspecies that represented the last wild wisent, eroded by poaching and forest destruction. The last wild Caucasian bison were poached in 1927.

In the 1930s the Soviet Union began reintroduction efforts in the Caucasus that used hybrids of lowland and Caucasian bison. Reintroductions continued into the 1970s with significant success, but the program began to collapse when the fall of the Soviet Union led to an increase in poaching in the 1990s, leaving only two herds in the Caucasus, one in Karachay-Cherkessia

and another in North Ossetia. Now, thanks to further Russian reintroduction efforts that started in the 2000s, three wisent subpopulations exist
in the Russian Greater Caucasus, though all are small in number. A herd
in the Kizgich Valley in the Arkhyz branch of Teberdinsky Nature Reserve
holds about forty animals, and the Tseisky Managed Nature Reserve in North
Ossetia holds about 110 animals. The most recent efforts, begun in 2018
at the Turmon Regional Managed Reserve, support about twenty animals.

Alongside these reintroductions of full-blooded European bison, in 1940
the Soviet Union translocated hybrids of European and American bison from
Askania-Nova Nature Reserve, in Ukraine, to an enclosure in the Kavkazsky
Strict Nature Reserve in the western Greater Caucasus. To this herd, in 1949,
the Soviet Union added hybrids of pure lowland wisent crossed with Caucasian
wisent. By 1955, all of these animals had been released into the wild, and they
now number more than 1,100 animals. As those wisent are hybrids, they are
not included in the European Bison Pedigree Book.

Besides the Russian reintroductions, in 2019 a wisent restoration initiative started on the southern slopes of the eastern Greater Caucasus in
Shahdag National Park. This program is a joint effort of the Azerbaijan government, World Wide Fund for Nature, European Association of Zoos and
Aquaria/European Endangered Species Programme (EAZA/EEP), International Dialogue for Environmental Action (IDEA) Public Union, and the
Tierpark Berlin, with the support of many European zoos and other partners. Since 2019, a total of twenty-six wisent have been successfully transported from European zoos (out of the EAZA/EEP) to the reintroduction
center in Shahdag National Park. Four calves were born in the reintroduction center within the first three years. In December 2021, the first group
of twenty wisent were released from the reintroduction enclosure into the
core zone of the national park. Until 2028, the project plans to bring up to
one hundred wisent from the EAZA/EEP. According to experts, Shahdag
National Park, with its 321,240 acres, can hold up to four hundred wisent.
To monitor the wisent, some cows have been fitted with GPS/VHF collars;
camera traps have been installed; and beginning in 2022 to 2023, annual
winter counting will be implemented by park rangers and wildlife biologists.

"The Ecoregional Conservation Plan for the Caucasus [ECP, 2020], a
conservation strategy developed and agreed to by all six range countries—
with the participation of governments, nongovernmental organizations,

and research institutes and with the support of the German government—provides an excellent instrument for joint conservation efforts such as the reintroduction initiatives in the Greater Caucasus, even in a conflict region, with clearly defined conservation targets not only for species-conservation programs (as for the wisent), but also for other locally or globally endangered species and other conservation initiatives on an ecoregional level," says Aurel Heidelberg, a forester and wildlife biologist who has been responsible for various conservation and reintroduction programs in the Caucasus ecoregion for the World Wide Fund for Nature–Germany since 2008. "Also, thanks to joint conservation efforts within the past two decades under the umbrella of the ECP, we still find huge, suitable ecosystems which are under protection and therefore provide habitats and enough space to build up viable populations of large mammals such as the wisent," Heidelberg adds. "Therefore, we believe that the Caucasus is a big opportunity for international wisent conservation and for free-ranging wisent herds. But to reach a viable population we need time and resources. It can be managed only with joint efforts of governments, international and national organizations, research institutes, and, last but not least, together with local communities."

Officials in Germany agree with this assessment of the project's importance. "It is very important to us to support this project again this year—despite all the hurdles we are facing," Berlin Zoological Garden and Tierpark Berlin director Andreas Knieriem declared on the zoo website. "Even if other topics currently dominate the news, endangered animal species still need our help in these times."

THE METHODS USED IN GATHERING AND RELEASING WISENT INTO RESTORation areas are reminiscent of early efforts in the United States, such as the release at Wichita Mountains, and at the same time distinctly modern, as outlined by Florian Sicks. The Tierpark Berlin, for which he is senior curator, started providing wisent for rewilding in 2018, when they offered five for a World Wide Fund for Nature project in Romania. "Only a small number of the wisents we send abroad are actually born in the Tierpark," he says. "They come from several different countries. We are the central clearinghouse for the animals. They are sent here, medically examined, and boxed up and sent to the airport." Individual animals have to meet certain criteria before they are transported, he says. For example, calves must be at least two years old and the cows should not be pregnant. Moreover, the European Endangered Species Programme, founded in 1985, sets mandatory breeding recommendations for zoos as part of an effort to keep genetic diversity as high as possible and to avoid inbreeding among captive "reserve" herds that serve as a backup should a catastrophe, such as disease, wipe out wild populations. The EEP coordinator selects breeding animals based on each animal's genetics and suitability, a process in which the pedigree book plays an important role.

Since 2019, the Tierpark Berlin, as a partner of the reintroduction program in Shahdag National Park, has been involved in transporting wisent to Azerbaijan—a good example of how bison are moved from place to place today. The World Wide Fund for Nature, EAZA/EEP, and the Tierpark Berlin are planning to transport up to ten wisent yearly to Azerbaijan. "We are getting ready to fly seven wisents to Azerbaijan," Sicks explains in November 2021. "We originally were planning on nine animals, but two from Belgium were pregnant, so we were left with seven. The next step: the wisents are vaccinated, examined, and tested for brucellosis and other diseases—they are put under anesthesia and a blood sample is taken. In addition, one animal is fitted with a GPS band [radio-transmitter collar] so we can follow the movements of the herd. We generally choose the leading cow for that. Then, about fourteen days later, they are loaded into large wooden boxes and taken to the airport." The entire transport, from fence to fence, should take no longer than twenty-four hours—nothing compared to the era when bison were transported across the United States in trains in the early 1900s. The average stay for these rewilding wisent at the Tierpark is around six months, between arrival and transport.

From the airport in Azerbaijan, the bison are transported in trucks. At reintroduction sites, bison enter enclosures where they can adjust to their new environment while being monitored by biologists, park rangers, and veterinarians. "We are bringing the bison to an area where they have not lived for a long time, and we have to make sure that they can cope here," Aurel Heidelberg says. After arrival at Shahdag, they are kept in a 300-hectare fenced area (about 740 acres) of the national park for a few months before the gates are opened and the wisent can leave of their own accord. After the release, the animals receive supplementary fodder (hay, acorns), in particular in winter, to make sure they can adapt slowly to winter conditions when food is scarce. This provision also ensures that they will not wander from a protected reintroduction site, helping them to avoid conflicts with local forest farmers. To monitor the herds, some animals are collared with GPS/VHF collars to allow park rangers and biologists to track them. "Monitoring is a key instrument to either prove success or adapt conservation measures," Heidelberg says. "An adequate natural food supply and the size of the area in the reintroduction area are important factors to assure that animals stay healthy, can reproduce and spread to reach as soon as possible a minimum viable population size. At the same time, we have to ensure that the national park staff is well trained and equipped to ensure the protection of the animals, but also to make sure that necessary wildlife-management measures can be applied, for example to mitigate human-wildlife conflicts (such as damages on surrounding meadows) caused by the wild cattle. Besides that, a regular dialogue between the reintroduction project and the inhabitants of surrounding local communities is a key component for smooth coexisting between human and wisent."

AS IN THE UNITED STATES OF AMERICA, BISON RESTORATION IN EUROPE FACES cultural and socioeconomic challenges. An example comes from one of the first bison releases in Germany: the Eleonorenwald project in 2005 on a 6,670-acre site in Niedersachsen. Within the site sprawled a 2,500-acre, privately owned, fenced area used for hunting for more than a century. Usually open to the public, the hunting preserve harbored red deer, fallow deer, roe deer, and wild boar. At the start of the reintroduction program, the state Ministry of Environment cooperated with the forest owners in efforts to release bison into the area, provided that public access would be limited only to guided tours. Then local politicians and officials stepped in and gave instructions to allow normal public access. However, none of the project partners wanted to take responsibility for the public, and the project ended three years after it began, with the bison removed to other reintroduction sites.

One of the primary concerns for wisent survival, says Florian Sicks, is "all about the question, How much space are people willing to allot to animals that were living here long before us?" According to Rewilding Europe, "On average the home range for a bison population is about 10,000 hectares [about 25,000 acres] and should thus be considered as minimum area for a 'true' reintroduction of bison living in the wild." Although finding such large expanses is a challenge, Sicks says, "I feel confident that the wisent will survive, certainly in those regions where space is less of a problem."

The IUCN outlines several key threats to wisent survival. According to a recent report, "several exacerbating factors" are expected "to continue across the current and next generation unless there are substantial multi-national adjustments in management of free-living European Bison." As outlined by the IUCN, these threats are:

- *Lack of viable breeding herds:* Most herds are too small to survive long into the future. Eighty-three percent include fewer than the 150 mature animals needed to sustain a herd; 34 percent include fewer than twenty-five bison.
- *Genetics:* Because all surviving Euro bison are descended from no more than a dozen animals, genetic variability is very low. For example, although nearly five hundred bison in Poland's Bialowieza Forest compose one of the largest herds, its genetic diversity makes it equivalent to a herd of only thirty animals.
- *Herd fragmentation:* Free-ranging bison herds are isolated from one another by physical obstacles or by the geographic distance between herds. According to IUCN data, 77 percent of forty-three free-living subpopulations are isolated from other herds, imposing limits on genetic diversity.
- *Artificial feeding and culling:* Restoration programs released wisent mostly into forests, which do not provide the animals with premium habitat. Consequently, all eight subpopulations greater than 150 animals are given supplemental food. When herds grow, some are culled—animals are removed—to reduce conflicts with landowners. Both of these measures, reports the IUCN, "could lead to unintended consequences, including unsustainable expense, reduced subpopulation viability, and disruption of the species evolved natural life history."
- *Conservation dependence:* Wisent survival depends heavily on such measures as supplemental feeding in winter and transport of animals from one breeding site to another. Governments are inconsistent in establishing policies for bison support and in conceiving programs that would allow the species to become truly free-living, truly wild. "Progress in

recovery of the European Bison through large-scale ecological restoration projects will depend on significant changes in its legal status and management as wildlife by governments, harmonisation of policies and activities among agencies at multiple levels, cooperation with environmental organisations, and public tolerance and support of free-living bison managed as wildlife on large landscapes," avows the IUCN.

Public tolerance has proved to be an elusive goal. Talking about resistance from foresters in North Rhine-Westphalia, Sicks says, "That is just the reality; not everyone has a heart for animals." Usually, private landowners who cultivate commercial forests do not think highly of the bison's proclivity for stripping bark from trees. "In forest under protection, such as national parks, this is not an economic problem," Aurel Heidelberg says. "But it is a natural process which opens forest stands and provides habitats for certain other species. It becomes a problem if you are in a managed forest or on agricultural land, where wisent can cause economic damages which affect landowner profits." Germany offers payments for damages, but not all forest owners see payment as full compensation for lost trees.

Ecologically, the bison benefit the habitat when gnawing bark from beech trees and opening up glades in the forest. Forest owners take a different view, tallying some 600,000 euros in tree damage during the ten years that the North Rhine-Westphalia project has been in effect, according to a report by the University of Veterinary Medicine Hannover. Legal battles over the bison, with forest owners suing conservationists, have run on for years. Forest owners are paid for damaged trees, but as one forester told a newspaper reporter covering the controversy, he felt that the compensation did not cover the losses. Moreover, he was not paid for the time he had to spend driving into the forest with appraisers and assessing damage. The one hope for forest owners and bison conservationists is construction of a fence that will contain bison while letting other species, such as deer, move freely. A proposed fence would hold the bison on 2,075 acres, at least temporarily, making captives of animals reintroduced to the wild in order to be wild.

Under the original plan for the ailing Rothaar restoration site, the bison were to roam on 10,625 acres donated by a local prince. The bison, however, were soon drifting across up to 34,600 acres belonging to other landowners.

Kaja Heising and her colleagues avoided conflicts with forest farmers by putting out hay and silage for wisent in winter so the animals would not need to search for food. They also used GPS transmitters to identify the animals' land use in order to implement measures as needed, such as selection of feeding sites.

The European bison today has been introduced or reintroduced to ten nations, with a total of forty-seven herds containing 6,819 free-ranging animals within historical range in Belarus, Bulgaria, Germany, Latvia, Lithuania, Poland, Romania, Russia, the Slovak Republic, and Ukraine, according to the Breeding Book 2020. Some 2,300 bison roam Poland alone, according to Wanda Olech. Another 2,292 bison were held in captivity, according to the book. The species' recovery is seen as a success, with the largest populations found in Poland, Belarus, and Russia, but only eight of the forty-seven herds are large enough to remain genetically viable into the future. The appeal of the animals has even resulted in the introduction of four wisent in summer 2022 to West Blean and Thornden Woods, a nature reserve near Canterbury, in England. Wisent have never occurred in England, but biologists are hoping the animals will remove encroaching conifer trees and restore more natural conditions dominated by birch trees.

The IUCN downlisted the wisent from vulnerable to near threatened in January 2021. However, Florian Sicks is cautious about the future. He says he can't imagine that wisent roaming truly wild can work in much of today's Europe. "I'm afraid that Western Europe is too densely populated for a stable bison population. Maybe the bison can be reintroduced locally—that it can settle as well as the wolf has done—but I think it is unlikely for reasons of space."

Bison biologists in Europe also inescapably face the dilemma that confronts bison managers in the United States, in Canada, in Mexico, and in Russia: How do you keep bison wild if they are being fed and fenced? Will the animals over time evolve to be little more than livestock? To better understand such issues, an inquiring mind should return to the place where it all more or less began: Yellowstone National Park.

CHAPTER 9

THE LAST REFUGE

Yellowstone National Park is the home base of a remarkable herd of bison, animals whose ancestry can be traced back to the few surviving buffalo that the army worked so hard to protect in the 1880s, 1890s, and early 1900s. Today's herd and its forebears make Yellowstone the only site south of the US-Canada border that has served as buffalo habitat since a time before history, making the saga of park bison representative of bison wherever they are found.

At about 5,450 animals in summer 2021, Yellowstone bison constitute the largest buffalo population on US public lands. They live in two more or less separate herds: 1,300 or so inhabit the park's central area, which offers a geyser basin where the animals can find a modicum of warmth in brutal winters; roughly 4,100 others range the warmer northern reaches of the park and, in rough winters, may cross the park boundary and drift onto lower, less frigid nonpark lands.

Although Yellowstone buffalo are arguably the last free-ranging bison in the United States, they don't roam entirely free, given that they can be shot if they wander outside the park or beyond certain designated, adjacent lands. This hunting pressure causes the animals to retreat into the safety of the national park rather than expand their range and wanderings. Making bison captive within the park could in itself have devastating effects on the herd, because Yellowstone, which rises more than 7,500 feet above sea level, is not prime bison habitat—it doesn't offer the sweep of rich grasslands that the Great Plains once did. Nevertheless, by preserving the descendants of the last wild US bison, the park is helping biologists to understand bison ecology, giving them a glimpse at how bison once lived, how they roamed, and how they interacted with one another and with their environment.

BISON ARE RELATIVELY EASY TO OBSERVE IN YELLOWSTONE: THEY FEED IN summer in the Lamar and Hayden Valleys, which are accessible during peak tourist season to motor vehicles; they're huge when fully grown, making them easy to spot; and they're social, forming scattered herds that average around twenty individuals in winter and two hundred in summer. During the mating season, in July and August, herds can exceed one thousand. Bulls stand out during this season, which is called the rut. They aggressively advertise their fitness and dominance by bellowing guttural roars that can travel long distances, by pawing the ground and throwing up clouds of dust, and, most overtly of all, by fighting other bulls. Once the rut ends, the excitement winds down, and mature bulls—generally more than six years old—leave the cow herds in favor of small, all-bull herds or a solitary existence. The large summer herds disperse, beginning in autumn and reaching a low ebb in March and April.

During winter, Yellowstone bison face several stresses, including temperatures sometimes falling far below zero; the withering of forage plants, which reduces their nutritional value; and the burying of forage under snow. Unlike other ungulates, which dig through snow with their front hooves, bison sweep deep snow aside with a sideways movement of their massive heads, backed with powerful muscles anchored to the prolonged vertebral spine that forms the hump. Although well adapted to cold, even bison cannot survive the miseries of particularly severe winters in Yellowstone without risking their lives and the lives of their young, so they sometimes attempt to leave the park for lower elevations. In this case, the bison are not seeking the most nutritional food plants. They are seeking areas with the least snow.

As spring begins to arrive, and snow to melt, sprouting vegetation forms a wave of new growth that begins in the warmer, lower elevations. The green wave follows the warmth, moving upward with the advance of spring. These young plants are highly nutritious, and bison graze the low-elevation areas from April through June. Most ungulates native to Yellowstone follow the rising tide of the green wave. In the earliest days of spring and new plant growth, bison leave winter ranges along with elk, deer, and other ungulates, but bison don't stick with the migration program. They let the wave flow past them, feeding intensively on low-elevation sites, eating freshly sprouting, nutritionally rich grasses and sedges. They cut down the plants over and over so that stems never reach more than a few inches tall.

Such trimming, clipping, and suppression would, at first glance, seem harmful to the new growth, but Yellowstone biologists have found quite the opposite. Bison create "grazing lawns," forcing plants to continue producing highly nutritional new growth. If the bison did not do this, the plants would grow to their full height earlier in the year, shortening the growing season and yielding less nutritional foliage. NASA satellite images show that heavily grazed areas become green earlier in the spring, more intensely, and for a longer time. The bison's "influence on the landscape affects the entire way that spring moves through the mountains and valleys of Yellowstone," according to the park website. "Bison are not just moving to find the best food; they are creating the best food by how they move."

Rick Wallen, who worked at Yellowstone for almost seventeen years as a wildlife biologist and as leader of the Bison Ecology and Management Team after previously working with bison in Grand Teton National Park, says he believes bison can detect which grasses have higher nitrogen content, a vital element to plant and soil ecology. The bison return the ingested nitrogen to the soil in urine and manure, providing nutrients for ants, beetles, and other animals that in turn make the nitrogen accessible to plants. "Bison keep grasses in a highly productive stage and keep grazing it until moisture disappears in autumn, making the land more productive than it would be without grazing," Wallen says. In such ways, bison not only eat plants but also contribute to Yellowstone's annual growth of 165 million to 172 million pounds of plant matter.

This behavior benefits other herbivores and the predators and scavengers that feed on the herbivores. Bison further serve the ecosystem by churning the soil with their hooves, keeping it from compacting as they move repeatedly between feeding sites and along migratory routes. Individual bison travel about one thousand miles yearly, more than any other park ungulate. A Canadian biologist calculated that the one thousand bison in Saskatchewan's Grasslands National Park leave about seven million hoofprints yearly, not only marking their movement but also stirring the soil.

He also calculated that one thousand bison would produce enough dung to cover 300 acres a year with a rich fertilizer.

In Yellowstone, calves are born from March through June, with about 80 percent of these births occurring between April 25 and May 25. Specifics depend on geography. Cows in the northern region of the park give birth about two weeks earlier than those that live in the more frigid central region. Although only a few miles separate the two herds, 72 percent of births in the northern herd occur before May 7, while 63 percent of births in the central area occur after May 8. The calving season marks the time of red calves dancing among the herds or following at their mothers' sides, bright evidence of a herd's vitality and its future. The color fades to brown by four months of age.

Births tend to coincide with the new growth of plants at the end of winter. This coordination—which means that milk production begins when plants high in protein are starting to sprout—is critical for calves to grow quickly and for cows to recover lost body fat and muscle mass. The cows need the extra nutrition to produce milk fat, which is derived from a cow's food, not from her body. However, because calves are born near the end of winter, when, for several months, the nutritional value of forage plants has been low, survival for cows can be a challenge in early spring. Larger cows tend to do better than smaller ones. Growth during summer is critical for calves, too, as larger calves are more likely to survive their first winter. According to *Yellowstone Bison: Conserving an American Icon in Modern Society*, the growth rate of bison calves and their body size at the start of their first winter "reflects the food available to their mothers for milk production."

Calves are generally able to stand and nurse within thirty minutes of hitting the ground. They soon are able to travel with their mothers and begin eating grass and drinking water when only a week old. They generally continue to depend on their mother's milk for seven to twelve months, though some may nurse for up to a year and a half. By the time a calf is weaned, it is familiar with the foods it will eat for the rest of its life, which could span another twenty years or more. Adults usually graze in meadows and plains, spending up to eleven hours a day eating the twenty-five or so pounds of grasses, sedges, and similar plants that make up 90 percent of their daily diet. They also nosh on forbs and various parts of woody plants, though they're less inclined to do so than are European bison.

Like elk, deer, moose, domestic cattle, and many other hoofed species worldwide, bison are ruminants, which means their digestive systems are complicated. Digestion begins when a grazing bison trims off sprigs of grass and other foods, chews them while simultaneously wetting them with saliva, and swallows. This bolus of vegetative material goes to a large digestive organ, the rumen, one of the bison's four stomachs, where the bolus sits and ferments while the bison continues grazing, adding more and more chewed, wet grass to the fermentation vat. When the bison has had enough, it may stand or lie down to chew its cud—a wad of grasses burped up from the rumen. The bison will add more saliva to the lump of vegetation and thoroughly grind it into slivers. The cud is swallowed and moves through the rumen and passes on to the second stomach, the reticulum, which continues the digestive process begun in the rumen before delivering the bolus to stomach number three, the omasum, where some nutrients are absorbed before the bolus enters the abomasum, which is equivalent to the stomach of a nonruminant. There, the plant matter and accompanying microbes are digested. The nutrients are absorbed as the digested material moves through the small and large intestines before leaving the body. The entire process takes about seventy-eight hours, a relatively long time among ruminants— cattle digest their food in about sixty-four hours—which means that bison can process low-quality flora more completely than some other hoofed, or ungulate, species, a distinct nutritional and ecological advantage that allows them to survive even in marginal habitat.

The rumen of an adult bison can hold about forty gallons of material, including a microbe population in the tens of millions of organisms per ounce. The microbes turn plant protein into essential amino acids for their own use, but the acids also are absorbed by the bison and help build body tissues. "In other words," according to experts, "energy is supplied to bison through the fermentation of dietary carbohydrates, while protein is supplied through the digestion of rumen microbes." The microbes themselves may fulfill 25 percent of a bison's protein need after they are digested in the abomasum.

Yellowstone bison have done well. Recent data indicate that 60 to 80 percent of calves born in April or May are still alive the following April, according to Wallen. About 90 percent of animals in this age-class survive from their first to second birthdays, he says. "All older female bison survive from year to year at a rate of about 95 to 98 percent. We don't have data for males, so we have to assume that they have a similar but likely not quite as good of a survival rate as females as they reach ten years old. Fighting during the rut reduces male survival probability as they age." When it comes to survival, buffalo outlast mule deer (94 percent chance of surviving at least a year), pronghorn (80 percent), and bighorn sheep (65 percent). So it's no surprise that the park's bison population is growing by 10 to 17 percent yearly.

Predators—which in this case means wolves and grizzly bears, the only park predators likely to attack an adult bison—do not kill a significant number of buffalo. Grizzlies are omnivores, eating a wide range of foods, from pine seeds to ground squirrels to ungulates. Wolves are ungulate specialists, but in one study, bison amounted to only 5 percent of their diet. Wolves prefer to hunt elk, which make up 90 percent of their kills. Wolves kill bison mostly in winter, when deep snows bog down the buffalo or they are weak from hunger or illness. The northern Yellowstone herd tripled in size after wolves were reintroduced to the park, a clear indicator that wolves are a small threat. Calves would be easy pickings, but bison as a group will defend threatened calves, sometimes forming a circle around them and facing out, brandishing their horns. Even wolves and bears find that wall of resistance discouraging.

THE RECOVERY OF YELLOWSTONE BISON IS TESTIMONY TO DECADES OF MAN-agcment that have benefited park wildlife. This management has reflected the burgeoning expertise of park administrators and biologists as knowledge of habitat, wildlife, and ecology has accrued through time. When Congress set aside Yellowstone as a park, the avowed goal was to protect its geological features, such as geysers and rock formations shaped by heat and water. From 1872 to 1883, area residents could cut trees for firewood or building material and kill wildlife without interruption. Wildlife protection didn't become an issue until after 1883, when poachers were jeopardizing the last wild bison south of the border with Canada, but it was not the sort of protection we know today. Species such as elk, deer, wild sheep, and bison were protected in the park, or at least an attempt was made to protect them. A similar attempt was not made to protect Yellowstone's wolves, bears, or mountain lions, which were generally perceived as threats to the favored game species and were targeted for extermination. This policy was successful with wolves, which were wiped out in the 1920s and did not occur again in the park until 1995, when wolves from Canada were introduced as part of an endangered species restoration project.

Despite the enactment of laws to protect Yellowstone bison in the late 1800s, poaching continued for various reasons—market hunting, trophies, meat, the fun of it (a.k.a. "sport"). An estimated six hundred park bison in 1880 were whittled down to perhaps twenty-three by 1902, thirty years after the park's creation. In that year, park managers augmented the herd with plains bison of Pablo-Allard and Charles Goodnight origins. The introduced bison were kept in a fenced pasture until 1907, when they were moved to the Lamar Buffalo Ranch in the Lamar River valley. Until at least 1915, the bison were treated as if they were ranch stock: closely herded during the day, moved into a fenced pasture each night. The bison grew accustomed to this life, it seems. Bulls that were released from the pasture or that broke out rarely if ever joined wild bison, and twenty bulls driven fourteen miles from the ranch in 1914 all came back on their own.

Meanwhile, the original wild herd, once it was protected from poaching, grew. Free-roaming bison—which might have included both former ranch bison and wild bison, as the two groups started mixing between 1915 and 1920—apparently doubled in number from 1903 to 1921 as poaching ground to a halt. Specific numbers were hard to ascertain because the park's bison were generally so wary that they were difficult to locate. By 1915, the official count was nearly one hundred. That year, the ranch bison were put out to pasture for the entire summer, free to mix with the wild bison. However, the wild bulls presumably did most of the breeding, because ranch bulls were routinely slaughtered, and more than half of male ranch calves were castrated. "As a result," wrote biologist Mary Meagher in *The Bison of Yellowstone National Park*, "the number of aggressive, dominant [ranch] bulls with the intermingled groups would have been considerably decreased."

During the next few years, park staff focused not on maintaining a wild bison population but on preserving bison in general, regardless of their domesticity or their wildness. This approach took the form, for example, of riders on horseback rounding up as many bison as they could find in late autumn and herding them—never an easy task—into the Lamar Valley, where the bison were fed through winter and culled if they surpassed the number managers thought the park could sustain. Staff killed any crippled, diseased, and aged bison and any others deemed unsuitable. The bison were treated to hay every winter through 1952.

A shift began in 1930 from ranching to preserving bison as wild and free-roaming. This shift became firmer in the wake of a 1932 ecological study of habitat conditions and the park's capacity for maintaining bison. At this time, indeed from 1929 through 1932, bison that wintered in the Lamar Valley numbered in excess of one thousand animals. The biologist who conducted the ecological study urged the Park Service to keep the bison under one thousand. One measure of the rudimentary state of 1930s ecological study is this: today, park staff think Yellowstone may be able to support ten times that number. However, the Park Service repeatedly lowered the maximum number in the years following the study. Aerial counts of park bison didn't begin until 1949. They were not done every year, and the canvassers did not strain to count all bison nor to search all the main herding sites each time. When the planes didn't fly, counts were accomplished on the ground. Either way, the data were not reliable, though perhaps they might have indicated population trends.

Culling, or removal, of bison became park policy in the wake of the 1932 ecological study. Culling was linked in part to winter, which in Yellowstone can be brutal even for bison. The northern region is relatively warm, with January temperatures averaging 18 degrees Fahrenheit and snow depths from 1 to 3.5 feet. The central part of the park is another matter, with January lows of minus 44 degress Fahrenheit and a snowpack that may reach 6 feet deep. In the pre-Columbian era, bison probably would have migrated out of the park during especially tough winters, but during the first century or so of Yellowstone National Park's existence, bison, so few in number, rarely left. This behavior led management to believe that bison moved out only when their numbers were so high that the park did not produce enough forage to sustain them. In effect, bison migration was interpreted as a symptom of an ecological ailment—overpopulation. This diagnosis, based more on intuition than on data, resulted in culling designed to keep the animals to only a few hundred head. By 1952, the Lamar herd was down to 143 animals. An aerial count in March 1967 turned up 397 bison in total for Yellowstone. The park population for years was "lower than at any time since the early years of the introduced herd," according to Mary Meagher. Some areas of bison habitat were emptied of this key grassland species. The park was more or less re-creating the devastation of the nineteenth century.

In 1969—as administrators segued into a new management style that treated the park less like a ranch and more like a wild place where natural ecology should be preserved—culling to control the population stopped. At that time, the northern herd numbered fewer than one hundred animals, and the central herd four hundred—a total population park-wide of around five hundred. Without culling, the bison rebounded to three thousand by 1990. This change in numbers brought changes in behavior. Before 1975, only a few bulls left the park, but as herds grew, they began to expand their winter range by crossing Yellowstone's northern and western boundaries. Naturally, they came into conflict with people, primarily livestock growers who saw these native ungulates as competitive grazers that should be, if not eliminated, at least greatly curtailed. "It's all about grass," says Mike Mease, campaign coordinator of Buffalo Field Campaign, a conservation group that seeks to reduce bison slaughter and increase bison mobility. Ranchers, he says, think all the grass is theirs.

Given the political clout of the livestock industry in the states surrounding Yellowstone, a revival of culling seemed almost inevitable. It was indeed revived by the early 1980s and continues to this day, one way or another. One of the most intensive collisions between bison and the livestock industry, in this case in Montana, occurred in the winter of 1996 to 1997, leading slowly to changes in bison management. State officials and spokesmen for the livestock industry alleged that what happened that winter had nothing to do with grass and everything to do with a perceived threat posed by bison to cattle.

BRUCELLOSIS IS A BACTERIAL DISEASE THAT CAN CAUSE ABORTIONS, INFER-tility, and lowered milk production in cattle and bison. The bacterium is not native to North America and was probably transmitted to Yellowstone bison by European cattle that shared a pasture with the bison at the Lamar Buffalo Ranch after 1915. It was first detected in the northern herd in 1917. The disease usually is transmitted during calving season—the bacteria accumulate in placentas and body fluids, and a buffalo or domestic cow that touches infected afterbirth or amniotic fluid with nose or tongue can catch brucellosis. Elk also carry the disease, which can infect humans too, though it rarely does so in the United States. In humans it takes the form of undulant fever. Rarely fatal and incapable of being passed from person to person, it can cause chronic fevers if not treated early. In 1934, the US Department of Agriculture initiated a program to eradicate brucellosis in cattle, a project that has cost $3.5 billion in federal and state taxes and private funds, with costs still mounting, though the disease has been documented in less than 0.0001 percent of US herds. The program wiped out the brucellosis bacterium across most of the nation, with the exception of feral hogs in Texas and of elk and bison in Yellowstone and the surrounding ecosystem.

With the start of the national eradication program, Yellowstone staff cooperated with the US Department of Agriculture in testing the bison herd. In the 1940s, the Park Service began to vaccinate bison calves and slaughter animals that tested positive for the disease. A major problem with these tests, then and now, is that animals that are infected and can transmit the disease and those that were infected but have recovered and can no longer transmit it both test positive, which for decades has been a death sentence.

When the Lamar Buffalo Ranch shut down in 1952, testing stopped, though it was revived in the mid-1960s. Brucellosis management focused on elk in the southern part of the Yellowstone ecosystem, which includes Grand Teton National Park and other federal and state lands beyond the park, and on bison in the northern boundary area, which abuts Montana.

To date, no case of bison infecting cattle in the field has been documented, even though 60 percent of adult Yellowstone bison cows have tested positive for exposure to brucellosis. No more than 30 percent of these bison can transmit the disease. Experts calculate that the risk bison pose as disease vectors to cattle is "negligible" for at least three reasons: federal land managers keep bison and cattle apart, bison calve before ranchers release cattle on summer range, and bison tend to move to higher pastures in national parks after the snow melts, places where cattle cannot go. The risk of bison spreading the disease to cattle is estimated at 1 percent, as opposed to 99 percent for transmission by elk. The three biologists who wrote *Yellowstone Bison* contend that "many of the approximately 450,000 cattle in the Greater Yellowstone Area are fed on private land holdings during winter and released on public grazing allotments during summer— but throughout the year they are allowed to mingle with wild elk. . . .

[M]anagement to suppress brucellosis in bison will not substantially reduce the far greater transmission risk from elk."

Brucellosis became a divisive issue after park staff announced they would stop shooting bison for population control in 1969. Until then, park authorities had shown limited interest in disease control and were not pressured by the livestock industry. Alarmed by the specter of an end to culling, officials from Montana, Idaho, and Wyoming protested that the bison population would expand outside the park if not controlled. The Park Service responded in 1968 by shooting bison that wandered close to the northern and western park boundaries. In the 1970s, park personnel shot two to eight bison in a succession of winters. None of this border control aroused public or political concern until the late 1980s, when Montana started a sport bison hunt outside the park. The bison did not retreat from the hunters, having had no experience with this threat. When media reports showed the bison being killed by sport hunters at close range, the shooting drew a certain amount of public opprobrium. By 1991, public controversy had led to Montana legislation that shut down the hunt. Hazing, or herding, bison away from border areas on horseback or vehicle had by then become a primary means for keeping bison inside the park.

Meanwhile, the US Department of Agriculture's Animal and Plant Health Inspection Service (APHIS)—which, among other responsibilities, certifies the health of US agricultural products—unintentionally added to the pressure to contain bison within the park when it declared Wyoming brucellosis-free in 1983, Montana in 1985, and Idaho in 1991. Officials in these three states, which surround Yellowstone Park, now feared that if bison weren't culled, the states would not be able to maintain their brucellosis-free status, which was achieved through great effort. For example, Montana earned its brucellosis-free status by running an aggressive campaign against the disease, beginning in 1952, at a cost of $30 million to the livestock industry.

In the first half of the 1990s, a barrage of lawsuits and complaints aimed by Montana livestock officials at federal agencies related to Yellowstone and to agriculture led to an agreement to develop an interim bison/brucellosis management plan that would take effect until the Park Service issued an official management plan, then in the works. This task was nothing that the service had not been working on for decades, testing various approaches to dealing with brucellosis in bison and elk. They tried or contemplated birth control and vaccination, but neither worked. The methods were not 100 percent effective, and anyway, trying to treat hundreds or thousands of wild animals roaming across millions of wild acres was prohibitive in several ways—expensive, labor intensive, unreliable. Instead, the Park Service stepped up its herd-reduction program, settling on two primary ways, along with hazing, for doing so: shooting bison that left the park, and capturing bison that were moving toward or across park borders, testing them for brucellosis, and shipping to slaughter those that tested positive, regardless of false positives. Between 1985 and 2000, about 3,100 bison learned that trying to leave the park in search of suitable habitat in tough winters was a fatal mistake. Some were shot by licensed sport hunters and by tribal hunters who had treaty rights. State agents killed hundreds. And some bison were rounded up and slaughtered, with the meat going to tribes or relief agencies. "Every bison was seen as a threat to the livestock industry," Rick Wallen says. "That was an extreme exaggeration." Regardless, the industry and a handful of politicians who kowtowed to them dominated state bison policy. "Small, specific interests were driving the philosophy of wildlife management," Wallen says.

In late 1996, Yellowstone's bison population stood at a record level—upward of 3,500 animals. Then winter struck with a vengeance, burying food plants beyond reach under alternating layers of early snow, rain that turned to ice, and more snow. Wildlife had to hoof through the layers, sinking into the snow, crashing through the ice, and sinking into deeper snow. Famished bison in search of forage moved toward lower elevations outside the park. When they crossed park boundaries, they encountered federal and state agents who shot or sent to slaughterhouses more than 1,000 of them as winter wore on. Buffalo that stayed in the park were unmolested, but more than 1,300 of them starved to death. The toll marked the largest incident of bison mortality in more than a century.

Shooting bison made for poor public relations even before winter was fully under way. The *Billings (MT) Gazette* reported in December 1996 that the "practice of shooting bison proved to be a controversy of national proportions." The *Gazette* went on to report details of how Montana livestock officials were capturing bison that wandered outside the park and testing them for brucellosis. The state had two pens outside the park into which agents lured bison with hay. Herded into a squeeze chute, which more or less immobilizes individual bison, cows were tested for pregnancy and all of the captives endured having blood withdrawn from beneath their tails. They left with a shiny souvenir—a metal tag in the left ear that indicated they'd been tested. They also were stained with a purple dye that would remain visible for up to a year. All bison that tested positive were sent off to slaughter-houses. Those that tested negative were released back into familiar habitat. The cost of the operation for the entire winter was estimated to run more than $200,000. The previous year, livestock officials killed four hundred bison at a cost of only $121,000. The state also presumed that more bison would still be shot in winter 1996–1997. Meanwhile, the Park Service was also capturing bison that wandered near park boundaries and shipping all that were caught to slaughter.

A court battle was raging at the time, meant to stop the bison slaughter. Filed by the Sierra Club along with four local conservation groups, the suit sought to block application of the interim bison-management plan to which the Park Service and state livestock officials had agreed earlier in the year and which required killing all pregnant bison and all that tested positive for bru-cellosis exposure that were captured near West Yellowstone from November 1, 1996, through April 30, 1997. The court in mid-December ruled against the groups. The testing and killing would continue. On December 29, the Park Service said that in the course of the winter perhaps hundreds of bison would be killed.

Transboundary bison were shot or captured throughout winter. The *Great Falls (MT) Tribune* reported in December 1996 that in one mid-December day, Montana livestock officials captured thirty-six bison and sent fourteen of them to slaughter, including ten pregnant cows. In Wyoming, sport hunt-ers were allowed to shoot ten bulls in the North Fork Valley, a spot east of Yellowstone National Park in which Wyoming allowed bison hunting if more than fifteen bulls grazed there. Ostensibly this measure was taken to protect grazing for other wildlife—wildlife that, presumably, had survived well in company with bison for tens of thousands of years without human intervention.

In mid-January, the *Ravalli Republic* (Hamilton, MT) reported that more than 600 bison had been slaughtered so far that winter, breaking the pre-vious record of 569 set in winter 1988–1989. Cattle raisers may have been pleased, but others were not. On January 22, 1997, the *Billings Gazette* ran a selection of letters the paper had received from people who thought the current policy was, as one correspondent wrote, "a direct slap at the idea that Yellowstone Park is a haven for Wildlife." Others expressed similar opinions, such as: "This is an environmental crime which cannot be forgiven. God's creatures have a right to survive as much as Montana's cattle industry has a right to exist." And: "I am totally outraged by the slaughter of the Yellowstone bison (or any free-roaming bison) that happen to cross the state line into Montana. I was under the mistaken impression that Montana cared for wildlife and the heritage of our country." And: "There is plenty of public forest land surrounding Yellowstone Park for bison, and much of this land was set aside specifically to meet winter habitat needs of Yellowstone's wildlife." And: "The slaughter of the last free-roaming herd of wild bison steals from Americans a part of our heritage. Allow for bison to migrate onto National Forest Lands surrounding Yellowstone."

Bison continued to leave the park during this particularly tough winter. By late February nearly one thousand bison had been shot or sent to slaughter. The US Secretary of the Interior, the US Secretary of Agriculture, two US senators from Montana, and one member of the US House of Representatives held urgent meetings to try to change course. The *Independent Record*, a newspaper in Helena, Montana, reported, "None of the participants indicated a solution to the bison problem was near, nor that the killing of the animals would halt." In March, Yellowstone biologist Mary Meagher reported that her aerial survey of the park had counted only 1,089 animals out of a herd that had started the winter at about 3,500.

At the same time, John Mundinger, a bison specialist with the Montana Department of Fish, Wildlife, and Parks, was reported by the *Great Falls Tribune* as saying that the state had been trying unsuccessfully since 1988 to get a cooperative, long-term agreement about bison management out of the National Park Service and other federal agencies. "Until an agreement is reached, it's going to be real difficult to do something more responsible than what you're seeing this winter," he said. The *Independent Record* pointed out the absurdity of the situation in an opinion piece that, among other things, declared, "More than 1,000 bison were shot this winter to prevent contact with cattle that were not even present." It also urged state and federal officials "to come to terms with the fact that Yellowstone Park is not a cattle ranch, and Yellowstone bison are not Herefords."

The treatment of bison as livestock seemed not only ecologically bankrupt but also bureaucratically corrupt when the *Missoulian* reported that state livestock inspectors had cleared for sale the meat of some 483 Yellowstone bison killed at slaughterhouses. The meat was sold at eight auctions, all dominated by one meatpacker from Rapid City, South Dakota, that hauled away "truckloads of bison meat." A year earlier such sales had been illegal, but a management agreement had approved of the commerce. A co-owner of the meatpacking company said that 70 percent of the meat was ground into burger and snack foods, and most of it was shipped to outlets in Los Angeles, Dallas, and Newark, New Jersey, with better cuts of meat sold nationwide. The *Missoulan* reported that, according to the spokesman, the products were not marketed as Yellowstone bison. "Frankly, we haven't been telling them where it comes from. It's pretty controversial." The Montana Department of Livestock grossed $154,500 from the auctions, with $35,000 going to various contractors, such as haulers. The rest was used to defray the cost of the program to the state.

Despite the shooting and slaughtering, the bison population continued to grow apace with the augmentation of state and federal pressure to keep brucellosis out of livestock. In the mid-1990s, the State of Montana triggered five years of litigation and mediation by suing the National Park Service for allowing bison to leave the park under the interim policy. The outcome: Montana and the federal government developed a final plan to guide bison management in and around the park. The Interagency Bison Management Plan (IBMP) was issued in 2000 by five cooperating agencies—the National Park Service, the US Forest Service, APHIS, the Montana Department of Livestock, and the Montana Department of Fish, Wildlife, and Parks—which were joined in 2009 by three tribal partners to help achieve park goals: the Confederated Salish and Kootenai Tribes, the InterTribal Buffalo Council, and the Nez Perce Tribe. The central goal was to sustain a wild, free-ranging bison population while reducing the risk of brucellosis transmission from bison to cattle. The chief means for doing so, embedded in a good deal of bureaucratic steps and conditions outlined in the plan, were separation of bison and cattle on the range; hazing of bison away from park boundaries and into the park by staff on horseback, on all-terrain vehicles, and in helicopters; and, if need be, the capture of bison that left the park, followed by testing for brucellosis and slaughter of bison that tested positive. Superficially, at least, it was more or less a continuation of the interim plan.

In the wake of the management plan, not a single case of bison transmitting brucellosis directly to cattle has occurred, even though the Yellowstone population, since the year 2000, has ranged from 2,500 to 5,500 buffalo. On the Yellowstone National Park website, Park Service officials stress that "the state of Montana now allows bison to occupy some habitat adjacent to the park that was previously off-limits, including year-round in some areas, which is a major conservation advancement. However, lack of tolerance for wild bison in most areas outside Yellowstone continues to limit the restoration of this iconic species. Large parts of their historic winter ranges are no longer available due to human development, and because states only allow limited numbers of bison in areas near the park." On the same webpage, Park Service officials make an enlightening admission:

> Many people don't like the fact that animals from a national park are sent to slaughter. We don't like it either. We'd like to see more tolerance for migrating bison on public lands in surrounding states; similar to deer, elk, and other ungulates. The park isn't big enough to let bison numbers increase without more available habitat to sustain them, but we cannot force adjacent states to tolerate more migrating bison.

Some observers reacted to continued culling with unveiled animosity. Two such people, the late Rosalie Little Thunder, a Lakota elder and community leader, and Mike Mease, a Montana videographer, concluded in 1997 that the bison were "in dire need of help." They founded a group called Buffalo Nations, known today as Buffalo Field Campaign, and began daily road patrols of areas where bison were being shot. Mease continues patrols today, hazing bison off of roads where they might be harmed, for example by vehicle traffic. The vague risk of brucellosis, Mease says, did not justify killing bison. In Grand Teton National Park, south of Yellowstone but within the Yellowstone ecosystem, he points out, "bison have carried brucellosis for the past forty-plus years, with diseased bison mixing with cows, and have had no transmission." In his view, as campaign coordinator of Buffalo Field Campaign, the attack on bison as a disease vector marks "a prejudice against Native Americans and the bison." Bison were wiped out, he says, to make room for cattle. The field campaign's primary goal is to achieve a legal status for bison that treats them as wildlife in the same way that elk are managed. "Bison are the only animals not allowed to leave the park," he says. Even grizzlies and wolves leave.

Meanwhile, accumulating data indicated that bison were a minimal threat to cattle. In 2010, the National Park Service published a report, *A Risk Analysis of* Brucella abortus *Transmission Among Bison, Elk, and Cattle in the Northern Greater Yellowstone Area,* which included new research on brucellosis. It underscored elk as more likely than bison to transmit the disease to cattle, in part because elk were more widespread than bison and had more contact with cattle "and are more tolerated by managers and livestock keepers on public grazing allotments. Thus, the predominant source of risk to cattle in the northern portion of the greater Yellowstone area [GYA] is from elk." Elk, the document said, "will continue to represent the vast majority of risk of *B. abortus* exposure to cattle grazing in the northern portion of the GYA. Therefore, brucellosis management efforts should focus more on the comingling of cattle and elk during the critical abortion period to more effectively decrease risk of transmission." And yet, as the report pointed out, "for decades, livestock and regulatory personnel have viewed Yellowstone bison as the highest priority wildlife source of transmission of pathogens for livestock in the GYA." As a result of "the intense focus on bison *B. abortus* management during the past decade, elk have received minimal brucellosis management attention until recently and often move freely across the ecosystem and come into close contact with cattle premises."

Unlike bison, elk are traditional quarry for today's sport hunters, which is a major reason that elk get a pass. "Elk have more political backing, especially from hunters and outfitters, than do bison," says James A. Bailey, coordinator of the Montana Wild Bison Restoration Coalition. Lee C. Jones, a biologist with the US Fish & Wildlife Service Wildlife Health Office in Montana, says, "Elk have been clearly documented as the primary driver of brucellosis in livestock, but everyone wants a lot of elk."

Around 2010 or 2011, Montana officials began to see that they were exaggerated in their concern about brucellosis and bison. Rick Wallen, one of the coauthors of the research papers included in the 2010 risk analysis, says, "They were losing credibility," given that there was no known case of cattle in pastures getting brucellosis from bison, and, in addition, bull bison were culled even though they are not capable of spreading the disease. "No bull bison has ever been pregnant," Wallen says unequivocally. "It's ludicrous that they would spread brucellosis." Research published in 2016, which included Wallen as a coauthor, again reported that data used in the research predicted that the greatest quantity of brucellosis transmission between any two species in the study would be from elk to livestock, whereas predicted bison transmission to livestock was "close to zero and no transmissions of brucellosis from wild bison to cattle have been detected." The study concluded that culling and other management measures "directed towards bison in Yellowstone NP may not affect brucellosis prevalence elsewhere in the [Greater Yellowstone Ecosystem]. Also, *B. abortus* appears to be persisting in elk outside of these locations, so under present conditions it is unlikely that bison are a necessary host for brucellosis persistence."

Adding insult to injury, bison often were being killed on public land—national forests—for the sake of private livestock. Some critics asked by what distorted sense of values do officials endorse killing public wildlife on public land to avoid a nonexistent risk to private livestock. But, progress: through time, the number of cattle on public land diminished because conservation groups bought allotments with no intention of installing cattle or the Forest Service left allotments vacant when leases ended. In addition, to reduce harm to state economies, APHIS in 2010 changed its certification policy. Until that time, when two or more herds had positive tests for brucellosis within a single state, or if one herd tested positive and was not destroyed within sixty days, APHIS would nullify the entire state's brucellosis-free status. After 2010, states are no longer declassified so long as the states investigate positive results and remove all cattle that test positive.

Surveys show that about 72 percent of Montana residents want free-roaming bison, Mease says. "Without a doubt, we can have free-roaming bison," he maintains. He urges a gradual progression toward letting buffalo roam farther and farther afield as they learn where to graze and where not to linger. A portion of the Madison River valley that lies beyond Yellowstone National Park's western border provides habitat for some five thousand elk, Mease says, and should be able to support bison as well. Ranchers who graze cattle in the area get a tax break for each head of cattle they put out. He suggests that if the ranchers who graze the five largest tracts in the area were given the same tax break for grazing bison, they might agree to conservation easements that would open the land to wildlife. The same arrangement could be made in other parts of Montana and on tribal reservations. "There is a lot of land in Montana," he says. "Once we get the state to want bison back, the solutions will appear. We can fence bison off the land of those who don't want them. There are so many solutions, it's just the *want* that's missing."

Conflicts centering on bison have been declining outside the park. Research has confirmed that separating bison and livestock helps to limit any jeopardy from brucellosis. Instead of trying to inoculate wild animals with vaccines, biologists have suggested that the cattle industry adopt the procedures that eradicated brucellosis in livestock across the United States—work with livestock. For example, ranchers could limit brucellosis exposure between cattle and bison by controlling the movement and location of cattle, rather than trying to reduce bison herds. Between 2000 and 2015, about 3,600 bison were removed from Yellowstone without reducing the prevalence of brucellosis. Extensive data indicate that bison outside the park do not increase the risk of brucellosis for livestock. Park authorities have reduced contact between cattle and buffalo by limiting bison to designated conservation zones—areas beyond park borders where buffalo are permitted to roam. Even though hundreds of bison range yearly across conservation zones beyond park borders, bison and cattle have not mixed there since 2013.

EVEN IF CONCERN ABOUT BISON TRANSMISSION OF BRUCELLOSIS HAS abated, Yellowstone still has to deal with limiting bison—the park and its surroundings, however vast, are painfully finite when it comes to the ability of bison herds to outgrow their habitat. One way to reduce bison that has received renewed attention is sport hunting. Bison hunting is illegal in Yellowstone National Park. The National Park Protective Act of 1894 (see chapter 1) banned hunting there and prohibited the possession or removal of wildlife from the park. Even driving wildlife out of the park is illegal. Managers also oppose hunting in the park because it would alter the behavior of many species and the visitor experience. However, the IBMP partners did agree to use hunting outside the park and capturing animals near the park boundary as tools to hold the park population at about five thousand bison. Hunts began during 2005 to 2006, with forty-four licensed Montana hunters. Seven tribes with treaty rights to hunt on public land outside the park also began to participate, dramatically increasing the number of hunters and the number of bison killed. By 2015, hunting had replaced hazing as the primary means for limiting the movement of bison beyond park borders.

Within five years, incidents of hazing dropped from about ninety per year to around ten. But hunting is no panacea for bison population control. For example, the partners agreed to reduce the population by six hundred to nine hundred animals in winter 2021–2022. Since hunters, including tribal hunters, kill only two hundred to four hundred bison during most winters, some animals must be captured to meet the targeted reduction.

While hunting reduces the number of animals sent to slaughter, it is encumbered by certain challenges. Montana issues only around forty bison-hunting permits yearly. Getting one, says Mease—who puts food on his table by hunting elk and deer—is "kind of a chance of a lifetime" as about seven thousand hunters apply. In the winter of 2021–2022, sport hunters shot about four bison and officials captured thirty-eight. More are always captured than shot, Mease says. Based on the outcome of brucellosis tests, twenty-seven of these animals were slaughtered and the rest were put into quarantine.

Hunting has evolved since 2006 as part of the bison control strategy. Now, Wallen says, there's so much hunting pressure that bison are not expanding out of the park as much as they could be. "You can see it in their behavior," Wallen says. "The animals don't push the boundary as hard as they used to." Park staff, Wallen says, "kept arguing that we shouldn't hunt them so hard, because the bison don't explore and expand." If killed or even if hunted intensively, the bison don't bring their young into new territory. Even those without calves become wary and leave the borderlands around the park, retreating into Yellowstone. When bison avoid heavily hunted zones, their numbers in those zones thin out. Eventually, hunters find other places where buffalo are congregating, and the pattern begins anew. The Park Service is cooperating with state agencies to make bison hunting work as it does for species such as elk and deer. To achieve this goal, managers must let bison disperse farther from Yellowstone, which requires greater tolerance for the animals in Montana.

The bison received a boost in 2015 when Montana governor Steve Bullock signed a state decision notice that opened 256,000 acres of grazing land for bison, most of it on the three-million-acre Custer Gallatin National Forest north and west of the park. Bison are now permitted to graze there year-round, the first time in more than a century that bison have been allowed to live full-time in Montana, though the area has been the central herd's calving area for twenty-five years, Mease says. The area is at a lower elevation than the park and allows bison to escape harsh winters. Hundreds of them do so, making the area critical winter range as well as calving grounds. Hunting is permitted there, but not with much success, Mease adds. Bison usually don't enter the area until spring, which is not a prime hunting season. As a bison refuge, however, this national forest, with 1.1 million roadless acres, can be threatened by plans to log and to build logging roads.

The treaty tribes involved, and state officials with wildlife responsibilities, each define their own hunting seasons, licensing, and regulations, though the US Forest Service wields the authority to close areas if hunting becomes unsafe. Hunting zones are established in units of one square mile, with the units separated from one another by two miles of nonhunting areas. Although Yellowstone staff helped develop habitat-suitability models that identified migration routes bison could use to move into areas outside the park, Montana law limits where bison can move beyond park borders. Given the number of entities involved, bison management is a balancing act that seeks to maintain a healthy bison population large enough to protect the ecology of the species and the natural processes that bison contribute to the greater Yellowstone area, but not so large that it could lead to mass migration and conflicts with ranchers and other landowners. Because most of the hunting occurs on conservation areas immediately outside the park and adjacent to private land, it leads to congestion, Wallen says. Several hunters may be shooting at bison from a single herd at the same time, reminiscent of the market hunters of old.

In another attempt to reduce bison slaughter, the National Park Service, APHIS, the State of Montana, and the Fort Peck Assiniboine and Sioux Tribes launched the Bison Conservation Transfer Program (BCTP). The Fort Peck Assiniboine and Sioux Tribes started their own herd of Yellowstone-descended bison with animals from a pilot study that ran from 2005 to 2012. The transfer program now certifies which captured bison do not have brucellosis and ships them to new habitats instead of slaughtering them like livestock. After eight years of negotiation among federal officials, agencies of the State of Montana, and the Fort Peck Assiniboine and Sioux Tribes, the program came to fruition in late August 2019, when the park transferred fifty-five bison to the Fort Peck Indian Reservation in northeastern Montana. Those bison had been held in a testing facility for seventeen months and had been tested twice to prove they did not have the disease. Under APHIS rules, proving that a bison was not infected required placing it in fenced quarantine pastures with similarly aged animals and repeatedly testing it for up to five years. "We went around and around with them," Wallen says, referring to efforts by himself and other park biologists to change the policy. APHIS is still insisting on three tests on every bison captured yearly. Most of the animals are two- or three-year-olds captured primarily in March, Wallen says. Wallen and other bison officials contended that the bison did not need to be tested so many times before being turned over to tribes. No bison that has continuously tested negative in the first ten months of capture has ever come up positive in subsequent tests, Wallen says. He believes that eventually the program should get an authorization for moving male animals to the final stage of assurance testing after November of the first year in quarantine. "A lot of professional opinions are going against each other," he says.

The Fort Peck herd in 2021 numbered upward of 400 bison that range across more than 18,000 acres of rolling hills and sheltered valleys. From 2019 to 2021, 154 bison arrived at the Fort Peck Reservation and 82 of them were turned over to the InterTribal Buffalo Council and sent to seventeen member tribes. Plans call for further transfers in the years ahead. The BCTP has led to the largest ever relocation of Yellowstone bison to Native American tribes. The program is so efficient at capturing and entering bison in the program that there is not enough space for all the bison that qualify. Only two facilities—one inside Yellowstone National Park and one leased by APHIS on private land near the park's northern boundary—can be used for the first and second phases of bison certification. However, park officials have cooperated with Yellowstone Forever, a National Park Service support group, and the Greater Yellowstone Coalition, which seeks to protect the lands, waters, and wildlife of the 20-million-acre Greater Yellowstone Ecosystem, to increase the capacity of the park facility from eighty to two hundred animals. Staff anticipate that further improvements will result in transferring about one hundred animals yearly to tribes. Park staff tried to get other agencies to take bison, but they were turned down by all but the Utah Division of Wildlife Resources, which holds a bison-hunting season, Wallen says. Tribes are invested in bison, he says, so they stand out as a natural partner in bison preservation. "I think the whole effort to reintroduce animals to tribal lands has a long-term future to show people we can live with wildlife," Wallen says.

To many tribal members, bison restoration to tribal lands is not only an alternative to slaughtering the animals but also a means to recover a missing part of themselves. Many tribes feel a unique link to Yellowstone bison because these buffalo, never completely wiped out within the park, are a direct tie to the bison their ancestors hunted and to the place where they hunted them—something no other bison herd offers.

To maintain a wild, migratory bison population, to send bison to other conservation areas instead of slaughtering them, and to support hunting outside the park, the National Park Service in 2022 initiated an updating of the Interagency Bison Management Plan, incorporating new information and accommodating changed conditions in the park. The agencies and tribes that provided input into the new plan are the same as those that cooperated on the 2000 plan, with Custer Gallatin National Forest representing the US Forest Service. The new plan will almost certainly involve bison management on lands outside the park in Montana, where the National Park Service has no control over such activities as hunting and can do little to engender tolerance for bison among communities beyond the park. The National Park Service is considering three preliminary management alternatives and has invited public comment on all of them. The minimal alternative could leave the current management plan in place, and the most innovative could allow the Yellowstone herd to number up to eight thousand bison after calving. A middle alternative falls in between. The chosen alternative could similarly change the hunting and slaughter of bison. At the time of this writing, no decision had been made.

Mease is already skeptical about the changes the new plan will produce. The Park Service, he notes, is suggesting that the park can maintain eight thousand bison, which he doesn't doubt, but he believes that the cattle industry and Montana officials will never agree to that number in the park. The three states surrounding the park, he says, have the most national forest, the most public lands, in the Lower 48 and could "really help wildlife, but they won't. They don't want bears, bison, and wolves." Elk are okay, because hunters kill thousands every year and are a strong political voice for the species. Nevertheless, one way to limit bison inside Yellowstone, Mease says, is to "let them out of the park." The national forests are lower-elevation land—elk winter habitat—which can be bison winter habitat. Once again, he says, "If we want bison back, we can help them come back."

Wallen agrees. "Montana has had a long history of not liking Yellowstone National Park and not liking the management philosophy of the park," he says. Even though the park brings in a lot of money, the idea among some Montanans has been that the federal government locked up commerce in the park: no logging, no mining, no livestock. This view represents the interests of elected officials who represent a small part of the state, Wallen says. They see wildlife as competition for forage. If you look at Montana residents, there's probably a lot of support for doing something for wildlife on public land, he says, "but the legislature has done a lot to block that." As a result, Yellowstone will always have to churn bison, letting the herd grow, then cutting it down. "There's always going to be a need to manage bison at the boundary of acceptability," Wallen says, meaning at the level that local politicians are willing to accept. "That's probably the future of bison management on public lands."

AFTER MORE THAN A CENTURY OF REINTRODUCTIONS AND OTHER MEASURES, the persistent question in bison conservation, restoration, and recovery remains whether the bison is a creature of the wild, or a form of livestock. Whether it will roam free, or remain forever inside fences, shot down when it reproduces too successfully or shows signs of recovering too vigorously. The saga of the bison is still an unfurling epic. "Bison are a wildlife icon in America, and Yellowstone bison represent one of the greatest wildlife conservation stories in our nation's history," declared Daniel N. Wenk, superintendent of Yellowstone National Park, in the preface to the 2015 book *Yellowstone Bison: Conserving an American Icon in Modern Society*. Yet even in Yellowstone the story is unfinished, and bison still have not recovered from the gruesome handiwork of the nineteenth century. The three biologists who wrote *Yellowstone Bison* make this point succinctly (some references and scientific species names have been removed to compress the text):

> Bison are the only wild North American ungulate that has not been recovered across significant portions of their historic range. Unlike bighorn sheep, caribou, deer, elk, moose, mountain goats, and pronghorn, bison receive little tolerance on private or public lands outside of national parks and refuges. Thus, they have failed to gain

legitimate status as wide-ranging wildlife and their conservation is constrained by real and perceived conflicts.

The questions surrounding Yellowstone are not, however, reserved for bison alone. You cannot consider the future of bison without asking how it predicts the destiny of other large animals that roam in herds, a question that comes down to this: If we can't save bison as a wildlife species, how can we hope to save such megafauna as African and Indian elephants, African Cape buffalo, and the towering giraffe? What promise does bison restoration hold for other beleaguered megafauna?

CHAPTER 10

BUILDING A FUTURE FOR BISON

Some three hundred mountain gorillas—the largest of the planet's apes, with males hitting up to four hundred pounds—inhabit the Democratic Republic of the Congo's Virunga National Park, which covers 3,000 square miles of tropical mountains, volcanoes, and savanna. The gorillas live in extended family groups that average ten members but can include up to thirty. The species shares the park with chimpanzees and eastern lowland gorillas, the only place where these three ape species live together. Of course, the mountain gorilla is vastly different from the bison and lives in a habitat that is a far cry from the Great Plains, and yet the ape faces some of the same challenges as the American buffalo. About 8 percent of the park has been taken over by agriculture, and the park lost almost 10 percent of its tree cover between 2017 and 2020. Nearly eight hundred rangers strive to protect the forested mountains and their wildlife from illegal logging, poaching, and militant political groups funded by selling meat from wildlife and charcoal made from forest trees. About one ranger is killed every month in the course of conservation work. Nevertheless, since 2008, the mountain gorilla population has doubled—a success with a dark side. Larger gorilla populations can mean more of the great apes looking for food in farmers' fields, of which there are many, as about eighty thousand people live in the park. The inevitable result: angry farmers, dead gorillas. The secret to saving the animals comes down to finding ways to make wildlife profitable for local residents.

A key means for achieving this goal is tourism. Mountain gorillas are a big attraction, with each animal potentially bringing in about $4 million in tourism trade throughout its lifetime. However, militant terrorist activity is undermining tourism.

Meanwhile, in the southeast African nation of Malawi, the managers of Liwonde National Park have learned in the past few years that Liwonde's more than 600 elephants—the beginning of an overpopulation—are damaging park vegetation and threatening its biodiversity, which includes more than 400 bird and mammal species. Breeding at a rate of 10 percent yearly, the elephants could harm the 211-square-mile park's woodlands, floodplains, and lagoons. In contrast, 236 miles to the north lies Kasungu National Park, with 810 square miles of habitat and a dearth of elephants as a result of poaching, which reduced the park's 1,200 elephants to perhaps 49 by 2015. In a remedy to both problems, Malawi's Department of National Parks and Wildlife—in cooperation with the International Fund for Animal Welfare and with African Parks, a nonprofit that manages and restores parks in partnership with governments and local communities—is translocating 250 elephants from Liwonde to Kasungu. In a project that would have astonished even William T. Hornaday, the park also is moving 405 other individual animals, including Cape buffalo, impala, sable, and warthogs. The elephants are darted with sedatives and taken by truck to their new home. Speaking with the Associated Press, Sam Kamoto of African Parks, which manages twenty protected areas in eleven African nations, said, "This will establish viable elephant populations, and ensure the prosperity of local communities living around the parks. It will also alleviate habitat pressure and reduce human-wildlife conflict." However, like bison in US parks and wildlife refuges, the elephants will be kept in line by a fence, in this case twenty-five miles of an elephant-proof barrier along Kasungu's eastern boundary designed to keep the pachyderms out of nearby farmland.

Protecting and restoring large aggregations of animals is one of wildlife conservation's greatest challenges today. Large herding mammals are among the most vulnerable animals on the planet. Usually, they breed relatively slowly and are easy for poachers to locate. For examples one need look no further than elephants, being slaughtered across Africa. Gestation for an African elephant—the time it takes one to develop from conception to birth— is about twenty-four months. Bulls usually don't become acceptable breeders until they are around forty years old—cows prefer older mates, though they themselves begin producing calves when in their teens. Poaching during the past decade or so has reduced some African elephant populations by 90 percent, particularly the forest elephants of West African rain forest. Savanna elephants also have been dying at the rate of nearly one hundred per day, killed for ivory. Other examples of challenges for conservation efforts spring to mind:

- Seemingly endless herds of wildebeest migrate semiannually between the Serengeti of Tanzania and the Masai Mara of Kenya, spreading from horizon to horizon on the long slopes of rolling hills. But today, political instability is eroding the tourism business in Kenya and other African nations, and poachers are inexorably cutting down wildebeest and other species. If current trends continue, these creatures are likely to be lost within fifty years.
- Giraffe numbers are shrinking rapidly across Africa because of poaching and habitat loss. According to figures from the Center for Biological Diversity, a private US conservation group, giraffe numbers have dwindled by 40 percent during the past thirty years. The center, allied with other groups, sued the US Fish & Wildlife Service for failing to consider the giraffe for protection under the federal Endangered Species Act and won in court. The service, as of this writing, is studying the potential for listing the giraffe and should announce a decision in 2023. Listing would allow the service to restrict the import of giraffe products into the United States, among other benefits.

DESPITE THE SHORTCOMINGS, CHALLENGES, AND CONFRONTATIONS SUR-rounding US bison recovery, its successes have inspired many biologists and wildlife enthusiasts worldwide. One team of biologists exploring the future of bison in the United States wrote, "We believe that the cause of bison ecological recovery will provide a rallying point for other species restoration efforts."

The federal Department of the Interior is the top US bison restoration agency. It includes the National Park Service, the US Fish & Wildlife Service, and the Bureau of Land Management, all of which play major roles in the orchestration of bison conservation not only in the United States but also internationally, through cooperative work with officials, agencies, and biologists from other countries. These three bison-management agencies are responsible for some eleven thousand bison in nineteen independent herds roving 4.6 million acres of grasslands spread across twelve states. Before the great slaughter, bison range in the Lower 48 states covered more than 36 billion acres and crossed forty-two of those states; it also accounted for about 28 percent of Canada's four western provinces. A report published in 2020 on the long-term viability of bison herds managed by the Department of the Interior called the agency "the primary national conservation steward of North American plains bison." To the other three agencies must be added Interior's Bureau of Indian Affairs, which plays a key role in supporting bison restoration on tribal lands.

The eight biologists who wrote the report—three of whom work for private conservation groups while the rest are federal employees—outlined the limitations of federal bison management. Most of the herds are relatively small and live on restricted and isolated ranges, confined by fences "and further bound by socio-political concerns that limit their ecological recovery." Small, isolated populations can fall victim to catastrophic events that can wipe out an entire herd. They lose genetic diversity more quickly than large populations, and can lose viability through inbreeding. However, according to the authors of the paper, the bison-managing agencies within the Interior Department "are now well equipped to implement a new approach to bison conservation: a cooperative, multi-scaled stewardship model to preserve and protect our national bison heritage and to promote ecological and cultural restoration of bison to North America." The report concluded that cooperative stewardship combined with bison population management "may prove to be one of the most important advances in federal bison conservation since the establishment of herds during the past century."

Of course, specific problems still challenge bison restoration. The challenges can be divided into two types: biological problems and management issues, though functionally the two categories intersect. One of the most complex challenges is maintaining bison genetic diversity. In the nineteenth century, bison ran into a genetic bottleneck when their vast number was cut to a pathetic handful. Various figures are bandied about for how many wild bison remained in North America at the end of the nineteenth century and became the ancestors, or founders, of all of today's plains bison. The figures cited by the Department of the Interior are as sound as those of any other source, keeping in mind that when it comes to counting bison, accuracy, starting with the earliest estimates for the number of bison that existed before the slaughter, is a victim of the vagueness of data, the elusiveness of bison, and occasional wishful thinking. According to the Interior, all of today's plains bison are descended from only thirty to fifty individuals from six captive herds along with an estimated twenty-five wild bison that survived at the lowest ebb in Yellowstone National Park, according to the report. However, the founding bison in the United States came from different herds in different areas around the nation with different genetic diversity, says Lee Jones, a biologist with the US Fish & Wildlife Service Wildlife Health Office in Bozeman, Montana, and one of the authors of the 2020 paper. "We got lucky with bison genetics," she says. The six herds drew on different genetic stock from Kansas, Texas, Montana, and Wyoming, so this small population contained a considerable amount of genetic diversity—more, for example, than that provided by the founders of today's European wisent.

When the Department of the Interior published the report on long-term bison viability, that handful of buffalo had turned into 334,000 buffalo scattered across mostly western North America. About 303,000 were in privately owned commercial herds, which means the animals may be subject to breeding plans and other behavioral modifications such as increased docility or greater growth for meat production (one slogan says, "More rump, less hump"). North American bison reserved for conservation totaled only about thirty-one thousand in 2017—and the number could be slightly more or slightly less today—including twenty thousand plains and eleven thousand wood bison, all living in a scattered string of sixty-eight conservation herds. These herds typically number fewer than five hundred bison each and are too isolated for interbreeding unless individual bison are moved from one herd to another by human intervention. In all of North America, only two herds of wild bison roam on unfenced range and exceed four thousand individuals in number, either persistently or in some years—the herds of the Greater Wood Buffalo National Park area in Canada and the herds of Yellowstone National Park, where "unfenced" is a somewhat distorted concept. In short, biologists seeking to restore bison have a total of about thirty-one thousand animals with which to work, animals scattered in little parcels from northern

Mexico to northwestern Canada. "While extinction is no longer an imminent threat," stated the 2020 report, "substantial work remains to more fully restore the species to its ecological and cultural role on appropriate landscapes within its historical range."

Federal agencies cooperating with private conservation groups on the report used genetic data from eighteen government-managed bison herds in the United States and Canada to assess the animals' genetic diversity and long-term viability. Various simulation models of individual bison herds suggest that, under 2020 management practices, all of the Interior Department herds will lose genetic diversity during the next two hundred years unless gene flow among the herds is restored and maintained. Herds of more than five hundred bison are likely to lose 3 to 7 percent of their genetic diversity, while herds under one hundred animals will lose 34 to 81 percent.

Exploration for a new approach for bison management began in 2008, when the Secretary of the Interior created the department's Bison Conservation Initiative to improve federal bison restoration. One of the first outgrowths of the initiative was a federal workshop on bison genetics. By 2010, Interior biologists had established that a minimum population size of one thousand bison is needed to maintain genetic variation for the next two centuries. However, the Interior herds, with the exception of Yellowstone National Park, were under one thousand individuals (as of 2022, the herd at Badlands National Park in South Dakota also exceeds one thousand). For administrative purposes, federal biologists in 2010 defined a wild bison herd as "one with a large enough population size to prevent loss of genetic variation and with low levels of cattle or subspecies [genes], and subject to some of the forces of natural selection, including competition for breeding opportunities." The department concluded that in the future, "management actions should maximize population size, minimize selection for docility and other traits related to domestication, strive for an even sex ratio considering differential survival, and minimally interfere with social behavior." Very importantly, the department added that its bison herds "must be increased in size to avoid negative genetic effects," with staff actively seeking cooperative management across jurisdictional boundaries to facilitate conservation of herds held in various states and administered by various state, federal, private, or tribal agencies.

By 2020, focus on bison conservation had sharpened ideas about bison preservation through metapopulation management. A bison metapopulation is one composed of several independent herds, often miles apart, that are managed as a single large herd, with individual bison moved from herd to herd periodically to maintain genetic diversity. This practice may help small herds to avoid the loss of various useful traits through inbreeding. At present, only the Yellowstone and Badlands National Park herds are large enough to exist on their own without genetic loss.

Department officials recognized that moving bison from place to place requires increased cooperation among management agencies, or what the 2020 report called "new and sustained levels of coordination and communication between DOI agencies and other bison conservation stakeholders." Plans also called for adapting traditional management processes so that they can accomplish "broad species conservation goals that support continental conservation across multiple jurisdictions while respecting the variations in local management purpose and capacity."

As early as 2014, Interior officials declared that "the most important bison conservation tool available to DOI continues to be collaboration amongst federal, state, local, and tribal partners." These officials hoped to find means for partnerships with landowners that would allow the weaving together of small stretches of bison habitat into combinations "large enough to cultivate the full interplay between bison and the surrounding ecology," thus increasing local biodiversity and restoring prairie ecosystems.

In this way, the federal bison agencies are in line with thinking that started with the Vermejo conference in 2008 (see chapter 5). This conference sought new avenues for bison restoration. In the ensuing years, says Eric W. Sanderson, a senior conservation ecologist with the Wildlife Conservation Society and senior author of the Vermejo Statement, progress has been made, if not on the ground, at least in the ideas that ultimately shape that progress. "Part of the conservation community is moving from a preoccupation with extinction into a preoccupation with recovery," he says. Bison need to survive not just as a species but as an ecological entity with a role to play in their specific habitats. This approach means more than saving bison as a species. It also means looking at ecotypes of bison, he says. All plains bison belong to one species, but herds live in various types of habitat. The behaviors, and potentially even the genetics, of bison living in different types of habitat may vary. Bison living in Alaska may differ from those in the arid Southwest, and those on the northern plains may differ from those in mountain areas. These different types of bison stem from the ecological demands of their habitat, hence they are ecotypes. To protect bison for the long term, managers need to consider ecotypes in their plans.

ANOTHER HAUNTING GENETIC CONCERN ABOUT WILD PLAINS BISON TODAY is whether they carry an influx, or introgression, of cattle genes. The story of how those genes got into bison begins with the crossbreeding of bison and cattle decades ago when ranchers tried to "toughen" domestic animals by turning them into catalo. Among the early private owners of bison herds, the idea repeatedly cropped up because bison were better adapted to the rugged plains country. Summer heat and, especially, winter cold and snow hammered domestic cattle, many breeds of which are poorly adapted to the slings and arrows of Great Plains blizzards. The plains bison, a species that walked in the shadow of the woolly mammoth when glaciers were carving the earth, uses its massive head to dig through heavy snow and find grass. It faces into blizzards and stands in place, rather than turning its back to the wind and drifting aimlessly across prairies, only to fall into snow-filled ravines and die, as did tens of thousands of cattle during severe winters in the late 1800s.

The ungulate genetic experiment even attracted the backing of Representative John Lacey, who, in the US House of Representatives in 1900, spoke in support of an early plan to restore bison to New Mexico: "There is another important feature connected with this experiment. Domestic cows can be placed on this range and crossed with the buffalo bulls. This is no longer an experiment. The product of this cross is an animal with a coat heavy enough to resist the severest western winter storm. This, however, is only an incident to the real purpose of the plan, as there would be no attempt made to breed from the female buffalo anything but the pure-blooded bison. The addition would be made by breeding domestic cows, and so the production of the pure bloods would not be in this manner decreased."

Charles Goodnight, among the first to try crossing bison with cattle, started by putting one of his bison bulls with two Angus cows given to him in 1885 by another rancher. They produced young, but with some ominous caveats. Bull calves were always stillborn during the first round of pairing a bull bison with domestic cows; sometimes the mother died too. Female crossbred calves, called catalo, did survive and later gave birth to live bull calves when bred with bull buffalo. However, the bull calves were infertile. Goodnight tried various crossing combinations. By 1917, he had forty head of catalo. He was pleased: "The breed seemed immune to disease, particularly blackleg, required less feed than domestic stock while gaining flesh faster, produced a sweeter and more uniformly marbled tallow, lived and multiplied to a much greater age than other breeds, and weighed heavier—the cows from eleven hundred to sixteen hundred pounds off Panhandle grass." However, as time went on, the cows began aborting frequently, costing Goodnight too much money, and he sold them off.

The idea to mate bison with cattle came to Buffalo Jones in March 1886, in the aftermath of a winter of harsh blizzards that killed hundreds of thousands of cattle across the West. Some ranchers lost 90 percent of their herds. Theodore Roosevelt, who was ranching in the Dakota Badlands that year, lost 60 percent and eventually had to quit the business. After Jones roamed the post-blizzard southern Kansas prairie, littered with dead cattle, he came to bison territory in Texas and found not a single dead one that had not been shot by hunters. In his 1899 autobiography he wrote, "I thought to myself, 'Why not domesticate this wonderful beast which can endure such a blizzard, defying a storm so destructive to our domestic species? Why not infuse this hardy blood into our native cattle, and have a perfect animal, one that will defy all these elements?'"

A few years later he put his plan to work. He wrote, "I have been very diligent during the past five years in endeavoring to produce a race of cattle equal in hardiness to the buffalo, with robes much finer, and possessing all the advantages of the best bred cattle." He concluded that after years of breeding, with both failures and successes, he had "succeeded in a remarkable degree in producing the very kind of animal my imagination dwelt upon while in western Texas in 1886."

Nevertheless, his experiment with catalo, a herd of which he put out along the north edge of the Grand Canyon, came to a crashing end. Hornaday wrote: "I regret to say that 'Buffalo' Jones's catalo experiment on the Kaibab Plateau seems to have met an untimely and disappointing fate. For three years the bison and domestic cattle crossed, and produced a number of cataloes; but in 1911, practically the whole lot was wiped off the earth by cattle rustlers!"

Though not *exactly* wiped off. Recent genetic studies have frequently found cattle genes in bison, immediately raising the question of whether a low percentage of cattle genes in a buffalo makes any biological difference. "It probably depends on what type of genes are involved," says Lee Jones.

Traditional tests for locating nuclear cattle genes in bison detect only fifteen genetic markers for cattle introgression out of the thousands that compose a bison's genetic makeup. Tests of bison at Grand Canyon National Park indicated that they carry at least five of the fifteen markers for cattle genes, with most containing mitochondrial DNA—a relatively heavy amount. The problem may be less profound at other sites. Tests of bison at Badlands National Park detected two of the fifteen markers. Bison at Fort Niobrara and Wichita Mountains National Wildlife Refuges carried one. Bison at Wind Cave National Park had none. Most herds managed by the US Fish & Wildlife Service, Jones says, have had one marker for cattle genes detected.

Proof of the occurrence of cattle genes in bison herds has been somewhat dubious, according to Jones. The tools that have been used until recently were not sensitive enough, she says, to indicate what percent of cattle genes occurs among an individual bison's full array of genes, or genome. She says that tests have been sensitive enough to ensure only that if a bison herd tested positive for cattle genes, it *probably* had cattle genes. "With herds that test negative," she says, "we probably just missed the cattle genes that were present. We simply didn't have the sensitivity to do this."

Under this regimen, bison managers and experts considered Yellowstone bison the gold standard for bison purity, as they showed no signs of cattle genes and can be traced in an unbroken line to the last wild bison known south of the border with Canada. But that status changed in 2022 with the publication of research that used newer, more sensitive tests of the genomes of nineteen modern and six historical bison from six distinct North American herds, "including Yellowstone, Wind Cave, and Elk Island (plains and wood bison) National Parks," which were "previously believed to be free from cattle introgression," and found that "all have detectable levels of hybrid ancestry with cattle."

Knowing that all bison herds include cattle genes could affect how government agencies move metapopulation herds for breeding purposes. "FWS has some small herds that will inbreed fast, so managers must move them," Jones says. "But we don't know the percent of cattle genes." She suggests that managers take a conservative approach and wait to move bison until even newer and more sensitive tests show which herds are carrying heavy cattle introgression and which are carrying light. For example, if a herd carries 6 percent cattle genes, should bison introduced to the herd also carry 6 percent cattle genes, or fewer, or more? Jones offers some solace: "Most Interior Department herds had already been reported with nuclear cattle genes in previous studies, so the inclusion of Yellowstone and Wind Cave National Parks as containing low levels of hybridization is not terribly surprising, especially given that experimental hybridization with cattle was done in the late 1800s," she says. "Attempts to remove animals containing the tiny fraction of cattle genes would risk losing important bison genes, and we have no evidence that the tiny portion of cattle genes has any negative impact on bison. Each Interior Department bureau may make slightly different decisions as we continue to learn more about bison genetics, but I suspect that we will continue to follow a don't-make-it-worse paradigm by avoiding importing animals from herds known to have high levels of cattle genes."

James A. Bailey, a Montana wildlife biologist with fifty years in the profession who serves as the coordinator of the Montana Wild Bison Restoration Coalition, believes that evolution will solve the problem of cattle introgression. "Natural selection in a wild environment will gradually purge the bison genome of such deleterious cattle genes," he wrote in a personal overview of bison conservation, *American Plains Bison: Rewilding an Icon.* "We can begin restoring wild bison with animals having no more than, say, 1-2 percent cattle introgression and let nature take its course in a wild environment." He contends that a standard that adheres to breeding only purebred bison "would greatly limit our options for source herds to use in bison restoration. Introgression of cattle genes in the bison genome is so widespread that we cannot simply discard all bison carrying cattle genes without sacrificing some bison alleles [gene variants] that are found only in animals with some introgression."

The Interior Department's long-term plan also is designed to protect bison from diseases such as brucellosis, maintain natural selection and breeding competition, allow bison to revive their ecological roles, and restore cultural connections to bison, especially among Native Americans. The department also plans to encourage states to create new bison herds for state management. Eleven states already manage their own herds. Interior biologists are looking at goals for habitat management to "ensure that healthy landscapes that support the character of wild bison are maintained and that the resource needs of other species are met." This strategy will help to restore entire native ecosystems, a vision never before attempted within the confines of bison management. The 2020 report concluded, "This new approach . . . may prove to be one of the most important advances in federal bison conservation since the establishment of herds during the past century." It will guide the translocation of bison between federally administered lands as well as donations of bison to tribes such as the new Wolakota Buffalo Range of the Rosebud Sioux Tribe reservation in South Dakota. Interior Department officials predict that by 2027 the Wolakota herd will include up to 1,500 bison on nearly 30,000 acres.

One obstacle to moving bison is disease, which could place significant limits on translocations within metapopulations, according to the 2020 report. Brucellosis, for example, disqualifies individual bison from being moved into other herds. The respiratory disease *Mycoplasma bovis*, which can kill bison and presently has no known cure, could hinder or stop translocations if it becomes widespread. Disease can also affect genetics in a more subtle way. Bison that are infected with brucellosis and those that have been infected but may have recovered from the disease and are free of it will both turn up positive on the tests used to detect brucellosis in Yellowstone bison. As a result, recovered bison, which presumably have a genetic endowment that allowed them to get over the disease, are slaughtered along with bison that are ailing. This practice could potentially remove individual bison with strong immune systems, essentially lowering or eradicating a herd's genes for brucellosis recovery. However, the US Fish & Wildlife Service and the National Park Service both have well-established wildlife-health programs staffed by veterinarians, some of whom have specific knowledge about bison. Continued research on diseases, detection, and cures holds the promise of ensuring bison health in the future.

Another concern about bison today involves an overlap of management and genetics. This issue is the potential domestication of wild bison. James Bailey spelled out his concerns for this threat in *American Plains Bison*. To see the difference between a wild animal and a domesticated one of a related species, consider, first, the wolf and the many breeds of dog that human selection of genetic traits has turned the wolf into. Bailey, hitting closer to home, compared bison with domestic cattle: "The bison is designed by natural selection to be strong, mobile, agile, fast, independent, competitive and wary. The domestic cow is designed by human selection to be calm, slow, tractable, directing as much energy as possible to producing body tissue, rather than to activity, and dependent upon humans to provide emergency food, to control disease and perhaps to assist at birthing time." Bailey is concerned that management even of conservation herds is driving bison toward domestication. "We are on our way to domesticating bison—to the extinction of wild bison, at least south of Canada," he wrote.

According to Bailey, human interventions that lead to domestication include small herd sizes; small units of habitat with little biological diversity; artificial water sources; supplementary feeding during winter and drought; selection of bulls (often for docility) for breeding; no effective predation to keep bison alert, strong, and aggressive; and maintaining herds with unnaturally young age distributions. If bison managers remove adult, rather than younger, animals from herds, genetic diversity is more likely to be lost, Lee Jones says. If each bison cow, bred through its whole life, produced fifteen calves, there is a larger chance that the herd's endowment of genes will be preserved, she says. Management is the key to preserving bison wildness and genetic diversity. Managers can add to the loss of genetic diversity and wildness by kicking out adults or culling out dominating, aggressive bison, Jones says, "or we can restore gene flow if we're smart about it."

Yellowstone bison have been subjected to selection pressures that can in effect domesticate them with the passage of time. Bailey cited several examples in his book, including limited herd size, reduction in average age through culling, blocking the species' usual migratory behavior, especially in severe winters, and the shooting of aggressive and nomadic individuals. "Unnatural selection, for a constrained suite of behavior traits, could result in a maladapted bison not fitted to the natural environment," wrote two of the United States' leading bison biologists, Keith Aune and Glenn Plumb. "Bison may be at risk for ecological extinction, where their primary function is no longer expressed in nature and they cannot be managed without major human interventions that further introduce an artificial selection pressure." In 2010, according to other bison biologists associated with the National Park Service, none of the Interior Department herds were "subject to the full range of historic natural selective forces that influence genetic variation."

Even good intentions can lead to negative effects. Controlling disease through vaccination, for example, can reduce the selection of individual bison with the strongest immune systems. Under natural conditions, bison with the weakest immune systems, or those that contract the most virulent form of a disease, arguably will produce few or no offspring. Natural selection favors animals with the strongest resistance and also favors disease pathogens that do the least damage to their hosts. In this way, the strongest bison and the least harmful pathogens survive and accommodate one another. "In reality, a sick animal is a natural component of a 'healthy,' evolving ecosystem," wrote Bailey. "In contrast, intervention with vaccines, antibiotics and vermicides can impede natural selection for resistance and accommodation. It may also cause loss of whatever disease resistance bison already carry."

The genetic and wildness issues come down to this, in Bailey's terms: "Herds with fewer than 2000-3000 bison have compromised evolutionary potentials. . . . and only the Yellowstone National Park herd is large enough to limit loss of genetic diversity to moderate levels in the long term." But even Yellowstone is not a strong foundation for the future of the bison because "the park is not the best possible habitat for retaining a sample of wild bison. Originally, this upper Yellowstone area supported a backwater population on the periphery of better plains bison habitat. It is a harsh habitat, at least at some seasons, for plains bison today. If we are to preserve examples of wild bison, we should do so in more than one place, and in some places with better bison habitat than Yellowstone National Park."

Bison also need more space for herd enlargement, as data on herd size and habitat indicate. The plains buffalo is a roving species, moving with the grass and the seasons. If they are to meet their full biological potential and use all their evolved adaptations to life in the wild, they cannot be bound up within a limited space, even in a place as large as Yellowstone National Park. Canadian conservationist Harvey Locke wrote, "To confine plains bison within a national park's boundary is to cheat ourselves of a great opportunity to right a historical wrong." We seem to be holding bison in a nineteenth-century pattern, ceding public prairie lands to cattle and shooting down and in other ways limiting bison numbers. During a severe winter, when bison might seek more temperate quarters, a fence can be as deadly as a gun. "It is unfortunate that in the United States, we have persisted in thinking of bison as an ancient relic, or livestock, to be viewed behind a fence but never fully experienced like other wildlife," contended veteran bison biologists Aune and Plumb in their 2019 book about Theodore Roosevelt and bison restoration. "The future for bison is dismal if these views remain entrenched in the American psyche."

Here is the problem for bison in a nutshell, according to the 2015 book *Yellowstone Bison: Conserving an American Icon in Modern Society* (some references and scientific species names have been removed to compress the text):

> *The restoration of wild bison has advanced more slowly, and with much greater debate, than nearly all other wildlife species over the past 150 years. Bison are massive animals that compete directly with humans and livestock for use of the landscape. Their preferred habitats include nutrient-rich valley bottoms where agricultural and residential developments occupy most of the land, while public lands are more likely to encompass mountainous areas. Given existing habitat loss and the constraints modern society has placed on the distribution of wild bison, it is unlikely many additional populations will be established and allowed to roam widely across the landscape.*

Biologists working at national parks and wildlife refuges with herds of relatively free-roaming bison face a serious challenge—as herds burgeon, they run out of space and food, jeopardizing their habitat. Are we to fence and cull them like livestock, sell their meat to butchers and grocery store chains? Turn them, inevitably, into livestock and render them more domestic as decades pass?

In 1987, Deborah Popper and Frank Popper, two environmental-planning professors at Rutgers University, proposed a solution to the problem of space for bison, though they had a bigger target in mind. They later wrote that they "published an article in *Planning*, a magazine for urban planners, in which we reviewed the past and prospects of one of the nation's major regions, the Great Plains. We recorded the Plains' boom-and-bust history and suggested that a new path lay about a generation ahead: a large-scale land restoration project that we called the Buffalo Commons."

The Poppers contended that agricultural use of the plains typically began with federally subsidized settlement plans during periods of high rain. People signed up for the programs, brought in livestock and plows, and put out more cattle and plowed more land than the arid prairies could support. As a result, the land eroded, and people moved out. Indeed, during the sixty-seven years prior to the Poppers' proposal, about a third of the human residents had left the area. The Poppers suggested that the federal government, over a fifteen-year period, buy nearly 140,000 square miles of the more arid portions of the plains and turn it into an almost fenceless neo-wilderness, the Buffalo Commons. It would span ten states from Mexico to Canada.

For those who saw this plan as a boon to wildlife, the commons conjured images and hopes of herds of bison, elk, deer, and pronghorn tracked by wolves, mountain lions, and bears, along with dreams of a park that would rival Africa as the world's premiere wildlife attraction. However, western residents generally resented the proposal. They didn't see a solution to the cycle of boom and bust but rather saw the Buffalo Commons "as a general assault on their way of life," the Poppers wrote. "Many Plains people intensely disliked the commons portion of the metaphor, associating it with collectivism and lack of choice, but even so the strength of their reaction helped achieve some community-building." When outlining the decline of population in the Great Plains, the proposal did not take into account the role of industrial farming in destroying jobs and forcing people to find work elsewhere. It also ignored such factors as the passing on of ranches and farms to descendants.

During the ensuing decade, the Poppers observed the plains and thought they saw the formation of the Buffalo Commons starting almost spontaneously, or at any rate without federal endorsement. "On private lands a noticeable number of ranchers switched to buffalo and prospered financially and ecologically," they wrote. "Membership in the National Bison Association, a membership group for buffalo professionals, has risen steadily; so has membership in the organization's state and regional chapters, especially in the Plains. Plains Indians have formed the InterTribal Bison Cooperative, a consortium of 44 Native American governments that trains Indian buffalo producers and tribal land managers and takes other steps to reinvigorate buffalo's [sic] historically central place in their cultures. The buffalo count on Indian land has at least tripled since 1992."

The Poppers were pleased to see North Dakota governor Edward Schafer promoting bison production and tourism as a means for economic growth. North Dakota's agricultural extension service offered technical assistance to bison ranchers, and banks offered them loans, something previously denied to bison growers. The Poppers also were encouraged that the US and Canadian governments expanded protection of grasslands. However, there continues to be resistance to the idea of more open buffalo habitat from residents throughout the region.

Although creation of the Buffalo Commons may be a long row to hoe at this point, an almost equally ambitious but more likely proposal concerns establishing pathways or corridors of wild lands between existing protected public areas. One group, Y2Y—Yellowstone to Yukon, created in 1993—calls for preserving a corridor that would connect large protected areas from Yellowstone National Park in Wyoming to the Arctic in Canada's Yukon, on the border with Alaska. This series of protected sites extends 2,100 miles across an area that varies in width from 310 to 496 miles—a total of 502,000 square miles of wildlife habitat. The target area crosses five states, two Canadian provinces, two Canadian territories, and the territories of at least seventy-five Indigenous tribes. The group's studies indicate that Y2Y has increased protected areas in the corridor by 80 percent since 1993.

One of the great dangers to wildlife that corridors help to avert is the isolation of parks and wildlife refuges within an ecological desert of developed lands, turning habitats into oases from which wildlife cannot escape. Corridors are pathways that allow animals such as wolves, bears, hoofed species, reptiles, and amphibians to find new range and locate mates. Y2Y and similar advocates work with landowners to protect areas suitable as pathways between protected sites. They also promote the building of highway overpasses and underpasses, designed with vegetative cover, so wildlife can traverse what would otherwise be death traps. At least 117 of these overpasses have been built in the Y2Y corridor, probably the most in any area in the world, according to the group. Banff National Park in Alberta includes more than forty overpasses and underpasses. Since their construction, collisions between motor vehicles and wildlife have declined 90 percent.

Another means of establishing suitably large places for bison, suggests Rick Wallen—the former leader of Yellowstone's Bison Ecology and Management Team—is to consolidate currently isolated units of bison habitat. Ted Turner took a step in the right direction when he started his chain of large bison ranches, Wallen says, but now "we need the next step." Bison need a large range to fulfill their ecological role and lead less human-manipulated lives. "For wildlife, bigger is better," he says. He suggests that conservation groups work out deals with ranchers who own adjacent properties, trading them for their land with more scattered land owned by the groups. This procedure would allow the consolidation of ranches into bigger units. He suggests that even the federal government could trade smaller, isolated national wildlife refuges for bigger plots of land to create bigger refuges. He also suggests that Ted Turner could trade two or three of his smaller Montana ranches for ranches near the Charles M. Russell National Wildlife Refuge, allowing him to create even bigger, contiguous bison range.

The Charles M. Russell National Wildlife Refuge, or the CMR, as it is commonly known, is managed by the US Fish & Wildlife Service. Long the center of controversy involving bison restoration, its vast grasslands could provide a release valve for burgeoning herds at Yellowstone and other parks and refuges. The CMR runs for about 125 air miles along both sides of the Missouri River, from the Fort Peck Dam west to the boundary with the Upper Missouri River Breaks National Monument. The refuge is composed of rolling grasslands, emerald green in spring and golden tan as autumn arrives. The American Prairie conservation group, which is attempting to put together 3 million acres of bison habitat (see chapter 5), already has control of prairie abutting the CMR. The refuge was prime bison habitat before the great slaughter. James Bailey, whose Montana Wild Bison Restoration Coalition is seeking to reintroduce bison to the refuge, wrote that it is the best and largest area of diverse, mostly contiguous public land in north-central Montana, along with the Upper Missouri River Breaks National Monument. Encompassing 1.1 million acres, the CMR is the second-largest national wildlife refuge in the Lower 48 states, exceeded only by Desert National Wildlife Refuge in Nevada, at 1.6 million acres. It lies a few miles from the Fort Belknap and Fort Peck Indian Reservations, where bison restoration has been ongoing for well over a decade and now sustains several hundred bison, including Yellowstone buffalo. The number of bison on the extensive prairies of the CMR: zero. Therein lies a tale.

About twenty-five years ago, the State of Montana sued the National Park Service, focusing on Yellowstone National Park, as Montana officials wanted the service to control bison movement out of the park. The court ordered the state and the service to work together on bison management, giving rise to the Interagency Bison Management Plan (see chapter 9), which is still in effect, and to a state environmental impact statement that outlined the effects of bison conservation measures.

In 2020, under Democratic governor Steve Bullock, the Montana Department of Fish, Wildlife, and Parks released a record of decision for a ten-year state environmental impact statement analyzing opportunities for restoring public herds of wild bison in Montana. The decision statement concluded that bison could be restored in Montana and requested site-specific proposals from the public for bison reintroduction sites. Bailey calls the document the "no-decision statement," as Governor Bullock's successor, Republican Greg Gianforte, shut down all plans for bison restoration, an edict "voiding a ten-to-twelve-year effort on bison restoration," Bailey says. Under the new governor, the state, says Bailey, "has decided not to restore any public-trust bison by transplant, anywhere in the state," an intention reinforced by two anti-bison laws enacted in Montana in 2021.

However, Bailey points out, federal law—specifically the National Wildlife Refuge System Improvement Act—requires the US Fish & Wildlife Service "to restore biodiversity and biotic integrity" on the lands it manages, putting federal law on the side of the Fish & Wildlife Service. On the website of the Montana Wild Bison Restoration Coalition, Bailey underscores that the Refuge Improvement Act declares that actions by refuge officials must be compatible with the mission of the National Wildlife Refuge System and with the purposes stated in the establishing legislation of individual refuges. In general, refuges are expected to provide for wildlife and plant conservation, habitat protection, biological integrity, and biodiversity. Refuges are legally permitted to "restore wildlife where appropriate," which includes reintroduction of vanished species. Moreover, the law does not lock refuge managers into dogged cooperation with state wildlife goals. Instead, refuge managers must cooperate with state and local rules only "to the extent practicable."

Restoring bison to the CMR, Bailey says, would "fulfill the mandates of Congress in the Refuge Improvement Act and would contribute to fulfilling the avowed goals of the Department of the Interior's Bison Conservation Initiative." These goals include a commitment to maintaining wildness and genetic diversity in large, wide-ranging bison herds on expansive landscapes. The CMR's own management plan states that without bison, "progress in restoring ecological processes would remain incomplete," while "bison restoration would bring back what was once a dominant herbivore and keystone species in the refuge landscape" and would be "a positive move toward restoration of natural ecological processes."

Despite the biological and legal elements supporting bison reintroduction to the CMR, the refuge's management plan concludes, "The Service will not consider reintroducing bison on the refuge unless Montana Fish, Wildlife & Parks initiates an effort." The plan also says that "any proposal for bison restoration would be conducted by a public process led by Montana Fish, Wildlife & Parks." Bailey, as stated on the coalition website, sees this approach as "an abdication of federal statutory and public trust responsibilities for federal lands and resources, despite the state's long failure, in not restoring wild bison, to fulfill its own Constitutional mandate and public trust responsibilities to the people of Montana." And so, while cattle graze on national forests and other federally administered lands, bison are locked out of a national wildlife refuge that was once their natural home. The issue is urgent. "Land for bison is the limiting factor, by far," Bailey says. "I don't accept private livestock 'everywhere' and public bison nowhere on all our federal public lands."

Bailey believes that, after decades of stalling on the part of state officials, the time has come for the US Fish & Wildlife Service to move ahead with CMR bison reintroduction without the permission of Montana officials. Of course, he says, the service would end up in court. Anyone familiar with the issue could well imagine that states' rights would be waved like a red flag. "So it's a very difficult thing for anyone in the government to do," he concedes. He has approached several national conservation groups, asking them to sue the service for its failure to meet its mandate and to force it into action, but no groups with which he has talked want to take up the banner.

At the heart of the matter with CMR is intolerance for bison. Human intolerance of wildlife is as much a challenge in conservation as more direct forms of destruction, such as poaching and habitat loss. In a seminal 2008 paper on bison conservation, the authors wrote, "Today the population size and distribution of most species are culturally determined . . . a simple consequence of the relative abundance of people and the depth and breadth of our mark on the planet. . . . People prefer some species and find coexistence with others perilous or inconvenient; bison have the luck of being both, and that tension plays out in the arguments for their conservation and management." Now, however, "the idea of large landscapes without fences is a key part of our notion of bison conservation," Eric Sanderson, one of the paper's authors, says. "We could have free-ranging bison herds tomorrow if we could just get people to agree, but they don't," he adds.

This conundrum is clear at Yellowstone National Park, a model for bison issues. The public land is there, in and around the park, but the cultural and social will is not. "Negotiating more tolerance for bison outside Yellowstone is going to take a long time," according to the National Park Service. "In fact, we may never find enough tolerance outside the park to eliminate the need for some population control. In the interim, identifying brucellosis-free bison and moving them to new homes may be part of the solution to giving bison more room to roam. It is the beginning of returning Yellowstone bison to the lands where they once roamed."

The destiny of bison everywhere perhaps may be foreseen at Yellowstone, where, according to *Yellowstone Bison: Conserving an American Icon in Modern Society*, administrators have two management models to choose from: let herds grow until bison must be slaughtered to a lower number or a severe winter reduces the herds, or let the population increase to a size where the bison leave the park yearly and are reduced by hunting or other removal—an approach that, several of the contributing experts wrote, "necessitates tolerance for bison outside of the park, especially during years when severe winter weather increases numbers of migrating animals."

BISON SURVIVAL IS INSTRUCTIVE FOR SAVING THIS BELEAGUERED SPECIES. Bison success, regardless of its limits, stems from a combination of conservation laws, enforcement of those laws, careful study of the beleaguered species, protection of habitat, and working with landowners and Indigenous peoples. These elements can be constituted into a road map for protecting and restoring wildlife anywhere. That's the good news.

On the other hand, the protection of bison also offers a warning. Is the intensive management to which the bison is subjected all that the future holds for rhinos, wildebeests, elephants, giraffes, zebras, and other large social species if they survive poaching? As human populations grow, will parks—pressured by surrounding development—transform from being the final refuge of large animals into a type of life imprisonment for each species? Will individuals of all these species one day wear ear tags and computer implants and be sold or slaughtered to reduce population size? When a species is largely confined to parklands and its populations artificially reduced, is it truly wild? Is a limited patch of natural habitat all that humanity will leave these creatures? Or will other forms of land protection prevail, such as corridor development or other, new approaches that use high-tech farming and industry to reduce human sprawl?

If I may enter the narrative at this late moment, please let me tell you a story that, for me, graphically illustrates the dire state of wildlife conservation in our time. Quite some years ago, when a game ranger from South Africa visited the National Audubon Society headquarters in New York City, I joined another editor of *Audubon* magazine in taking him to lunch. He talked about how he was assigned the culling of elephants in areas where biologists concluded the animals were too numerous. He said that, armed with a rifle, he flew over a herd in a helicopter, rounding up the animals. The younger elephants ran to a stand of trees, seeking cover, it seemed, while the older matriarchs of the herd stood out in plain sight, as if, he said, they were saying, "Kill us, but let our young live." Culling operations killed entire herds, however, and did that day. Can that be the future for large, group-living animals? Kill them off—to save them and their habitat, to keep them from overeating the plants that sustain them, and to keep them from raiding farmland? Conservation by firearms? Richard Leakey, when he was head of the Kenya Wildlife Service, told me during an interview that solving the poaching problem—which has proved intractable over the years—was easier than solving the land problem, the space problem, the habitat problem for elephants and, by implication, other species.

The mixed fate of the bison suggests that wildlife managers across the globe should be working to preserve genetic diversity in other dwindling species right now, while their numbers and distribution are still healthy enough to provide varied genetic endowment. This task is big, far more difficult than the effort to save random bison in the 1890s. Wildlife managers also need to plan now for corridors to connect Africa's and Asia's protected wildlife refuges and need to involve Indigenous peoples in any management process to ensure their cooperation and to access their expertise.

The saddest truth about the bison—and its greatest alarm for other species—is that, in the judgment of at least some biologists, it is ecologically extinct, meaning that its numbers are so low, so scattered, that it no longer fulfills any ecological role. Once a keystone species in Europe and North America, it is now biologically irrelevant, the only native wildlife species that, south of Canada, does not roam freely, as do deer, elk, and moose. Bison cannot hide in the shadows like wolves and even grizzly bears, quietly leading lives of recovery and population growth while shadowing the edges of cities and subsisting, if need be, on human garbage. Wild bison herds need large reaches of untrammeled habitat—grasslands, prairies, meadows, rivers. The same is fundamentally true for giraffes and elephants, rhinos and wildebeest, Cape buffalo and the massive gaur of Asia—species dwindling in the face of habitat loss from land development and fencing. If we can't restore the bison in the United States and Canada—nations with entrenched conservation values and open space—can we hope to save these other charismatic species?

RICK WALLEN, FORMER LEADER OF YELLOWSTONE'S BISON ECOLOGY AND Management Team, offers solutions to the bison conundrum. His comments can generally be applied to other large species that live in groups. We can live with bison, he suggests, if we:

- Accept that there will probably always be areas where we can't have bison, such as moderate to large urban areas and highways. But we can make roadways safer for bison by, for example, lowering speed limits where large animals occur and by putting wildlife tunnels or overpasses across freeways. "Human society will have to spend a little money" to keep an increasingly human environment suitable, or at least relatively safe, for roaming wildlife.
- Allow slow, incremental expansion of conservation areas for wildlife, with conservation groups raising money to help local people do such things as lowering speed limits and building fences along highways. One way to get people to like bison is to put up money to help. Living with bison can be inconvenient for residents of bison habitat, however much the bison might be a pleasure for visitors from other areas.
- Pay livestock raisers a little more per pound for livestock on the hoof, yielding them a higher profit so they can do what needs to be done to

cover the costs of providing wildlife a home on ranchland. If enough people want wildlife, they will have it.

- Identify individuals or groups that can engage in social media and create public discussion around how we preserve large animals. Radicals on the fringe of bison issues have false assumptions of what can and can't occur. The radical conservationists who think Yellowstone wildlife should be allowed to expand unfettered by any constraints aren't seeing the problems residents face in dealing with park wildlife, he contends. On the other side of the issue stand the anti-wildlife people who see everything as a threat to valuable cattle and to the agricultural community. Increasingly, however, people are recognizing that bison are not the threat that was feared in 1995 and that not every bison is going to knock down fences. They are generally peaceful.

- Undertake "a little work to build an industry around wildlife." Moose, elk, and bison are big components of hunting, which brings in a lot of money. Some ranchers don't oppose elk, which have a large hunter constituency. Greater opportunities for bison hunting would improve relations for wild bison.

- Augment the tourist industry, which already brings in billions of dollars across the nation. Having wildlife such as bison more widespread on the landscape, both inside and outside the parks, would be valuable. If people could see bison, bears, and other animals without having to go into Yellowstone, they'd save a lot of effort as well as money, he says. Yellowstone, with close to four million visitors yearly, can become a stagnant traffic jam in summer.

To Wallen's thoughts, Mike Mease, one of the two founders of Buffalo Field Campaign (see chapter 9), would add this: list the bison under the federal Endangered Species Act. The current management plan, in Montana, he says, is conducted by the state veterinarian, "a strong advocate for the cattle industry." A similar pattern exists in other western states that encompass vast tracts of potential habitat for bison and other prairie species. Presently, bison are confined to about 15 percent of their 7,720-square-mile historical range in the Yellowstone area, according to the field campaign. Listing would require protection of former habitat and the writing of a federal recovery plan that would set goals for bison distribution, numbers, and habitat protection, perhaps opening the gates to the Russell wildlife refuge. More broadly, listing would take bison out of state control, something to be underscored, because the states around Yellowstone are the same ones that, when given control of gray wolves after their recovery under federal management, immediately opened hunting on the popular canines. This policy is killing hundreds yearly, jeopardizing the success of wolf recovery, and systematically destroying a species of premium interest to park visitors. At Buffalo Field Campaign, Mease says, "we always knew listing bison was the end game." In June 2022, the field campaign and its allies—Western Watersheds Project and Friends of the Animals—after eight years of petitioning the Fish & Wildlife Service to list wild bison as threatened or endangered, finally won acknowledgment from the service that "substantial scientific or commercial information" indicated that listing the bison may be warranted. The service pledged to consider listing within twelve months.

LISTING THE BISON IS A SWEEPING BUREAUCRATIC GOAL THAT WOULD HAVE immense impact on bison restoration. But there are smaller steps that can also have an incalculable impact. As a teen, I worked on a ranch in the Sandhills of western Nebraska. One day back then, while we were taking a break from tearing down a fifty-year-old barbed-wire fence and building a new one, I scanned the surrounding country—knee-deep grass, long slopes piling up into a high ridge to the north, the valley before us stretching eastward toward a dark hay meadow. Black Angus cattle dotted the emerald hills, shadows of scattered clouds glided over sun-swept landscape, but I imagined a different scene, a dream of the Old West, of nature at its richest, and I asked the rancher with whom I worked if he would ever put buffalo in this pasture. He said he'd like to, but that they would walk through a barbed-wire fence like it wasn't there.

Recently I visited the area, and friends took me to the old ranch, where I asked if I could see the fence I'd helped build fifty years before. One of our companions said that the fence was gone. Media innovator Ted Turner had bought this rich, intact grassland and torn down the fence. He'd encircled his land with stronger fencing and, as part of his restoration of western prairies, had released bison on land adjacent to the very pasture where I had pictured the animals roaming.

We went to see the buffalo, and luck was with us. On a spread of thousands of acres there they were, maybe one hundred yards beyond the new fence—a scattering of unmistakable, dark brown, front-loaded animals silhouetted against the spring grass, moving slowly south, grazing, at home. The sight gave me chills. Bison are a component of intact prairies, a vanishing habitat—land development has shrunk US tallgrass prairies to about 1 percent of their original extent. A grassland that can support bison is a healthy grassland.

When struggles on behalf of the bison seem intense and never-ending, I would suggest that we heed perhaps the most salient lesson we have inherited from the early conservationists, some of whom wanted to kill a buffalo before they were all gone: We should never give up. The bison shows that a species reduced from millions to a few hundred can stage a comeback. All it needs is our cooperation.

Acknowledgments

First I want to thank the experts who served as both sources of information and reviewers of my text: James A. Bailey, coordinator of the Montana Wild Bison Restoration Coalition; Jason Belcourt, Chippewa Cree tribal sustainability coordinator; David Carter, former executive director of the National Bison Association (a great source of weekly-newsletter information on bison); Gerardo Ceballos, a wildlife biology professor at the National Autonomous University of Mexico's Institute of Ecology and a member of the IUCN's North American Bison Specialist Group; Galen Crum, former chairman of the Osage Ranch Board; Phillip Evans, chief communications officer, Turner Enterprises; Rob Ferguson and Mike Sipes, co-owners of the Virginia Bison Company at Cibola Farms; Nina Gandl, project officer for bison and moose with the World Wide Fund for Nature–Germany and part of LosBonasus-Crossing!, whose review of the chapter on European bison proved invaluable; Jason George, business development specialist for the Osage Nation Department of Natural Resources; Aurel Heidelberg a forester and wildlife biologist who has been responsible for various conservation and restoration programs in the Caucasus ecoregion for the World Wide Fund for Nature–Germany and whose revisions of the text about Russia and related topics was extremely helpful; Kaja Heising, scientific coordinator for Wisent-Welt, who helped refine my coverage of the wisent facility where she works; Lee Jones, with the Wildlife Health Office of the US Fish & Wildlife Service Natural Resource Program Center, who proved indispensable at refining my understanding of bison genetic studies; Mark Kossler, vice president of ranch operations for Turner Enterprises; Rurik List, also a wildlife biology professor at the National Autonomous University of Mexico's Institute of Ecology and a member of the IUCN Bison Specialist Group; Mike Mease, founder and campaign coordinator of Buffalo Field Campaign, which now has a twenty-five-year history of bison advocacy; Cristina Mormorunni, director of the conservation advocacy group Indigenous Led, founder of the conservation-strategy consulting group TERRAMAR, and a great source of help throughout the process of writing this book; Wanda Olech, a biologist with the Department of Genetics and Animal Protection at the Institute of Animal Sciences, a part of the Warsaw University of Life Sciences, who was a great help with the European bison chapter; Wes Olson, whose thirty-two years as a national park warden in Canada, working mostly with bison, has resulted in his own wonderful book, *The Ecological Bison*; Eric W. Sanderson, senior conservation ecologist with the Wildlife Conservation Society; Andrew V. Sandoval, wildlife biologist and consultant for a global corporation in Mexico; Florian Sicks, senior curator and deputy zoological director of the Tierpark Berlin; and Rick Wallen, former leader of the Yellowstone Bison Ecology and Management Team.

I am deeply indebted to my friend and former National Audubon Society colleague Page Chichester, who, as a resident of Germany, conducted the interviews for the chapter on European bison, making it a thorough examination of what is going on with bison in Europe and points east. I couldn't have done it without his extensive help.

I also owe heartfelt thanks to the editors who worked on my book with a deft and gentle touch and offered cogent comments: Kate Rogers, Janet Kimball, and Melissa Ousley. I offer a deep bow to proofreader Laura Larson, who in my estimation functioned also as a fact-checker and rescued my text from authorial blunders. Special thanks go to Alice Speilburg, my agent, for her stick-to-itive-ness and confidence; to Jill Walling, irreplaceable friend and colleague, for her comments and encouragement during multiple readings of the manuscript; to Rob Schuweiler, Seattle musician and painter, for his optimistic outbursts regarding my manuscript; to Caroline O'Connell, Los Angeles publicist and my mentor of marketing; and to my spouse, Jeanne, for her uncomplaining tolerance of my absences while working on this book.

Notes

Information derived from interviews with the sources mentioned in my acknowledgments appears throughout the text. In addition, selected notes and resources are listed here.

INTRODUCTION: BACK FROM THE BRINK

p. 10 **"While feeding, they are often"**: Dr. Godman, "The Bison, or Bonassus of North America," *Saturday Magazine*, November 2, 1833.

p. 11 **In 1872, these scavengers shipped**: All of the statistics in this paragraph are from William T. Hornaday, *The Extermination of the American Bison*, pp. 445–46.

p. 12 **Pawing the earth, a group of fifteen or twenty bulls**: John C. Frémont, *Frémont's First Impressions: The Original Report of His Exploring Expeditions of 1842–1844*, p. 25. During his expedition across Nebraska in 1842, John C. Frémont saw a cloud of dust rising over the prairie some distance away and rode over to see what was causing it. He found about twenty buffalo bulls fighting and pawing up dust.

p. 12 **80 percent of calves are born**: James A. Bailey, *American Plains Bison: Rewilding an Icon*, pp. 65–66.

p. 13 *[A]bout a dozen brown and white wolves*: Stanley P. Young and Edward A. Goldman, *The Wolves of North America*, pp. 225–28.

p. 13 **By 1800, mounted Plains Indians**: Bailey, *American Plains Bison*, pp. 25–26.

p. 14 **One famed rifleman, Vic Smith**: Hornaday, *The Extermination of the American Bison*, p. 510.

p. 15 **"a blood-lustful debauch"**: Lincoln A. Lang, *Ranching with Roosevelt*, pp. 24–25. On the other side of the equation, one former buffalo hunter said that "any one of the families killed and homes destroyed by the Indians would have been worth more to Texas and to civilization than all the millions of buffalo that ever roamed from the Pecos River on the south to the Platte River on the north." (Michael Punke, *Last Stand: George Bird Grinnell, the Battle to Save the Buffalo, and the Birth of the New West*, pp. 90–91.)

p. 15 **"The business-like, wholesale slaughter"**: Hornaday, *The Extermination of the American Bison*, pp. 520–21.

p. 16 **They have tamed it with their barrows**: "Passing of the Prairie," under the heading "Poems Old and New," *St. Joseph (MO) Gazette*, October 25, 1907, credited to *The New York Times*. As we will find in chapter 3, the week of October 18–25, 1907, was a fateful one for bison.

CHAPTER 1: IN THE BEGINNING

p. 19 **"the cougars are noxious"**: Theodore Roosevelt, *Outdoor Pastimes of an American Hunter*, p. 295.

p. 19 **Hunting in Idaho in spring 1889**: Theodore Roosevelt, *Hunting Trips of a Ranchman & The Wilderness Hunter*, pp. 569–72. A portion was also told by Sylvia Jukes Morris in *Edith Kermit*

Roosevelt, p. 119. Wildlife conservation was in a strange state in the late 1800s, when one of the leading advocates of wildlife protection could with pride kill a healthy member of a vanishing species.

p. 20 **"While the slaughter of the buffalo"**: Roosevelt, *Hunting Trips*, pp. 242–43.

p. 21 **His distinguished family tree**: For details of Grinnell's life, see Albert Kenrick Fisher, "In Memoriam: George Bird Grinnell," *The Auk* 56, no. 1 (January 1939): pp. 1–12, and John F. Reiger, ed., *The Passing of the Great West: Selected Papers of George Bird Grinnell*, p. 57.

p. 22 **The federal government set it aside**: George Bird Grinnell, introduction to vol. 1 of *The Works of Theodore Roosevelt*, ed. Hermann Hagedorn, p. xiv.

p. 22 **"still often sufficiently numerous"**: George Bird Grinnell, writing as "Ornis," "Buffalo Hunt with the Pawnees," *Forest and Stream*, December 25, 1873.

p. 23 **Grinnell's first experience with Yellowstone**: Kenneth H. Baldwin, "The Rude Hand of Man: The Ludlow Reconnaissance of 1875," in *Enchanted Enclosure: The Army Engineers and Yellowstone National Park; A Documentary History* (Washington, DC: Historical Division, Office of the Chief of Engineers, US Army, 1976). Available online at www.nps.gov/parkhistory/online_books/baldwin/index.htm.

p. 23 **"It may not be out of place"**: George Bird Grinnell, "Zoological Report," in *Report of a Reconnaissance from Carroll, Montana Territory, on the Upper Missouri, to the Yellowstone National Park, and Return, Made in the Summer of 1875*, by William Ludlow, p. 61. Quoted in Punke, *Last Stand*, p. 102.

p. 23 **"It is estimated that during the winter"**: Fisher, "In Memoriam," pp. 4–5.

p. 23 **In 1880, P. W. Norris, the park superintendent**: P. W. Norris, *Annual Report of the Superintendent of the Yellowstone National Park to the Secretary of the Interior for the Year 1880*, p. 38.

p. 23 **In 1885, the number was about two hundred**: D. W. Wear, *Annual Report of the Superintendent of the Yellowstone National Park to the Secretary of the Interior* (1885), pp. 3–5.

p. 23 **"take a leading position"**: *New York Times*, July 13, 1885. The review was correct: The book is still in print in several different editions. It also proved successful overseas—the January 16, 1886, issue of the London *Spectator* took up the *New York Times* anthem, calling the book "bright and fresh and full of good reading." Cited in Carleton Putnam, *Theodore Roosevelt*, vol. 1, *The Formative Years, 1858–1886*, p. 519.

p. 24 **"There is, I suppose, no country in the world"**: Robert G. Athearn, *Westward the Briton*, p. xv.

p. 24 **Grinnell would later recall**: Grinnell's recollections about this conversation were recounted in his introduction to vol. 1 of *The Works of Theodore Roosevelt*, pp. xiv–xvi.

p. 24 **he and Roosevelt agreed to create an organization**: Paul Russell Cutright, *Theodore Roosevelt: The Making of a Conservationist*, p. 169; Punke, *Last Stand*, pp. 165–66; James B. Trefethen, *Crusade for Wildlife: Highlights in Conservation Progress*, pp. 16–19.

p. 25 **who in Roosevelt's mind epitomized**: Theodore Roosevelt, "The Boone and Crockett Club," *Harper's Weekly*, March 18, 1893.

p. 25 **It was the first US organization**: Punke, *Last Stand*, p. 166.

p. 25 **"The preservation of forests"**: Theodore Roosevelt and George Bird Grinnell, eds., *American Big-Game Hunting: The Book of the Boone and Crockett Club*, p. 326.

p. 25 **"a vigorous and masterful people"**: Ibid., pp. 14–15.

p. 25 **"killed with the rifle in fair chase"**: Roosevelt, "The Boone and Crockett Club."

p. 26 **The club also was instrumental in passage**: Trefethen, *Crusade for Wildlife*, p. 48.

p. 26 **Presidents Grover Cleveland, Benjamin Harrison:** Sean Dennis Cashman, *America in the Gilded Age: From the Death of Lincoln to the Rise of Theodore Roosevelt*, 3rd ed., p. 311.

p. 26 **The first reserve set aside:** Trefethen, *Crusade for Wildlife*, p. 48.

p. 27 **the park came under military control:** Lieutenant Elmer Lindsey, "A Winter Trip Through the Yellowstone Park," *Harper's Weekly*, January 29, 1898.

p. 27 *The geysers, in the slow process of centuries:* Ludlow, *Report of a Reconnaissance*, pp. 26–27, 36. Also see Baldwin, "The Rude Hand of Man," www.nps.gov/parkhistory/online_books/baldwin/chap5a.htm. Despite his concern about the park, Ludlow was optimistic about its future, writing, "The day will come, and it cannot be far distant, when this most interesting region, crowded with marvels and adorned with the most superb scenery, will be rendered accessible to all; and then, thronged with visitors from all over the world; it will be what nature and Congress, for once working together in unison, have declared it should be, a national park" (Ludlow, p. 37).

p. 28 **Ludlow's advice was ignored:** Trefethen, *Crusade for Wildlife*, pp. 30–31.

p. 28 **Conservationists such as John Muir:** For details of the military intervention and responses to it, see Karl Jacoby, *Crimes against Nature: Squatters, Poachers, Thieves, and the Hidden History of American Conservation*, pp. 99–104; quotations pp. 100, 132.

p. 29 **complained that hunters were setting forest fires:** Moses Harris, *Annual Report of the Superintendent of the Yellowstone National Park to the Secretary of the Interior* (1886), pp. 7, 13.

p. 29 **"As it is now, the Park is placed":** George Bird Grinnell, "Our National Parks," *Forest and Stream*, December 3, 1891.

p. 29 **Twenty years earlier, he had ridden:** George S. Anderson, "A Buffalo Story," in Roosevelt and Grinnell, *American Big-Game Hunting*, p. 22.

p. 30 **In his report to the Secretary of the Interior:** George S. Anderson, *Annual Report of the Superintendent of the Yellowstone National Park to the Secretary of the Interior* (1892), pp. 9–11.

p. 30 **Anderson also set his sights on:** Punke, *Last Stand*, p. 182.

p. 30 **On March 14, 1894, US Army scout:** Sources for the Howell arrest: George Bird Grinnell, "The Capture of Howell," *Forest and Stream*, March 31, 1894; Jacoby, *Crimes against Nature*, pp. 123–29; Trefethen, *Crusade for Wildlife*, pp. 37–40.

p. 32 *It is the simplest thing in the world:* "Park Poachers and Their Ways," *Forest and Stream*, May 26, 1894. Quoted in Jacoby, *Crimes against Nature*, p. 131.

p. 33 *The man Howell, who has just been arrested:* George Bird Grinnell, "A Premium on Crime," *Forest and Stream*, March 24, 1894. Quoted in Jacoby, *Crimes against Nature*, p. 124.

p. 34 *I have ordered Howell's tepee and supplies burned:* E. Hough, "*Forest and Stream*'s Yellowstone Park Game Exploration: The Account of Howell's Capture," *Forest and Stream*, May 5, 1894. Quoted in Trefethen, *Crusade for Wildlife*, p. 39.

p. 34 **Among those who, in 1894:** L. H. Pammel, ed., *Major John F. Lacey: Memorial Volume*, pp. xviii–xix.

p. 34 **"I love the people who love birds":** Ibid., p. 149.

p. 34 **"the first American congressman":** William T. Hornaday, "John F. Lacey," in Pammel, *Major John F. Lacey*, p. 12.

p. 34 **"The extermination of the buffalo":** Pammel, *Major John F. Lacey*, p. 71.

p. 34 **As head of the House Committee on Public Lands:** Ibid., pp. 96–97, 106. Lacey scathingly said of game hogs that they "should have rather hired out or volunteered to stick pigs for two days for the meat packers, where they might have glutted their appetite for gore in a more creditable way."

pp. 34–35 **On May 7, President Grover Cleveland**: *Congregationalist*, August 24, 1893; Grinnell, "The Capture of Howell" and "A Premium on Crime"; "Park Poachers and Their Ways," *Forest and Stream*; Pammel, *Major John F. Lacey*, p. 60; Punke, *Last Stand*, p. 216; George S. Anderson, *Annual Report of the Acting Superintendent of the Yellowstone National Park to the Secretary of the Interior* (1895), pp. 11–12.

p. 35 **"The act of May 7, 1894"**: Anderson, *Annual Report of the Acting Superintendent* (1895), pp. 11–13.

p. 35 **Meanwhile, poachers are going unarmed**: "Killing Park Buffalo," *Forest and Stream*, December 7, 1895. Quoted in Jacoby, *Crimes against Nature*, p. 128.

p. 35 **In 1896, hunters kill ten bison**: Anderson, *Annual Report of the Acting Superintendent* (1896), pp. 11–13.

p. 35 **hovering always around fifty**: Oscar J. Brown, *Annual Report of the Acting Superintendent of the Yellowstone National Park to the Secretary of the Interior* (1899), p. 7.

p. 35 **To balance the losses from poaching**: Jonathan Pitcher, *Annual Report of the Acting Superintendent of the Yellowstone National Park to the Secretary of the Interior* (1902), pp. 9–10; (1903), p. 6; (1904), p. 6; (1905), pp. 8–9; (1906), p. 8; S. B. M. Young, *Annual Report of the Acting Superintendent of the Yellowstone National Park to the Secretary of the Interior* (1907), p. 14.

p. 35 **Finally, local poachers are**: Jacoby, *Crimes against Nature*, pp. 107–9.

p. 36 **Howell continues working**: Ibid., p. 129.

p. 36 *Slaughter was the order of the day:* Hornaday, "John F. Lacey," p. 13.

CHAPTER 2: WHEN SCIENCE FAVORS EXTINCTION

p. 37 **"the Museum was actually without"**: Hornaday, *The Extermination of the American Bison*, p. 529.

p. 38 **At the fort in late September 1886**: Hunt details are from Hornaday, *The Extermination of the American Bison*, pp. 508–9, 530–48. See this text for the full story.

p. 38 **Hornaday was born December 1, 1854**: For details on Hornaday's life, see Stefan Bechtel, *Mr. Hornaday's War: How a Peculiar Victorian Zookeeper Waged a Lonely Crusade for Wildlife That Changed the World*.

p. 39 **"wild and rugged butte country"**: This and the following quotes about the hunt are from Hornaday, *The Extermination of the American Bison*, pp. 535–36, 542–46.

p. 41 **One afternoon, when the taxidermists**: This account of the capture of the calf leans heavily on Bechtel, *Mr. Hornaday's War*, pp. 31–32, 34.

p. 41 **But the orphaned calf**: The display was exhibited at the Smithsonian for many years and is now exhibited at the Museum of the Northern Great Plains in Fort Benton, Montana.

p. 41 **Sandy may have helped give rise**: For details on the development of the National Zoo, see Bechtel, *Mr. Hornaday's War*, pp. 131–38.

p. 42 **One day in March 1888**: Bechtel, *Mr. Hornaday's War*, pp. 49–51.

p. 42 **Hornaday resigned**: Ibid., pp. 147–49.

p. 43 **"The big game that is hunted and killed"**: William T. Hornaday, *Our Vanishing Wild Life: Its Extermination and Preservation*, p. 395.

p. 43 **"can only be achieved by wise laws"**: Roosevelt, *Outdoor Pastimes of an American Hunter*, pp. 289–90.

p. 44 **By 1892, the politically powerful**: Anderson, *Annual Report of the Superintendent* (1892), p. 9; Grinnell, "Our National Parks." Much of the account of the 1892 fight given here is also adapted from Punke, *Last Stand*, pp. 186–91, and from Trefethen, *Crusade for Wildlife*, pp. 34–36.

p. 45 **Wyoming senator Francis Warren**: For more about Senator Warren, see Kerry Drake, "Francis E. Warren: A Massachusetts Farm Boy Who Changed Wyoming," WyoHistory.org, November 8, 2014, https://wyohistory.org/encyclopedia/francis-e-warren-massachusetts -farm-boy-who-changed-wyoming.

p. 45 **"would be detrimental to all"**: Grinnell, "Our National Parks."

p. 45 **"If one such railroad franchise"**: Ibid.

p. 45 **"all public spirited Americans"**: Quoted in Punke, *Last Stand*, pp. 188–89.

p. 46 **The proposed bill died**: Hornaday, *The Extermination of the American Bison*, p. 514.

p. 46 **"inquire into the expediency"**: Ibid., p. 514.

p. 46 **Two days later, Senator Henry Wilson**: See "Henry Wilson: A Featured Biography," US Senate, www.senate.gov/senators/FeaturedBios/Featured_Bio_Wilson_Henry.htm.

p. 47 **The bill imposed strict limits**: Details on the legislative battle and Hornaday's views on it are found in Hornaday, *The Extermination of the American Bison*, pp. 319–20, 435, 438, 514–20.

p. 48 **"There is, perhaps, no fact"**: This quote and the one that follows are from Pammel, *Major John F. Lacey*, pp. 154–55.

pp. 48–49 **The fundamental legal question**: This brief survey about early federal wildlife law is based on Michael J. Bean, *The Evolution of National Wildlife Law*, pp. 9–47.

p. 49 **"At that time, few large men in public life"**: Hornaday in Pammel, *Major John F. Lacey*, pp. 12–13, 202.

p. 49 **This legislation marked the federal government's**: Bean, *The Evolution of National Wildlife Law*, p. 18; Douglas Brinkley, *The Wilderness Warrior: Theodore Roosevelt and the Crusade for America*, pp. 365–67.

p. 50 **"the United States government has tardily"**: This and the following two quotes are from Pammel, *Major John F. Lacey*, pp. 155–59.

pp. 50–51 **"I desire again to urge upon the Congress"**: "President's Annual Message," 39 Cong. Rec. p. 15 (December 6, 1904).

p. 51 **the coyotes averaged about thirty pounds**: Roosevelt, *Outdoor Pastimes of an American Hunter*, p. 106.

CHAPTER 3: WHERE BUFFALO ROAM, AGAIN: EARLY RESTORATION

p. 53 **Theodore Roosevelt began pushing the idea**: For details on the creation of the Bronx Zoo, see Brinkley, *The Wilderness Warrior*, pp. 276–87.

pp. 54–55 **a White House conference on conservation**: For details of the governors' conference, see William J. McGee, *Proceedings of a Conference of Governors in the White House, Washington, D. C., May 13–15, 1908*, ed. Newton C. Blanchard et al.

p. 55 **Meanwhile, in 1904, Ernest Harold Baynes**: Harold P. Danz, *Of Bison and Man*, p. 125. See also useful and hard-to-find information about Baynes online at "Harold E. Baynes," All About Bison, https://allaboutbison.com/bison-in-history/h-e-baynes.

p. 55 **Hornaday sent J. Alden Loring**: Brinkley, *The Wilderness Warrior*, pp. 412, 624.

p. 56 **Some did it to preserve an element**: For a discussion of the motivations of bison breeders, see Danz, *Of Bison and Man*, pp. 139–42.

p. 56 **about half a dozen men**: Valerius Geist, *Buffalo Nation: History and Legend of the North American Bison*, p. 103.

p. 56 **a Pend d'Oreille or Kalispel Indian named Samuel Walking Coyote**: David A. Dary, *The Buffalo Book: The Saga of an American Symbol*, pp. 222–24.

p. 56 **All but two of the calves:** Different sources give different numbers for the bison calves and how many survived.

p. 57 **They continued to maintain the herd:** Ken Zontek, *Buffalo Nation: American Indian Efforts to Restore the Bison*, pp. 56–57.

p. 57 **Allard's other son sold his share:** Dary, *The Buffalo Book*, pp. 224–25.

p. 57 **Pablo offered to sell his bison:** "Moving a Herd of Buffalo," *Brooklyn (NY) Citizen*, October 31, 1909.

p. 58 *And this is all done to make room:* The story, "Moving a Herd of Buffalo," appeared on October 31, 1909, in the *Brooklyn Citizen* and in the Knoxville, Tennessee, newspapers the *Tribune* and the *Journal*; presumably it appeared in other newspapers that day, as the bison was now a species of national interest.

p. 59 **James McKay—born and raised in western Canada:** Irene M. Spry and Heather Conn, "James McKay," in *The Canadian Encyclopedia*, last edited March 8, 2019, www.thecanadian encyclopedia.ca/en/article/james-mckay.

p. 60 **One of the most successful pioneers of bison preservation:** Details about Charles Goodnight are from J. Evetts Haley, *Charles Goodnight: Cowman and Plainsman*, pp. 3–12.

p. 61 **"As the end of the first year's branding":** Goodnight's recollections about his business are from Emanuel Dubbs, "Charles Goodnight," in Charles Goodnight et al., *Pioneer Days in the Southwest from 1850 to 1879*, pp. 11–13, 22–28.

p. 62 **"Western men were not squeamish":** Laura V. Hamner, *The No-Gun Man of Texas*, p. 158.

p. 62 **"would probably average a hundred and twenty-five":** Haley, *Charles Goodnight*, p. 437.

p. 62 **In the 1920s, he was still selling:** Dubbs, "Charles Goodnight," p. 9.

p. 63 **When he died, the ranch passed into the hands:** "Goodnight Ranch Bison Herd Has New Protector," *Kerrville (TX) Times*, June 16, 1938; "Bison Hunt Stirs Wrath of Texans," *Salt Lake Tribune*, October 4, 1931. Both archived online at All About Bison, https://allabout bison.com/bison-in-history/texas-history/charles-goodnight-bison-herd.

p. 63 **announced he would allow the bison herd:** "Buffalo Bill Passes Both Houses Aug. 12," *Canyon (TX) News*, August 13, 1931; and "Bison Hunt Stirs Wrath of Texans," *Salt Lake Tribune*, October 4, 1931. Both archived online at All About Bison, https://allaboutbison.com/ bison-in-history/texas-history/charles-goodnight-bison-herd.

p. 63 **Since the 1990s, some of the land:** For details, see "Charles Goodnight Bison Herd," All About Bison, https://allaboutbison.com/bison-in-history/texas-history/charles-good night-bison-herd. The descendants of the Goodnight herd and their genetic issues are discussed in Chapter 10.

p. 63 **Today, descendants of the Goodnight herd:** Donnis Baggett, "How Did They Get There? The Texas State Bison Herd at Caprock Canyons State Park," *Bison World*, Summer 2022, pp. 18–19.

p. 64 **Born in Illinois in 1844, Charles Jesse Jones:** Details about Jones's life are from Charles Jesse Jones, *Buffalo Jones' Adventures on the Plains*, ed. Henry Inman, pp. 5–6, 15, 19–22, 256.

p. 66 **"I am positive it was the wickedness":** Ibid., p. 285.

p. 66 **"They instinctively know their doom":** Details on Jones's expeditions, attempts at ranching, and advocacy work are from Jones and Inman, *Buffalo Jones' Adventures on the Plains*, pp. 80, 202, 204, 220–23, 262–65, and Dary, *The Buffalo Book*, pp. 222–24, 226–27.

p. 66 *was rushing over the prairie:* Jones and Inman, *Buffalo Jones' Adventures on the Plains*, p 204.

p. 67 **That year he corralled in Yellowstone**: Pitcher, *Annual Report of the Acting Superintendent* (1902), pp. 9–10; (1903), p. 6; (1904), p. 6; (1905), pp. 8–9; (1906), p. 8; S. B. M. Young, *Annual Report of the Acting Superintendent* (1907), p. 14.

p. 68 **After he publicly criticized**: Dary, *The Buffalo Book*, pp. 227–28.

p. 68 **By 1908, six years after Conrad's death**: "Charles E Conrad," All About Bison, https://allaboutbison.com/bison-in-history/charles-e-conrad.

p. 68 **Similarly, Austin Corbin**: "Austin Corbin Park," All About Bison, https://allabout bison.com/austin-corbin-park.

p. 69 **American Express, Wells Fargo**: "National Herd of Buffalo in Its New Home," *St. Louis Post-Dispatch*, October 22, 1907.

p. 69 **"snorted and bellowed their disgust"**: "Buffalo Family Will Rule in Wild Wichita Mountains," *Cleveland Enterprise*, October 25, 1907.

p. 69 **"bumped and jerked and hauled"**: Ibid.

CHAPTER 4: AMERICAN BISON STEP OUT OF THE ER

p. 72 **"In ravines and water courses"**: "To Preserve the Buffalo on Flathead Reservation," *Great Falls (MT) Tribune*, March 23, 1908.

p. 73 **"it is thrown open to settlement"**: "Bison Range Seems Assured," *Missoulian*, May 29, 1908.

p. 73 **These properties would prove too small**: For an account of the land-allotment schemes, see Robert M. Utley, *The Last Days of the Sioux Nation*, pp. 40–59.

p. 73 **"instituted a kind of progressive poverty"**: T. H. Watkins, *Righteous Pilgrim: The Life and Times of Harold L. Ickes, 1874–1952*, pp. 532–33.

p. 74 **The federal government promptly bought**: Zontek, *Buffalo Nation*, pp. 61–62.

p. 74 **People from twenty-nine**: Hornaday, *Our Vanishing Wild Life*, p. 242.

p. 74 **"not one red cent"**: Danz, *Of Bison and Man*, p. 126.

p. 74 **The Northern Pacific Railroad**: "Buffalo to Arrive in October," *Missoulian*, September 1, 1909; "Railway Builds Spur for Bison Reserve," *Missoulian*, September 21, 1909; "Buffalo Stockade Nearly Done," *Missoulian*, September 29, 1909; and "Getting Reserve Ready for Reception of Bison," *Anaconda (MT) Standard*, September 21, 1909.

p. 74 **The fence was completed**: "Bison Herd for State of Mont. [sic] Is Complete," *Bismarck (ND) Tribune*, October 23, 1909.

p. 74 **By then, Hornaday had selected**: Hornaday, *Our Vanishing Wild Life*, pp. 242–43.

p. 74 **"given their liberty"**: "Buffaloes Are Turned Loose on New Range Near Missoula," *Anaconda Standard*, October 18, 1909.

p. 74 **"Five years ago it would have been impossible"**: "Montana's Bison Herd," *Anaconda Standard*, June 7, 1908. Fur seals, like bison, were being slaughtered for hides throughout their range and would likely have become extinct had not last-minute measures cut back on the mayhem. Side story: Anaconda Copper fought the progressive Republican Joseph Dixon and his attempted reforms, stifling him as a one-term US senator and a one-term Montana governor.

p. 75 **The cost of $40,000 for setting up**: Stephen Fox, *The American Conservation Movement: John Muir and his Legacy*, p. 168.

p. 75 ***We hope these eleventh-hour efforts***: "Bison Range in Montana," *Goodland (KS) Republic* and *Goodland (KS) News*, October 22, 1909. The article that included this quotation also appeared in the *Daily Sun* (Gainesville, FL), October 17, 1909, under the headline "National Bison Range Located in Montana," so presumably it was syndicated nationwide.

p. 76 **in this case $32,000:** "Bill Provides Wind Cave Game Preserve," *Black Hills Weekly Journal* (Rapid City, SD), April 26, 1912.

p. 76 **Accompanying them were the zoological society's:** "Bison Herd on Way to Hot Springs," *Weekly Pioneer Times Mining Review* (Deadwood, SD), December 4, 1913.

p. 76 **A report from the preserve for 1921:** "Game Herd Is Increasing," *Queen City Mail* (Spearfish, SD), February 22, 1922.

p. 76 **in October 1928, school officials asked:** "North Dakota 'U' Wants Wind Cave Park Buffalo for Bison Day Festivity," *Argus-Leader* (Sioux Falls, SD), October 20, 1928.

p. 76 **A fifth early preserve:** For history on this refuge, see "Niobrara Reserve," All About Bison, https://allaboutbison.com/bison-in-history/niobrara-reserve.

p. 77 **The oldest federal wildlife agency:** This section on the historical origins of federal agencies draws on Roger L. Di Silvestro, *Reclaiming the Last Wild Places: A New Agenda for Biodiversity*, pp. 102–68, as well as other sources cited below.

p. 79 **"He was exuberant, warm":** Horace M. Albright, *The Birth of the National Park Service: The Founding Years, 1913–33*, as told to Robert Cahn, p. 16.

p. 80 **"I'm not asking you to sit":** Ibid., p. 16.

p. 80 **"to conserve the scenery and the natural":** Bean, *The Evolution of National Wildlife Law*, p. 172.

pp. 80–81 **He also advocated reducing or ending predator control:** For early progressive thoughts on predator control, see Aldo Leopold, *Game Management*, pp. 230–52.

p. 81 **Early conservation measures were focused:** Curt Meine, *Aldo Leopold: His Life and Work*, p. 147.

p. 81 **In June 1915, he assumed responsibility:** Details on Leopold's views and work come from Meine, *Aldo Leopold*, pp. 144–46, 149, 150, 307.

p. 81 ***North America, in its natural state:*** Aldo Leopold, *USFS Game and Fish Handbook*, p. 9. Quoted in Meine, p. 146.

p. 82 **"To speak plainly, I do not know":** Quoted in Meine, p. 152.

p. 82 **"Game management is the art":** Leopold, *Game Management*, p. 3.

p. 83 **"The thought was that restriction":** Ibid., pp. 16–17, 21.

p. 86 **"For a parallel to this":** Fox, *The American Conservation Movement*, p. 114.

p. 87 **Refuge staff also conduct an annual roundup:** For current information on the timing of bison roundups, visit "Fort Niobrara Wildlife Refuge," National Park Service, www.nps.gov/places/fort-niobrara.htm.

p. 87 **"Based on today's knowledge of genetics":** Bailey, *American Plains Bison*, p. 159.

CHAPTER 5: PRIVATE HERDS: HOPES, ASPIRATIONS, ROADS TO RECOVERY

p. 89 **From the 1930s to the 1960s, bison numbers:** Bailey, *American Plains Bison*, p. 158.

p. 95 **"incentives for expansion of tribal/First Nation":** For more on the Bison 1 Million initiative, visit the National Bison Association website, https://bisoncentral.com.

p. 96 ***Over the next century, the ecological recovery:*** Eric W. Sanderson et al., "The Ecological Future of the North American Bison: Conceiving Long-Term, Large-Scale Conservation of Wildlife," *Conservation Biology* 22, no. 2 (May 2008): p. 252, https://doi.org/10.1111/j.1523-1739.2008.00899.x.

p. 97 **This mission would be achieved:** Ibid., p. 255.

p. 97 **"a new forward-thinking vision"**: Keith Aune and Glenn Plumb, *Theodore Roosevelt and Bison Restoration on the Great Plains*, p. III.

p. 97 **The western part of that range**: Sanderson et al., "The Ecological Future of the North American Bison," pp. 252–66.

p. 97 **"provides a lasting resource of experts"**: Aune and Plumb, *Theodore Roosevelt and Bison Restoration*, p. III.

p. 98 **"the most significant expansion"**: Ibid., p. 113.

pp. 98–99 **"willing to bear all the expense"** and **"Out of the 600,000,000 acres remaining"**: Representative John Lacey in support of House bill H.R. 10590, April 10, 1900, in Pammel, *Major John F. Lacey*, pp. 157–58.

p. 99 **One conservation group that has had significant success**: The information on The Nature Conservancy and their reserves, as well as the quoted material from conservancy managers, comes from the organization's website: "Where We Work," www.nature.org/en-us/about-us/where-we-work; "How to Help," www.nature.org/en-us/get-involved; and "Who We Are," www.nature.org/en-us/about-us.

p. 101 *Mate selection, with the dominance of large:* Bailey, *American Plains Bison*, p. 146.

p. 101 **American Prairie (formerly the American Prairie Reserve)**: Information on American Prairie is online at www.americanprairie.org; quoted material is at "Hunting and Conservation," www.americanprairie.org/news-blog/hunting-and-conservation.

p. 103 **a request by the reserve staff in 2021**: "BLM Extends Comments Period on APR's Bison Grazing Proposal," *Ravalli Republic*, (Hamilton, MT), July 14, 2021.

p. 103 **Turner told one of his biographers**: With the exception of quotes from Mark Kossler, which came from an author interview, information about Ted Turner and his ranch operations is from Todd Wilkinson, *Last Stand: Ted Turner's Quest to Save a Troubled Planet*, pp. 13–14, 26, 28, 33, 44–45.

p. 105 **"Rural communities see bison restoration"**: This source wishes to remain anonymous so they can speak freely. They are quoted here without attribution.

p. 107 **"We live in a time of minimal expectations"**: Sanderson et al., "The Ecological Future of the North American Bison," p. 264.

CHAPTER 6: TRIBES: FINDING HOME

p. 109 **"If any animal was ever designed"**: Hornaday, *The Extermination of the American Bison*, p. 437.

p. 109 *Soon I was mixed up in the dust:* Luther Standing Bear, *My Indian Boyhood*, p. 63.

p. 109 **"We trained our pony to walk"**: Ibid., p. 25.

p. 110 **"usually an Indian on horseback preferred"**: Frank H. Mayer and Charles B. Roth, *The Buffalo Harvest*, p. 32.

p. 110 **"Mayer, there's no two ways about it"**: Ibid., pp. 29–30.

p. 111 **"I would not seriously regret"**: Quotes here and below attributed to Columbus Delano, General William T. Sherman, General Philip Sheridan, Frank Mayer, and Colonel Richard Dodge were cited in Geist, *Buffalo Nation*, pp. 85, 91.

p. 112 **"The buffalo served his mission"**: Mayer and Roth, *The Buffalo Harvest*, pp. 28–29.

p. 112 **"All the danger and hardships suffered"**: Emanuel Dubbs, "Personal Reminiscences—Part II," in Goodnight et al., *Pioneer Days*, pp. 89–90.

p. 113 *My sun is set:* James R. Walker, *Lakota Belief and Ritual*, pp. 137–39.

p. 113 **Within twenty years, about twenty-five tribes**: Zontek, *Buffalo Nation*, pp. 68–70.

p. 114 **Tribes worked alone, and many lacked expertise**: Ibid., pp. 75–76.

p. 114 **"to the Indian nations in a manner"**: Online at www.ncai.org/conferences-events/ncai-events/Land_and_Natural_Resources_Committee_-_Inter_Tribal_Buffalo_Council_Presentation.pdf.

p. 114 **A key goal is the distribution**: Information on ITBC goals and management is from Zontek, *Buffalo Nation*, pp. 75, 78–79, 87.

p. 115 **In 2008, the Blackfeet of north-central Montana**: Aune and Plumb, *Theodore Roosevelt and Bison Restoration*, pp. 63–65.

p. 116 **In the new effort, which has relied heavily**: "CSKT Donate 5 Bison to Chippewa Tribe (From Associated Press), *Weekly Update* (e-newsletter), National Bison Association, November 5, 2021, p. 8.

p. 119 **It began in 2016 when the Osage Nation**: Online version of *The Land Report: The Magazine of the American Landowner*, posted July 3, 2017, at https://landreport.com/2017/01/2016-land-report-100-ted-turner.

p. 120 **"The biggest and strongest bulls will run"**: Jessica Brent, "Osage Nation Ranch Doubles Bison Herd," *Osage News*, November 8, 2021, https://osagenews.org/osage-nation-ranch-doubles-bison-herd.

p. 121 **The Blackfeet Nation abuts Glacier National Park**: For more information on the Blackfeet, Cristina Mormorunni recommends Jack McNeel, "10 Things You Should Know about the Blackfeet Nation," *Indian Country Today*, April 6, 2017, www.indiancountrytoday.com/archive/10-things-you-should-know-about-the-blackfeet-nation.

p. 122 **The main goals of the initiative**: The information here on the initiative comes from former Wildlife Conservation Society regional director Cristina Mormorunni and from "Blackfeet Buffalo Program," Blackfeet Nation, www.blackfeetnation.com/iinnii-buffalo-spirit-center.

CHAPTER 7: LOST HERDS: MEXICO AND CANADA

p. 127 **In 1987, nearly ten years after the bison roundup**: The story about Ceballos's trip in 1987 is based on Krista Schlyer, "The Lost Herd of Janos-Hidalgo," *Wildlife Conservation*, January/February 2009, pp. 48–55.

p. 129 **While en route from Monterrey**: This story is related in Neil B. Carmony and David E. Brown, eds., *Mexican Game Trails: Americans Afield in Old Mexico, 1866–1940*, pp. 11–12, 23–27.

p. 129 **"an integral part of southwestern grasslands"**: Rurik List et al., "Historic Distribution and Challenges to Bison Recovery in the Northern Chihuahuan Desert," *Conservation Biology* 21, no. 6 (December 2007): p. 1489. https://doi.org/10.1111/j.1523-1739.2007.00810.x.

pp. 129–130 **"Apparently bison were extirpated"**: Ibid., p. 1490.

p. 130 **On November 28, 2009, twenty-three bison**: Rurik List et al., "The Janos Biosphere Reserve, Northern Mexico," *International Journal of Wilderness* 16, no. 2 (August 2010): pp. 37–38

p. 130 **The story of the nation's complex system of land ownership**: Text about Mexico's land ownership and wildlands is from an article by Rurik List and Patricia Manzano-Fischer, "Conserving Wildlands in Mexico," *Wild Earth* 12, no. 2 (Fall 2002): pp.46–55.

p. 131 **Today, List says, the once-sprawling prairie dog**: At the same time that the US Fish & Wildlife Service and various state agencies are trying to save North America's rarest mammal species, the black-footed ferret—which is almost completely dependent on prairie dogs for food—the US Department of Agriculture's Wildlife Services is poisoning prairie dogs by the thousands every year at the behest of ranchers. If Wildlife Services proves successful at eradicating prairie dogs, eventually the chubby-looking ground squirrels will be rare enough to need listing under the Endangered Species Act. Our tax dollars at work.

p. 132 **Studies show that the border wall:** Robert Peters et al., "Nature Divided, Scientists United: US-Mexico Border Wall Threatens Biodiversity and Binational Conservation," *BioScience* 68, no. 10 (October 2018): pp. 740–43, https://doi.org/10.1093/biosci/biy063.

p. 133 **it was first documented in bison in 2013:** Mitch Smith, "Microscopic Killer Decimates Buffalo Herds and Baffles Scientists," *New York Times*, March 13, 2022.

p. 134 **"Eighteen eighty-three was the last year of buffalo":** Harvey Locke, ed., *The Last of the Buffalo: Return to the Wild*, pp. 11–12, 17–18, 73. This excellent and beautifully designed book, featuring essays by Locke, George Colpitts, Jennifer Rutkair, Leroy Little Bear, and Norman Luxton, is the source of the following discussion of plains bison in Canada, unless cited otherwise.

pp. 135–36 ***The Canadian Bison Herd:*** William T. Hornaday, "Notes on the Census," in *Annual Report of the American Bison Society, 1905–1907*, by the American Bison Society, p. 75.

p. 136 **Two years later, Canada reported:** Information from the Canadian reports is from Locke, *The Last of the Buffalo*, p. 31, and the Canadian Government, "Canada's Part in the Preservation of the Buffalo," in *Fourth Annual Report of the American Bison Society, 1911*, by the American Bison Society, p. 40.

p. 137 **produced a book on bison ecology:** The book referred to is Wes Olson and Johane Janelle, *The Ecological Buffalo: On the Trail of a Keystone Species*.

p. 138 **Ranching expanded from Texas:** Ibid., p. 62.

p. 139 **The two animals also display some behavioral:** Aune and Plumb, *Theodore Roosevelt and Bison Restoration*, p. 124.

p. 139 **as it ranged through large portions of northern Alberta:** Environment and Climate Change Canada, *Recovery Strategy for the Wood Bison* (Bison bison athabascae) *in Canada*, pp. 10–11.

p. 139 **the Royal North-West Mounted Police in 1897 took charge of protecting:** Zontek, *Buffalo Nation*, p. 120.

p. 139 **between 1925 and 1928 the federal government moved:** Environment and Climate Change Canada, *Recovery Strategy for the Wood Bison*, p. 11.

p. 140 **"in part due to the introduction of Plains Bison":** Ibid., p. 12.

p. 140 **However, a bison expert at the University of Alberta:** Dary, *The Buffalo Book*, p. 51.

p. 140 **In 1963, 168 of these bison found themselves:** Environment and Climate Change Canada, *Recovery Strategy for the Wood Bison*, p. 12; Zontek, *Buffalo Nation*, p. 121.

p. 140 **The Elk Island population and other:** Information about wood bison recovery in this section is based on Environment and Climate Change Canada, *Recovery Strategy for the Wood Bison*, pp. 12–13, 25, 43.

p. 142 **Bison have become an increasingly valued:** Committee on the Status of Endangered Wildlife in Canada, *COSEWIC Assessment and Status Report on the Plains Bison* Bison bison bison *and the Wood Bison* Bison bison athabascae *in Canada*, p. 14.

p. 142 **The reintroduction of wood bison into former habitat:** Zontek, *Buffalo Nation*, pp. 122–23, 126–27. The following discussion of Canadian laws that empowered First Nations as wildlife managers also stems from this source.

p. 144 **the decision was turned over to the new Northern Buffalo Management Board:** The specifics in this narrative regarding dates, along with the protections under Canada's Species at Risk Act, can be found in Ludwig N. Carbyn, Nicholas J. Lunn, and Kevin

Timoney, "Trends in the Distribution and Abundance of Bison in Wood Buffalo National Park," *Wildlife Society Bulletin* 26, no. 3 (Fall 1998): pp. 463–70.

p. 145 **In April 2022, about forty bison**: Kanishka Singh, "Dozens of Canada's Wood Bison Moved to Alaska for Long-Term Survival," Reuters, April 21, 2022, www.reuters.com/world/americas/dozens-canadas-wood-bison-moved-alaska-long-term-survival-2022-04-21.

CHAPTER 8: THE WAY OF THE WISENT

p. 146 **In August 1915, as the First World War enters**: The historical information here is from Rewilding Europe's *Bison Rewilding Plan, 2014–2024* and the Wikipedia entry for wisent, https://en.wikipedia.org/wiki/European_bison.

p. 146 **The following April, the remains of a poached**: Wanda Olech and Kajetan Perzanowski, *Best Practice Manual for Protection of European Bison* [in Polish], p. 6.

p. 147 **In the years ahead, the tsars stocked**: Das-Tierlexikon.de, "Wisent: Wiederansiedlung in Deutschland und Europa" [Wisent: Resettlement in Germany and Europe], www.das-tierlexikon.de/wisent.

p. 147 **At various times in the past, the wisent ranged**: G. Plumb, R. Kowalczyk, and J. A. Hernandez-Blanco, Bison bonasus, *European Bison*, p. 4.

p. 148 **the wisent is Europe's largest land animal**: Throughout this chapter, information on bison natural history comes from Olech and Perzanowski, *Best Practice Manual*. Discussions of natural history, bison social life, wisent reintroduction, local economics, and the restoration projects in the Rothaar Mountains and the Eleonorenwald are based on Rewilding Europe's *Bison Rewilding Plan, 2014–2024*, except as otherwise cited. The discussion of wisent habitat and diet relies on www.rewildingeurope.com and a February 9, 2021, blog post, "The European Bison: A Gastronomic Giant" (www.rewildingeurope.com/blog/the-european-bison-a-gastronomic-giant).

p. 149 **Bison particularly benefit dung beetles**: Anne Jeschke, "Umstrittene Kolosse" [A strident dispute], *Zeit Online* (Germany), September 29, 2021, www.zeit.de/2021/40/wilde-wisente-rothaargebirge-rinder-wildtiere-urteil-waldbauern-artenschutz.

p. 149 **In some areas, wildlife managers feed**: Ironically, because of these feeding stations, some people do not accept bison as wildlife, even though roe and red deer also are fed and commonly accepted by the public as wild animals (Kaja Heising, personal communication with author). A similar situation occurs in Yellowstone National Park, where elk are fed in Jackson Hole during winter and widely accepted as wildlife, while bison that feed alongside the elk are commonly treated as livestock in surrounding states.

p. 151 **"In the wild bison in Poland"**: Brigitte Osterath, "Die Wisente kehren nach Deutschland zurück" [The bison are returning to Germany], DW.com (Germany), April 11, 2013, www.dw.com/de/die-wisente-kehren-nach-deutschland-zur%C3%BCck/a-16248800.

p. 151 **"For biodiversity, it is very important"**: Interviews for this chapter with Florian Sicks, Wanda Olech, Nina Gandl, Kaja Heising, and Aurel Heidelberg were handled by Page Chichester, a former colleague of the author's when they both worked for the National Audubon Society's TV department. Page has lived in Germany for more than thirty years.

p. 158 **Nevertheless, a bull that drifted out of Poland**: For details on the bison shooting, see Lucinda Watts, "Germany's 'First Wild Bison in 250 Years' Shot by Authorities," *The Local* (Germany), September 18, 2017, www.thelocal.de/20170918/endangered-bison-shot-by-police.

NOTES

p. 160 **A herd in the Kizgich Valley**: Information about this herd and the herd at the Turmon Regional Managed Reserve is from P. J. Weinberg, "European Bison Monitoring in North Ossetia-Alania," unpublished report, World Wide Fund for Nature, 2019.

p. 160 **By 1955, all of these animals**: "Bison herds have reached the population limits of the Caucasian Reserve" [in Russian], TASS, October 22, 2018, https://tass.ru/v-strane/5705483.

p. 161 **says Aurel Heidelberg, a forester and wildlife biologist**: I must mention, with many thanks, that without Aurel Heidelberg's patient revisions and additions to this section of this chapter, beginning with the discussion of the Caucasus, this material would have been less well informed.

p. 161 **"It is very important to us to support"**: Tierpark Berlin, "Auswilderung trotz Hinernissen" [Release despite obstacles], press release, November 25, 2020, www.tierpark-berlin.de/de/aktuelles/alle-news/artikel/auswilderung-trotz-hindernissen.

p. 162 **At reintroduction sites, bison enter enclosures**: This description of a soft release and quotes from Aurel Heidelberg are adapted from Tierpark Berlin, "Auswilderung trotz Hinernissen."

p. 164 **"several exacerbating factors" are expected**: Plumb, Kowalczyk, and Hernandez-Blanco, Bison bonasus, *European Bison*, pp. 2–3, 10–11.

p. 166 **The European bison today has been introduced**: From the Breeding Book 2020, as cited by Kaja Heising during an interview for this book.

p. 166 **The appeal of the animals has even resulted in**: Adam Vaughan, "Wild Bison Roam in the UK for the First Time," *New Scientist*, July 23, 2022, p. 14.

p. 166 **The IUCN downlisted the wisent**: "The European Bison Is No Longer a Vulnerable Species," WWF-Romania, January 12, 2021, www.wwfcee.org/news/the-european-bison-is-no-longer-a-vulnerable-species.

CHAPTER 9: THE LAST REFUGE

p. 167 **This hunting pressure causes the animals**: Data on bison in Yellowstone National Park are derived from "Bison," Yellowstone National Park, National Park Service, last updated February 18, 2022, www.nps.gov/yell/learn/nature/bison.htm. See this site also for more information on bison social life.

p. 168 **Once the rut ends, the excitement winds down**: This same pattern of males leaving their birth herds and roaming alone or in all-male herds occurs in a wide range of species, from African elephants to sperm whales, suggesting it is a good strategy for the survival of herding species, though I've never seen any speculation or hypothesizing about why.

p. 168 **These young plants are highly nutritious**: Online at "Bison," www.nps.gov/yell/learn/nature/bison.htm, and also in P. J. White, Rick L. Wallen, and David E. Hallac, eds., *Yellowstone Bison: Conserving an American Icon in Modern Society*, pp. 71–80, 98–99.

p. 168 **follow the rising tide of the green wave**: The green-wave discussion comes from "Bison," www.nps.gov/yell/learn/nature/bison.htm, and "Bison Engineering a Better Yellowstone," Yellowstone National Park, National Park Service, last updated May 13, 2022, www.nps.gov/yell/learn/management/bison-engineering-a-better-yellowstone.htm (additional information in this chapter about the bison's impact on the Yellowstone ecosystem also comes from the latter source). See also P. J. White, Robert A. Garrott, and Glenn E. Plumb, eds., *Yellowstone's Wildlife in Transition*, pp. 156–59.

p. 169 **A Canadian biologist calculated that the one thousand bison:** Olson and Janelle, *The Ecological Buffalo*, pp. 50, 89.

p. 170 **Cows in the northern region of the park:** Natural history of bison in this section is derived from White, Wallen, and Hallac, *Yellowstone Bison*, pp. 84, 100–101, 103.

p. 171 **Digestion begins when a grazing bison:** The information in this section is based on Olson and Janelle, *The Ecological Buffalo*, pp. 50, 87–88. See this source for a discussion of rumination in bison.

p. 171 **"In other words," according to experts:** White, Wallen, and Hallac, *Yellowstone Bison*, pp. 98–99.

p. 172 **Wolves are ungulate specialists, but in one study:** White, Garrott, and Plumb, *Yellowstone's Wildlife in Transition*, pp. 104–5. This book offers an in-depth discussion of the evolution of management at Yellowstone; some of its thinking (pp. 14–21) is borrowed for the following section.

p. 172 **From 1872 to 1883, area residents:** Railroad companies were often instrumental to the creation of early parks, promoting them as scenic destinations to which they could carry passengers. Within that context, protection of scenery was also the principal goal for the designation of other early parks, such as Glacier and Grand Canyon National Parks.

p. 173 **An estimated six hundred park bison in 1880:** Margaret Mary Meagher, *The Bison of Yellowstone National Park*, p. 17.

p. 173 **The introduced bison were kept in a fenced pasture:** The material on early bison management is from Meagher, *The Bison of Yellowstone*, pp. 26–33.

p. 173 **"the number of aggressive, dominant":** Ibid., p. 29.

p. 174 **The northern region is relatively warm:** The January average is from Meagher, *The Bison of Yellowstone*, p. 8. The rest of the data is from White, Wallen, and Hallac, *Yellowstone Bison*, p. 7. According to the website of the conservation group Yellowstone Forever, the record low for the park is minus 66 degrees Fahrenheit, measured at the west entrance on February 9, 1933 ("Yellowstone Weather," www.yellowstone.org/experience/visitor-information/yellowstone-weather).

p. 174 **In the pre-Columbian era, bison probably:** Meagher, *The Bison of Yellowstone*, p. 85.

p. 174 **This behavior led management to believe:** White, Garrott, and Plumb, *Yellowstone's Wildlife in Transition*, p. 37.

p. 174 **"lower than at any time since":** Meagher, *The Bison of Yellowstone*, p. 32. The study she is referring to is, I believe, the one she conducted in the late 1960s and early '70s that resulted in this 1973 monograph.

p. 175 **At that time, the northern herd numbered:** White, Wallen, and Hallac, *Yellowstone Bison*, p. 49; White, Garrott, and Plumb, *Yellowstone's Wildlife in Transition*, p. 21.

p. 175 **Without culling, the bison rebounded:** White, Wallen, and Hallac, *Yellowstone Bison*, p. 14.

p. 175 **Brucellosis is a bacterial disease:** This discussion of brucellosis stems from "History of Bison Management," Yellowstone National Park, National Park Service, last updated February 22, 2022, www.nps.gov/yell/learn/management/bison-history.htm. Other sources are cited throughout.

p. 175 **The bacterium is not native to North America:** C. Cormack Gates and Len Broberg. *Yellowstone Bison: The Science and Management of a Migratory Wildlife Population*, pp. 79–82.

p. 176 **In 1934, the US Department of Agriculture initiated:** White, Wallen, and Hallac, *Yellowstone Bison*, p. 23.

NOTES

p. 176 **The program wiped out the brucellosis**: White, Garrott, and Plumb, *Yellowstone's Wildlife in Transition*, p. 227; White, Wallen, and Hallac, *Yellowstone Bison*, p. 23.

p. 176 **To date, no case of bison infecting cattle**: This paragraph is informed by White, Wallen, and Hallac, *Yellowstone Bison*, pp. 23–24, 26. Author's note: Bison that are infected with brucellosis and are sick from it will, of course, test positive and can pass on the bacteria. By contrast, those that survive brucellosis, or that were infected but never fell ill, may no longer carry the bacteria within their bodies and therefore cannot pass on the disease. However, they may still have antibodies for the disease in their blood, which will cause them to test positive, too. These animals—the ones whose immune systems were able to fight off brucellosis—are the animals one would want in a herd, because they are not susceptible to the illness. But when all animals that test positive are destroyed, the herd loses those with presumably strong immune systems that can fight off the bacteria.

p. 177 **When media reports showed the bison**: Gates and Broberg. *Yellowstone Bison: The Science and Management*, pp. 80, 90.

p. 177 **when it declared Wyoming brucellosis-free**: White, Wallen, and Hallac, *Yellowstone Bison*, p. 23.

p. 178 **The methods were not 100 percent effective**: For a detailed discussion of the failings of vaccination and birth control, see White, Wallen, and Hallac, *Yellowstone Bison*, pp. 29–43.

p. 178 **Wildlife had to hoof through the layers**: "Yellowstone's Bison Management Has Wandered for 100 Years," *Missoulian*, January 27, 1997.

p. 178 **"practice of shooting bison proved to be"**: "Corrals Await Wandering Yellowstone Bison," *Billings Gazette*, December 5, 1996.

p. 179 **Filed by the Sierra Club along with four**: "Judge Upholds Yellowstone Bison Plan," *Independent Record* (Helena, MT), December 20, 1996.

p. 179 **On December 29, the Park Service said**: "Slaughter of Errant Park Bison to Begin Soon," *Independent Record*, December 29, 1996.

p. 179 **in one mid-December day, Montana livestock officials**: "Another 36 Park Bison Captured Near West Yellowstone," *Great Falls (MT) Tribune*, December 12, 1996.

p. 179 **In Wyoming, sport hunters were allowed to shoot**: "Bull Bison Hunting Is Authorized," *Billings Gazette*, December 15, 1996.

p. 179 **more than 600 bison had been slaughtered**: "Brucellosis Is a Public Health Issue," *Ravalli Republic* (Hamilton, MT), January 21, 1997.

p. 180 **"None of the participants indicated"**: "Talks Bring No Solutions about Park Bison," *Independent Record*, February 28, 1997.

p. 180 **"Until an agreement is reached"**: "Advocacy Group Protests Killing of Bison," *Great Falls Tribune*, March 15, 1997.

p. 180 **"More than 1,000 bison were shot"**: "Focus on the Wildlife," *Independent Record*, June 20, 1997.

p. 181 **"truckloads of bison meat"**: "Yellowstone Bison Meat Showing Up All Around the United States," *Missoulian*, March 18, 1997.

p. 181 **The Interagency Bison Management Plan**: For information on the 2000 plan, go to www.ibmp.info/Library/IBMP_FED_ROD/3%20-%20Federal%20ROD.pdf.

p. 182 **"the state of Montana now allows bison"**: Online at "History of Bison Management," www.nps.gov/yell/learn/management/bison-history.htm.

p. 182 **"in dire need of help"**: "History," Buffalo Field Campaign, www.buffalofieldcampaign.org/history.

p. 184 **"close to zero and no transmissions"**: Pauline L. Kamath et al., "Genomics Reveals Historic and Contemporary Transmission Dynamics of a Bacterial Disease among Wildlife and Livestock," *Nature Communications* 7 (May 11, 2016): pp. 5–7, 11448, https://doi.org/10.1038/ncomms11448.

p. 184 **In addition, to reduce harm to state economies**: White, Wallen, and Hallac, *Yellowstone Bison*, p. 27.

p. 185 **Conflicts centering on bison**: Chris Geremia et al., *Bison Conservation Update, November 2020*, pp. 12–13, www.nps.gov/yell/learn/management/upload/BISON-Conservation-Update-2020.pdf.

p. 185 **Instead of trying to inoculate**: White, Wallen, and Hallac, *Yellowstone Bison*, pp. 38–41.

p. 185 **Yellowstone still has to deal with limiting bison**: Information in this section about Yellowstone's efforts to manage the bison population, regulate hunting, and open more public land for grazing is derived from "History of Bison Management," www.nps.gov/yell/learn/management/bison-history.htm; "Bison Management," Yellowstone National Park, National Park Service, last updated June 7, 2022, www.nps.gov/yell/learn/management/bison-management.htm; and Geremia et al., *Bison Conservation Update, November 2020*, pp. 11–13.

p. 186 **Montana governor Steve Bullock signed**: "Bullock Allows Bison to Roam Outside Yellowstone,"*Great Falls Tribune*, December 22, 2015.

p. 187 **The Fort Peck Assiniboine and Sioux Tribes**: "Bison Management," www.nps.gov/yell/learn/management/bison-management.htm.

p. 187 **The transfer program now certifies**: This discussion of the bison transfer program, with other sources individually cited, is derived from "Bison Management," www.nps.gov/yell/learn/management/bison-management.htm.

p. 189 **To many tribal members, bison restoration**: Information on bison restoration to tribal lands and the update of the Interagency Bison Management Plan is derived from "Bison Management," www.nps.gov/yell/learn/management/bison-management.htm, and Yellowstone National Park, "National Park Service Begins Environmental Impact Statement for Bison Management at Yellowstone National Park and 30-Day Public Comment Period," news release, January 31, 2022, www.nps.gov/yell/learn/news/22005.htm.

CHAPTER 10: BUILDING A FUTURE FOR BISON

p. 192 **Some three hundred mountain gorillas**: Adam Popescu, "Virunga Power," *New Scientist*, June 11, 2022, pp. 42–46.

p. 193 **Liwonde's more than 600 elephants**: Associated Press, "How Do You Move 250 Elephants to Their New Home? Very Carefully," NPR, July 14, 2022, www.npr.org/2022/07/14/1111555644/elephants-moved-malawi.

p. 194 **"We believe that the cause of bison"**: Sanderson et al., "The Ecological Future of the North American Bison," p. 264.

p. 195 **responsible for some eleven thousand bison in nineteen independent herds roving 4.6 million acres**: Cynthia Hartway et al., *Long-Term Viability of Department of the Interior Bison under Current Management and Potential Metapopulation Management Strategies*, p. xi. According to James A. Bailey, a Montana wildlife biologist with extensive experience in bison conservation, some changes have occurred in numbers and herds of bison managed by the Department of the Interior since this report was published. "With the recent transfer of the [National] Bison Range herd to tribal ownership, and considering primary herd management under current practice by the states of Alaska, Wyoming, and Utah with the Ute Tribe, the Department of the Interior exercises primary responsibility for managing thirteen herds with under 9,500 bison, over half of which are in Yellowstone National Park," he said in an interview with the author.

p. 195 **Before the great slaughter, bison:** Olson and Janelle, *The Ecological Buffalo*, p. 2.

p. 195 **A report published in 2020:** Hartway et al., *Long-Term Viability*, pp. xi, xiii, 1, 3, 36, 64, 69.

p. 196 **turned into 334,000 buffalo scattered:** Hartway et al., *Long-Term Viability*, pp. 1, 15. Other sources say there are about 450,000 bison in North America today, or 500,000, with "wild" plains bison still accounting for 20,000. The numbers metamorphose from source to source, but the orders of magnitude adhere closely to one another.

p. 197 **By 2010, Interior biologists had established:** Peter A. Dratch and Peter J. P. Gogan, *Bison Conservation Initiative: Bison Conservation Genetics Workshop; Report and Recommendations*, p. 2.

p. 198 **As early as 2014, Interior officials declared:** Department of the Interior, *DOI Bison Report: Looking Forward*, pp. 1, 17.

p. 199 **"There is another important feature":** Representative John Lacey in support of House bill H.R. 10590, April 10, 1900, in Pammel, *Major John F. Lacey*, p. 159.

p. 200 **"The breed seemed immune to disease":** Haley, *Charles Goodnight*, pp. 444–45.

p. 200 **"I thought to myself":** Jones and Inman, *Buffalo Jones' Adventures on the Plains*, pp. 47–48, 243, 245.

p. 200 **"I regret to say that 'Buffalo Jones's catalo":** Hornaday, *Our Vanishing Wild Life*, p. 343.

p. 201 **Tests of bison at Grand Canyon:** Lee Jones interview with the author. See also M. L. N. Terwilliger et al., *Management of the Kaibab Plateau Bison Herd in Grand Canyon National Park: 2018–2019 Operations Report*, Natural Resource Report NPS/GRCA/NRR—2020/2167 (Fort Collins, CO: National Park Service, 2020), https://doi.org/10.36967/nrr-2278108.

p. 201 **"including Yellowstone, Wind Cave":** Sam Stroupe et al., "Genomic Evaluation of Hybridization in Historic and Modern North American Bison (*Bison bison*)," *Scientific Reports* 12 (April 16, 2022): 6397, https://doi.org/10.1038/s41598-022-09828-z.

p. 203 **"ensure that healthy landscapes that support":** Hartway et al., *Long-Term Viability*, pp. 35, 66–67, 69.

p. 203 **Interior Department officials predict that by 2027:** "Bison Conservation Initiative Fact Sheet," National Park Service, last updated May 6, 2020, www.nps.gov/articles/bison-conservation-initiative-fact-sheet.htm.

p. 204 **"subject to the full range of historic natural":** Dratch and Gogan, *Bison Conservation Initiative*, p. 2.

p. 205 **"To confine plains bison within":** Harvey Locke, foreword to Olson and Janelle, *The Ecological Buffalo*, p. xii. Locke is a world leader in the conservation of parks and wilderness and cofounder of the Yellowstone to Yukon Conservation Initiative (Y2Y), which seeks to link the Yukon of far northwestern Canada with the Greater Yellowstone Ecosystem via a series of corridors of wildlife habitat.

p. 206 *The restoration of wild bison has advanced:* White, Wallen, and Hallac, *Yellowstone Bison*, p. xiv.

p. 206 **proposed a solution to the problem of space:** A later article by Deborah E. Popper and Frank J. Popper, outlining their proposal—"The Buffalo Commons as Regional Metaphor and Geographic Method"—can be found on the Great Plains Restoration Council website at https://gprc.org/research/buffalo-commons/the-buffalo-commons-as-regional-metaphor-and-geographic-method.

p. 208 **One group, Y2Y—Yellowstone to Yukon:** Material about this corridor is drawn from the Y2Y website at https://y2y.net.

p. 208 **Banff National Park in Alberta includes:** Katharine Gammon, "Animal Crossing: World's Biggest Wildlife Bridge Comes to California Highway," *Guardian*, April 9, 2022, www.theguardian.com/environment/2022/apr/09/wildlife-bridge-california-highway-mountain-lions.

p. 209 **The Charles M. Russell National Wildlife Refuge:** The CMR is named after Charles M. Russell, painter and sculptor of the American West, who was brave enough or crazy enough to make this comment while addressing civic boosters in Great Falls, Montana, in the 1920s (quoted in Geist, *Buffalo Nation*, p. 114): "In my book a pioneer is a man who turned all the grass upside down, strung bob-wire over the dust that was left, poisoned the water and cut down the trees, killed the Indian who owned the land, and called it progress. If I had my way, the land here would be like God made it, and none of you sons of bitches would be here at all."

pp. 210–211 **"progress in restoring ecological processes":** "Management of Wildlife on Federal Lands," Montana Wild Bison Restoration Coalition, https://mtwildbison.org/mgmtwildlife.htm.

pp. 211–12 **"Today the population size and distribution":** Sanderson et al., "The Ecological Future of the North American Bison," p. 263.

p. 212 **"Negotiating more tolerance for bison":** "Bison Management," www.nps.gov/yell/learn/management/bison-management.htm.

p. 212 **"necessitates tolerance for bison outside of":** White, Wallen, and Hallac, *Yellowstone Bison*, p. 95.

p. 215 **Presently, bison are confined to about 15 percent:** Buffalo Field Campaign, "ESA Victory! Buffalo Field Campaign Wins Candidate Status for Yellowstone's Bison under the Endangered Species Act," press release, June 6, 2022, www.buffalofieldcampaign.org/press-release-esa-victory-buffalo-field-campaign-wins-candidate-status-for-yellowstones-bison-under-the-endangered-species-act.

p. 216 **"substantial scientific or commercial":** Ibid.

Bibliography

Albright, Horace M. *The Birth of the National Park Service: The Founding Years, 1913–33*. As told to Robert Cahn. Salt Lake City: Howe Brothers, 1985.

Anderson, George S. "A Buffalo Story." In Roosevelt and Grinnell, *American Big-Game Hunting*, pp. 19–25.

———. *Annual Report of the Acting Superintendent of the Yellowstone National Park to the Secretary of the Interior*. Washington, DC: US Government Printing Office, 1895; 1896.

———. *Annual Report of the Superintendent of the Yellowstone National Park to the Secretary of the Interior*. Washington, DC: US Government Printing Office, 1892.

Athearn, Robert G. *Westward the Briton*. New York: Charles Scribner's Sons, 1953.

Aune, Keith, and Glenn Plumb. *Theodore Roosevelt and Bison Restoration on the Great Plains*. Charleston, SC: History Press, 2019.

Baggett, Donnis. "How Did They Get There? The Texas State Bison Herd at Caprock Canyons State Park." *Bison World*, Summer 2022.

Bailey, James A. *American Plains Bison: Rewilding an Icon*. Helena, MT: Sweetgrass Books, 2013.

Bean, Michael J. *The Evolution of National Wildlife Law*. Rev. and expanded ed. New York: Praeger, 1983.

Bechtel, Stefan. *Mr. Hornaday's War: How a Peculiar Victorian Zookeeper Waged a Lonely Crusade for Wildlife That Changed the World*. Boston: Beacon Press, 2012.

Brinkley, Douglas. *The Wilderness Warrior: Theodore Roosevelt and the Crusade for America*. New York: HarperCollins, 2009.

Brown, Oscar J. *Annual Report of the Acting Superintendent of the Yellowstone National Park to the Secretary of the Interior*. Washington, DC: U.S. Government Printing Office, 1899.

Canadian Government. "Canada's Part in the Preservation of the Buffalo." In *Fourth Annual Report of the American Bison Society, 1911*, by the American Bison Society, pp. 37–41. New York: American Bison Society, 1911.

Carbyn, Ludwig N., Nicholas J. Lunn, and Kevin Timoney. "Trends in the Distribution and Abundance of Bison in Wood Buffalo National Park." *Wildlife Society Bulletin* 26, no. 3 (Fall 1998): pp. 463–70.

Carmony, Neil B., and David E. Brown, eds. *Mexican Game Trails: Americans Afield in Old Mexico, 1866–1940*. Norman: University of Oklahoma Press, 1991.

Cashman, Sean Dennis. *America in the Gilded Age: From the Death of Lincoln to the Rise of Theodore Roosevelt*. 3rd ed. New York: New York University Press, 1993.

Committee on the Status of Endangered Wildlife in Canada. *COSEWIC Assessment and Status Report on the Plains Bison* Bison bison bison *and the Wood Bison* Bison bison athabascae *in Canada*. Ottawa: COSEWIC, 2013.

Cutright, Paul Russell. *Theodore Roosevelt: The Making of a Conservationist*. Urbana: University of Illinois Press, 1985.

Danz, Harold P. *Of Bison and Man*. Niwot: University Press of Colorado, 1997.

Dary, David A. *The Buffalo Book: The Saga of an American Symbol*. New York: Avon Books, 1975

Department of the Interior. *DOI Bison Report: Looking Forward*. Natural Resource Report NPS/NRSS/BRMD/NRR—2014/821. Fort Collins, CO: National Park Service, 2014.

Di Silvestro, Roger L. *The African Elephant: Twilight in Eden*. New York: John Wiley & Sons, 1991.

———. *The Endangered Kingdom: The Struggle to Save America's Wildlife*. New York: John Wiley & Sons, 1989.

———. *In the Shadow of Wounded Knee: The Untold Final Chapter of the Indian Wars*. New York: Walker, 2005.

———. *Reclaiming the Last Wild Places: A New Agenda for Biodiversity*. New York: John Wiley & Sons, 1993.

———. *Theodore Roosevelt in the Badlands: A Young Politician's Quest for Recovery in the American West*. New York: Walker, 2011.

Dratch, Peter A., and Peter J. P. Gogan. *Bison Conservation Initiative: Bison Conservation Genetics Workshop; Report and Recommendations*. Natural Resource Report NPS/NRPC/BRMD/NRR—2010/257. Fort Collins, CO: National Park Service, 2010.

Dr. Godman. "The Bison, or Bonassus of North America." *Saturday Magazine*, November 2, 1833.

Dubbs, Emanuel. "Charles Goodnight." In Goodnight et al., *Pioneer Days*, pp. 7–28.

———. "Personal Reminiscences—Part II." In Goodnight et al., *Pioneer Days*, pp. 61–99.

Environment and Climate Change Canada. *Recovery Strategy for the Wood Bison* (Bison bison athabascae) *in Canada*. Species at Risk Act Recovery Strategy Series. Ottawa: Environment and Climate Change Canada, 2018.

Fisher, Albert Kenrick. "In Memoriam: George Bird Grinnell." *The Auk* 56, no. 1 (January 1939): pp. 1–12.

Forest and Stream. "Killing Park Buffalo." December 7, 1895. Quoted in Jacoby, *Crimes against Nature*.

———. "Park Poachers and Their Ways." May 26, 1894. Quoted in Jacoby, *Crimes against Nature*.

Fox, Stephen. *The American Conservation Movement: John Muir and his Legacy*. Madison: University of Wisconsin Press, 1981.

Frémont, John C. *Frémont's First Impressions: The Original Report of His Exploring Expeditions of 1842–1844*. Lincoln: University of Nebraska Press, 2012.

Gates, C. Cormack, and Len Broberg. *Yellowstone Bison: The Science and Management of a Migratory Wildlife Population*. Missoula: University of Montana Press, 2011.

Geist, Valerius. *Buffalo Nation: History and Legend of the North American Bison*. Stillwater, MN: Voyageur Press, 1996.

Geremia, Chris, Rick Wallen, Lauren McGarvey, Ramon Perez, and Doug Blanton. *Bison Conservation Update, November 2020*. YCR-2021-01. Yellowstone National Park, WY: National Park Service, 2021. www.nps.gov/yell/learn/management/upload /BISON-Conservation-Update-2020.pdf.

Goodnight, Charles, Emanuel Dubbs, John A. Hart, et al. *Pioneer Days in the Southwest from 1850 to 1879*. 2nd ed. Guthrie, OK: The State Capital Company, 1909.

Grinnell, George Bird. "The Capture of Howell." *Forest and Stream*, March 31, 1894.

———. "Hunting Trips of a Ranchman." *Forest and Stream*, July 2, 1885.

———. Introduction to vol. 1 of *The Works of Theodore Roosevelt*, edited by Hermann Hagedorn, pp. xiv–xvi. New York: Charles Scribner's Sons, 1926.

———. "Our National Parks." *Forest and Stream*, December 3, 1891.

———. "A Premium on Crime." *Forest and Stream*, March 24, 1894. Quoted in Jacoby, *Crimes against Nature*.

Grinnell, George Bird, writing as "Ornis." "Buffalo Hunt with the Pawnees." *Forest and Stream*, December 25, 1873.

———. "Zoological Report." In Ludlow, *Report of a Reconnaissance*, pp. 59–92. Quoted in Punke, *Last Stand*.

Haley, J. Evetts. *Charles Goodnight: Cowman and Plainsman*. New ed. Norman: University of Oklahoma Press, 1949.

Hamner, Laura V. *The No-Gun Man of Texas*. Amarillo, TX: published by the author, 1935.

Harris, Moses. *Annual Report of the Superintendent of the Yellowstone National Park to the Secretary of the Interior*. Washington, DC: US Government Printing Office, 1886; 1887.

Hartway, Cynthia, Amanda Hardy, Lee Jones, Brendan Moynahan, Kathy Traylor-Holzer, Blake McCann, Keith Aune, and Glenn Plumb. *Long-Term Viability of Department of the Interior Bison under Current Management and Potential Metapopulation Management Strategies*. Natural Resource Report NPS/NRSS/BRD—2020/2097. Fort Collins, CO: National Park Service, 2020.

Hornaday, William T. *The Extermination of the American Bison*. Washington, DC: US Government Printing Office, 1887.

———. "John F. Lacey." In Pammel, *Major John F. Lacey*, pp. 12–15.

———. "Notes on the Census." In *Annual Report of the American Bison Society, 1905–1907*, by the American Bison Society, pp. 75–78. New York: American Bison Society, 1908.

———. *Our Vanishing Wild Life: Its Extermination and Preservation*. New York: New York Zoological Society, 1913.

Hough, E. "*Forest and Stream's* Yellowstone Park Game Exploration: The Account of Howell's Capture." *Forest and Stream*, May 5, 1894. Quoted in Trefethen, *Crusade for Wildlife*.

Jacoby, Karl. *Crimes against Nature: Squatters, Poachers, Thieves, and the Hidden History of American Conservation*. Berkeley: University of California Press, 2001.

Jones, Charles Jesse. *Buffalo Jones' Adventures on the Plains*. Edited by Henry Inman. Lincoln: University of Nebraska Press, 1970. First published 1899 as the first part of *Buffalo Jones' Forty Years of Adventure* (Topeka: Crane).

Kamath, Pauline L., et al. "Genomics Reveals Historic and Contemporary Transmission Dynamics of a Bacterial Disease among Wildlife and Livestock." *Nature Communications* 7 (May 11, 2016): 11448. https://doi.org/10.1038/ncomms11448.

Lang, Lincoln A. *Ranching with Roosevelt*. Philadelphia: JB Lippincott, 1926.

Leopold, Aldo. *Game Management*. Madison: University of Wisconsin Press, 1986. First published 1933 by Charles Scribner's Sons (New York).

Lindsey, Lieutenant Elmer. "A Winter Trip Through the Yellowstone Park." *Harper's Weekly*, January 29, 1898.

List, Rurik, Gerardo Ceballos, Charles Curtin, Peter J. P. Gogan, Jesús Pacheco, and Joe Truett. "Historic Distribution and Challenges to Bison Recovery in the Northern Chihuahuan Desert." *Conservation Biology* 21, no. 6 (December 2007): p. 1489. https://doi.org/10.1111/j.1523-1739.2007.00810.x.

List, Rurik, and Patricia Manzano-Fischer. "Conserving Wildlands in Mexico." *Wild Earth* 12, no. 2 (Fall 2002): pp. 46–55.

List, Rurik, Jesús Pacheco, Eduardo Ponce, Rodrigo Sierra-Corona, and Gerardo Ceballos. "The Janos Biosphere Reserve, Northern Mexico." *International Journal of Wilderness* 16, no. 2 (August 2010): pp. 37–38.

Locke, Harvey. Foreword to Olson and Janelle, *The Ecological Buffalo*, pp. xi–xii.

Locke, Harvey, ed. *The Last of the Buffalo: Return to the Wild*. Banff: Summerthought, 2016.

Ludlow, William. *Report of a Reconnaissance from Carroll, Montana Territory, on the Upper Missouri, to the Yellowstone National Park, and Return, Made in the Summer of 1875*. Washington, DC: US Government Printing Office, 1876.

Mayer, Frank H., and Charles B. Roth. *The Buffalo Harvest*. Union City, TN: Pioneer Press, 1995. First published 1958 by Sage Books (Denver).

McGee, William J. *Proceedings of a Conference of Governors in the White House, Washington, D. C., May 13–15, 1908*. Edited by Newton C. Blanchard, John Franklin Fort, John C. Cutler, James O. Davidson, and Martin F. Ansel. Washington DC: US Government Printing Office, 1909.

Meagher, Margaret Mary. *The Bison of Yellowstone National Park*. Washington, DC: US Department of the Interior, National Park Service, 1973.

Meine, Curt. *Aldo Leopold: His Life and Work*. Madison: University of Wisconsin Press, 1988.

Morris, Sylvia Jukes. *Edith Kermit Roosevelt*. New York: Vintage Books, 1990.

Norris, P. W. *Annual Report of the Superintendent of the Yellowstone National Park to the Secretary of the Interior for the Year 1880*. Washington, DC: US Government Printing Office, 1881.

Olech, Wanda, and Kajetan Perzanowski. *Best Practice Manual for Protection of European Bison*. [In Polish.] Warsaw: Center for Coordination of Environmental Projects, 2014. docplayer.pl/12372217-Podrecznik-najlepszych-praktyk-ochrony-zubra.html.

Olson, Wes, and Johane Janelle. *The Ecological Buffalo: On the Trail of a Keystone Species*. Regina, SK: University of Regina Press, 2022.

Pammel, L. H., ed. *Major John F. Lacey: Memorial Volume*. Cedar Rapids: Iowa Park and Forestry Association / Torch Press, 1915.

Peters, Robert, et al. "Nature Divided, Scientists United: US-Mexico Border Wall Threatens Biodiversity and Binational Conservation." *BioScience* 68, no. 10 (October 2018): pp. 740–43. https://doi.org/10.1093/biosci/biy063.

Pitcher, Jonathan. *Annual Report of the Acting Superintendent of the Yellowstone National Park to the Secretary of the Interior*. Washington, DC: US Government Printing Office, 1902; 1903; 1904; 1905; 1906.

Plumb, G., R. Kowalczyk, and J. A. Hernandez-Blanco. Bison bonasus, *European Bison*. The IUCN Red List of Threatened Species, 2020. Assessment available online at dx.doi.org/10.2305/IUCN.UK.2020-3.RLTS.T2814A45156279.en.

Popescu, Adam. "Virunga Power." *New Scientist*, June 11, 2022.

Punke, Michael. *Last Stand: George Bird Grinnell, the Battle to Save the Buffalo, and the Birth of the New West*. New York: HarperCollins, 2007.

Putnam, Carleton. *Theodore Roosevelt*. Vol. 1, *The Formative Years, 1858–1886*. New York: Charles Scribner's Sons, 1958.

Reiger, John F., ed. *The Passing of the Great West: Selected Papers of George Bird Grinnell*. Norman: University of Oklahoma Press, 1985.

Rewilding Europe. *Bison Rewilding Plan, 2014–2024*. Nijmegen, Netherlands: Rewilding Europe, 2014. www.rewildingeurope.com/wp-content/uploads/publications/bison-rewilding-plan-2014-2024/html5.

Roosevelt, Theodore. *An Autobiography*. New York: Macmillan, 1913.

———. "The Boone and Crockett Club." *Harper's Weekly*, March 18, 1893.

———. *Hunting Trips of a Ranchman & The Wilderness Hunter*. New York: The Modern Library, 2004. *Hunting Trips of a Ranchman* first published 1885 and *The Wilderness Hunter* 1893 by G. P. Putnam's Sons (New York).

———. *Outdoor Pastimes of an American Hunter*. Mechanicsburg, PA: Stackpole Books, 1990. First published 1905 by Charles Scribner's Sons (New York).

———. "President's Annual Message." 39 Cong. Rec. pp. 10–21 (December 6, 1904).

Roosevelt, Theodore, and George Bird Grinnell, eds. *American Big-Game Hunting: The Book of the Boone and Crockett Club*. New York: Forest and Stream, 1893.

Sanderson, Eric W., et al. "The Ecological Future of the North American Bison: Conceiving Long-Term, Large-Scale Conservation of Wildlife." *Conservation Biology* 22, no. 2 (May 2008): 252–66. https://doi.org/10.1111/j.1523-1739.2008.00899.x.

Schlyer, Krista. "The Lost Herd of Janos-Hidalgo." *Wildlife Conservation*, January/February 2009.

Seton, Ernest Thompson. *Lives of Game Animals*. Vol. 3, pt. 2, *Hoofed Animals*. Boston: Charles T. Branford, 1953.

Standing Bear, Luther. *My Indian Boyhood*. Lincoln: University of Nebraska Press, 1988. First published 1931.

Stroupe, Sam, David Forgacs, Andrew Harris, James N. Derr, and Brian W. Davis. "Genomic Evaluation of Hybridization in Historic and Modern North American Bison (*Bison bison*)." *Scientific Reports* 12 (April 16, 2022): 6397. https://doi.org/10.1038/s41598-022-09828-z.

Trefethen, James B. *Crusade for Wildlife: Highlights in Conservation Progress*. Harrisburg, PA: Stackpole; New York: Boone and Crockett Club, 1961.

Utley, Robert M. *The Last Days of the Sioux Nation*. New Haven and London: Yale University Press, 1963.

Vaughan, Adam. "Wild Bison Roam in the UK for the First Time." *New Scientist*, July 23, 2022.

Walker, James R. *Lakota Belief and Ritual*. Lincoln: University of Nebraska Press, 1991. Published in cooperation with the Colorado Historical Society.

Watkins, T. H. *Righteous Pilgrim: The Life and Times of Harold L. Ickes, 1874–1952*. New York: Henry Holt, 1990.

Wear, D. W. *Annual Report of the Superintendent of the Yellowstone National Park to the Secretary of the Interior*. Washington, DC: US Government Printing Office, 1885.

Weinberg, P. J. "European Bison Monitoring in North Ossetia-Alania." Unpublished report, World Wide Fund for Nature, 2019.

White, P. J., Robert A. Garrott, and Glenn E. Plumb, eds. *Yellowstone's Wildlife in Transition*. Cambridge, MA: Harvard University Press, 2013.

White, P. J., Rick L. Wallen, and David E. Hallac, eds. *Yellowstone Bison: Conserving an American Icon in Modern Society*. Yellowstone National Park: Yellowstone Association, 2015.

Wilkinson, Todd. *Last Stand: Ted Turner's Quest to Save a Troubled Planet*. Guilford, CT: Lyons Press, 2013.

Yellowstone Center for Resources. *A Risk Analysis of* Brucella abortus *Transmission Among Bison, Elk, and Cattle in the Northern Greater Yellowstone Area*. Technical Report to the National Park Service, October 2010. YCR-2012-02. Mammoth Hot Springs, WY: National Park Service, 2012.

Young, S. B. M. *Annual Report of the Acting Superintendent of the Yellowstone National Park to the Secretary of the Interior*. Washington, DC: US Government Printing Office, 1907.

Young, Stanley P., and Edward A. Goldman. *The Wolves of North America*. New York: Dover, 1964.

Zontek, Ken. *Buffalo Nation: American Indian Efforts to Restore the Bison*. Lincoln: University of Nebraska Press, 2007.

Resources

Would you like to partner with organizations working with bison and bison habitat? Below are sources of information on bison history and conservation, including organizations working to restore bison as well as sites where you can observe the animals. A map of bison ranges on page 6 also shows where you can see bison.

WORKING WITH BISON

All About Bison: A clearinghouse for an exhaustive amount of information on bison, from natural history to history in general. If you have a question about bison, allaboutbison.com is a good place to look for answers.

American Prairie: This innovative group changes its name so often that it is hard to keep up, but it also is moving at a rapid pace on its plan to set aside 3 million acres of private and public lands as a vast prairie reserve in the northern reaches of the West. It has scored successes with leases on federal grazing lands and with limiting the distribution of cattle on public lands and opening those lands to bison. The group also physically restores land within its administration. Find them at americanprairie.org.

Buffalo Field Campaign: In business now for a quarter of a century, this Montana-based group puts activists on the ground in the Yellowstone National Park area to help guide tourist traffic during seasons when bison are lingering on local roads. The group also works on bison policies and issues, such as listing the bison under the US Endangered Species Act. They can be reached at buffalofieldcampaign.org.

The Center for Biological Diversity: This group would have won the allegiance of William T. Hornaday, as the staff is not shy about fighting court battles on behalf of wildlife species and wildlife habitat. They cover a wide range of species and geography, outlined at biologicaldiversity.org.

Defenders of Wildlife: Founded in the late 1940s, this organization based in Washington, DC, has dedicated decades of work to the protection and restoration of such prairie natives as the black-footed ferret, mountain lion, grizzly bear, whooping crane, and bison. They are at defenders.org.

The Greater Yellowstone Coalition: Headquartered in Bozeman, Montana, and with offices in Idaho and Wyoming, the coalition has worked to protect the world's first national park for nearly forty years. See what they are up to at greateryellowstone.org.

Montana Wild Bison Restoration Coalition: Relatively new, this organization started in 2018 to urge bison-management procedures designed to keep the species wild and to fend off measures that might lead, however inadvertently, to domestication. The group also works to open the Charles M. Russell National Wildlife Refuge to bison. See their goals at mtwildbison.org.

National Audubon Society: Founded by George Bird Grinnell in the 1880s, Audubon traces its roots to the early years of wildlife conservation. As a premiere bird-conservation group, Audubon is often at the forefront of efforts to protect prairies in the United States and Canada, and it is focusing some of its energy on cooperative programs with ranchers to ensure the protection of wildlife and habitat. Visit the group at audubon.org.

National Bison Association: This organization serves the interests of bison while also serving the interests of bison ranchers. The association puts an emphasis on education, teaching bison ranchers the finer points of raising bison without the risk of domesticating the animals. The organization publishes a bimonthly magazine and weekly digital newsletters that are always informative about bison issues. Drop into their site for more information at bisoncentral.com.

Wildlife Conservation Society: In an earlier incarnation, this organization, which runs the Bronx Zoo in New York City, was called the New York Zoological Society. Today it boasts a staff of myriad biologists working around the world on species ranging from elephants and gorillas to snow leopards and Bengal tigers. It has had a long focus on bison conservation, dating to the early 1900s when Theodore Roosevelt was a major impetus for the founding of the zoo and the society. Learn more about this world-class conservation group at wcs.org.

World Wildlife Fund/World Wide Fund for Nature: Generally speaking, these two names refer to the same group, with the former name used in the United States and the latter more or less everywhere else. It is a leader in prairie and bison protection in North America and in wisent protection in Europe and points east. Find out all you need to know at worldwildlife.org.

Yellowstone to Yukon Conservation Initiative: This organization seeks to build specially designed bridges and tunnels so wildlife can cross major highways that are often death traps for animals. Check it out at y2y.net.

PLACES TO SEE BISON

Caprock Canyons State Park and Trail: The 15,360 acres of Caprock Canyons State Park have a historic link to frontier rancher and bison enthusiast Charles Goodnight. The park is located in the Texas Panhandle, straight north of Lubbock and straight west of Oklahoma City. A motor trail allows visitors to view bison. Find out more at https://tpwd.texas.gov/state-parks/caprock-canyons

Custer State Park: This 71,000-acre unit is South Dakota's largest state park and is home to around 1,400 bison. The annual bison roundup occurs at the end of September, and visitors can watch either in person or via live stream. The park sells some 300 bison yearly to limit herd size. Learn more at https://gfp.sd.gov/buffalo-roundup.

Elk Island National Park: Located thirty-five miles east of Edmonton, Alberta, this 48,000-acre park is relatively small but possesses profound historical significance for bison conservation. It offers visitors access to bison as well as 250 bird species and, seasonally, viewing of the aurora borealis. Check it out at www.pc.gc.ca/en/pn-np/ab/elkisland.

Fort Niobrara National Wildlife Refuge: At 19,200 acres, this refuge, managed by the US Fish & Wildlife Service, is home to 360 bison. An annual roundup is open to public viewing. The refuge is located near Valentine, Nebraska, on the edge of the Sandhills region, a vast grassland area; the refuge is one of six within the Sandhills National Wildlife Refuge Complex. Visitors can drive through the refuge and see a variety of prairie species, including pronghorn and elk. More of its treasures are revealed at www.fws.gov/refuge/fort-niobrara.

Fort Peck (Assiniboine-Sioux) Reservation: Also known as Nakota (or Nakona or Nakoda) and Dakota Tribes, respectively, the people of this 2-million-acre reservation in northeastern Montana have been building a herd of bison for several years. Visitors can see herds moving across natural prairie habitat. Before visiting, check out the reservation website and ask about access: https://tribalnations.mt.gov/fortpeck or 406-768-2300. The Assiniboine and Gros Ventre Tribes of the Fort Belknap Reservation in north-central Montana also are building a bison herd on their 652,000 acres of prairie. More information on accessibility can be found at https://tribalnations.mt.gov/fortbelknap or 406-353-2205.

Henry Mountains: The federal Bureau of Land Management administers some 2 million acres encompassing part of Utah's Henry Mountains and nearby desert. These public lands are home to 250 to 400 free-ranging, wild bison and feature an annual sport bison hunt. The area is rugged and remote and rarely patrolled by authorities. Officials warn visitors to bring along plenty of water and a reliable motor vehicle. Learn more at www.utah.com/destinations/natural-areas/henry-mountains.

The Nature Conservancy sites: Headquartered in Virginia just outside Washington, DC, the conservancy is one of the largest (it's active in seventy-nine nations and territories) and best-funded (it has an annual budget in excess of $1.2 billion) conservation groups. It has used its clout to establish bison reserves in several western states, from Illinois to Oklahoma to the Dakotas. These reserves are home to some 5,500 bison. The conservancy also works with tribes and with federal and state agencies to restore bison to the central plains. For details, go to www.nature.org.

Osage Nation: The Osage Nation is a federally recognized government headquartered in Pawhuska, a town in northeast Oklahoma. The Osage lands include a 43,000-acre ranch on which the tribe is building a bison herd, currently in excess of two hundred animals. The ranch is open to public visitation. For information, go to www.osagenation-nsn.gov/services or call 1-800-320-8742 or 918-287-5555.

Santa Catalina Island, California: If you happen to be in Los Angeles and in the mood for a side trip that will bring you within proximity of bison, catch a ferryboat ride to Santa Catalina Island, during which you may see flying fish. Bison were brought to the island in the 1920s to appear in two Western films. Whether they made it to the screen is uncertain, but there is no question that when the film crews cleared out, the bison remained. Today, about a hundred of them range across island grasslands. Explore the possibilities at www.visitcatalinaisland.com.

Theodore Roosevelt National Park: This park in the Badlands of western North Dakota is the very place where Roosevelt first went bison hunting and then set up two ranching operations. His original ranch house is preserved at the park, where you are also likely to see bison near roads, as well as herds of free-ranging horses. There's more at www.nps.gov/thro/index.htm.

Wichita Mountains National Wildlife Refuge: Located in the heart of Oklahoma, near the town of Lawton, this refuge is an important historic site in the world of bison conservation, as it was the first place where captive bison were released in a restoration program. Today the refuge—a mix of grasslands punctuated with the remnants of ancient granite mountains—provides habitat for prairie dogs, about 1,000 elk, and some 650 bison. Find answers to your questions about the refuge at www.fws.gov/refuge/wichita-mountains.

Wind Cave National Park: Along with its 33,847 prairie acres, this park in southwest South Dakota offers one of the most complex cave systems in the United States, as well as elk, pronghorn, and 250 to 400 bison. According to Lakota Indian traditional beliefs, Wind Cave was the place from which both bison and people first entered the upper world. The National Park Service offers information on the park and bison at www.nps.gov/wica/index.htm.

Wood Buffalo National Park: At more than 11 million acres, Wood Buffalo National Park has plenty of room for the wood bison to roam. Located on the border of Alberta and the Northwest Territories, this site is for dedicated bison enthusiasts, as roads in the area are mostly gravel and can prove dangerous in winter. Check out conditions at www.pc.gc.ca/en/pn-np/nt/woodbuffalo.

Yellowstone National Park: This is the premiere bison site in the Lower 48 states, with the herd varying in number but presently around 4,000. The park crowds badly during the summer tourist season and can be hard to negotiate in the dead of winter, with deep snow, but in spring and autumn, and with careful planning, you can avoid those challenges. The National Park Service provides info at www.nps.gov/yell/index.htm.

PROPER ETIQUETTE FOR BISON ENCOUNTERS

Bison often seem oblivious to their surroundings as they graze or rest, tempting tourists to draw near. But bison are finely attuned to what is going on around them, and getting too close is dangerous. To avoid confrontations, keep the following tips in mind.

- When on a trail where bison may be hidden around the next bend or when within sight of bison, however far away, be alert. Bison can switch from placid to aggressive very quickly, especially if startled. Always stay at least 75 feet away and avoid eye contact and sudden movements. If you encounter bison on a trail, turn around and slowly retreat or, if conditions allow, go far around them.
- Watch for warning signs of aggression or for situations likely to lead to aggression, particularly around cows with calves and with bulls during the spring mating season. One bison rancher told me that cows have charged him from all the way across a wide pasture, even though he was nowhere near their calves. If a bull in your vicinity is pawing up dust, bawling, shaking his head, and keeping his tail raised, or if you find yourself near peacefully grazing bison and notice that one or more stop eating and begin watching you, recognize that they may be alarmed and are assessing you as a possible threat. Retreat immediately.
- If you want to observe bison up close, do so from a motor vehicle or through binoculars. Keep in mind that a bison may ram a motor vehicle and can cause extensive damage with a single blow, so even in a vehicle, watch for signs of aggressive behavior or warnings of irritation.

For more information, try these three useful sites:

- wildlife.utah.gov/news/utah-wildlife-news/1223-stay-safe-around-bison.html
- nps.gov/yell/planyourvisit/safety.htm
- nps.gov/yell/planyourvisit/viewanim.htm

Index

A

Albright, Horace, 79–80, 84
Allard, Charles, 57, 135
American Bison Society, 55, 72, 75–76, 96, 137
American Plains Bison: Rebuilding an Icon (Bailey), 202, 203–204
American Prairie, 96, 101–103
Anderson, Captain George S., 29–30, 32, 34, 35
Animal & Plant Health Inspection Service (APHIS), 177, 184
Atatitsa (Peregrine Falcon Robe), 134
Audubon, John James, 22, 40
Audubon, Lucy, 22
Audubon group, 24–25
Audubon Society, 48–49
Aune, Keith, 97, 204, 207

B

Badlands National Park's herd, 197, 198
Bailey, James A., 87, 100–101, 183, 202, 203–204, 205, 210, 211
Baird, Spencer F., 37, 38, 41
Baynes, Ernest Harold, 55, 68
Bedson, Colonel Samuel L., 60, 66–67, 68
beefalo, 90
Belcourt, Jason, 116–118, 119
Bergmann's rule, 138, 139
Bialowieza National Park, Poland, 151, 153, 154, 157, 164
bibliography, 239–244
biosphere reserves, 131–132
bird protection, conservation, 48–49
bison
    breeding and calving, 12–13, 92–93
    vs. buffalo, 8
    calving season of, 12, 170, 171–172
    campaign to save the, 36, 70
    vs. cattle, 91–92, 117–119, 178, 180–181, 183
    culling of, 174–175
    diets, 94
    digestion of, 171
    diseases, 133, 138, 140, 143, 151, 175–185, 203
    European. *See* wisent (European bison)
    extermination of, 21, 34, 111–113
    genetic diversity, 204
    hunting, 178–180, 185–186
    hybridization, 140, 202
    influence on the landscape, 169–170
    last big herd, 14–15
    leather, skulls, 94
    near-extinction of, 9–10, 23, 24–25, 27–28, 50
    Plains Indians and the, 108–113
    poaching of, 10, 28–29, 30–34, 35, 193–194, 213
    predators, 172
    in prehistory, 9–10
    ranges of, 6, 10
    reintroduction, 75–77
    restoration of the, 95–98, 116–124, 133–134, 141–142, 145, 163–166, 172–175, 189, 205, 210–212, 216–217
    slaughter of, 14–16
    subspecies of, 10, 138–139, 148
    threats to, 164–165
    vaccination, 205
    wallows, 11–12, 149
Bison 1 Million initiative, 95
Bison Conservation Initiative, 197
Bison Day Festival, 76
Bison of Yellowstone National Park, The (Meagher), 173
Bison Rewilding Plan, 2014-2024, 150
Bison Working Group, Dept. of the Interior, 97
Blackfeet Confederacy, 115, 121–122
Blue Mountain Forest and Game Preserve, New Hampshire, 55, 68
Boone and Crockett Club, 19, 25–27, 44, 45, 53, 54, 69
bovine tuberculosis, 138, 140, 143
breeding season of bison, 12, 92
Bronx Zoo, 56, 68, 120
brucellosis, 138, 140, 143, 175–185, 203
buffalo and bison, 8
Buffalo Commons, 206, 208
Buffalo Harvest, The (Mayer & Roth), 12, 63, 111
Buffalo Nation: American Indian Efforts to Restore the Bison (Zontek), 143–144
Buffalo National Park, Canada, 136, 137, 139, 140
Bullock, Governor Steve, 186, 210
Bureau of Land Management, 86–87, 194–195
Burgess, Felix, 30, 31

C

calving season of bison, 12, 170, 171–172
Canadian herds, 134–145
Cárdenas, President Lázaro, 131
Carter, David, 89–90, 92, 95
catalo, 199, 200
cattle
    crossbred with bison, 199–202
    vs. bison, 91–92, 117–119, 178, 180–181, 183
Caucasian bison, 148, 159–160
Ceballos, Gerardo, 127, 128, 129, 132
Charles M. Russell National Wildlife Refuge, 101, 102, 118, 209, 211
Cheyenne River Lakota, 114
Chippewa Cree people, 116, 119
Cleveland, President Grover, 26, 35, 67

INDEX

Cole, Senator Cornelius, 46
Comanche people, 69
Confederated Salish & Kootenai Tribes, 123, 181
Congo's Virunda National Park, 192–193
Conrad, Charles E., 57, 68
Conrad herd, 74
conservation herds, 104
Corbin, Austin, 55, 68
Corbin herd, 74
cows. See cattle
Coyote, Samuel Walking, 56–57
Cree people, 142, 143
crossbreeding of bison and cattle, 199–202
Crow Indians, 113
Crum, Galen, 120–121
Custer, George Armstrong, 22, 115, 124
Custer State Park, 58

D
Dakota Badlands, 18, 20
Daugherty, Charlotte, 61
Daugherty, Hiram, 60–61
Dawes Act of 1887, 73
Delano, Columbus, 111
Department of Interior, 97, 194–195, 202–203
Department of Living Animals of the National Museum, 42
Di Silvestro, Roger L., 255
Division of Economic Ornithology & Mammalogy, Dept. of Agriculture, 77–78
Dixon, Senator Joseph M., 71–72
dung beetles, 149
Dupree, Frederic & Pete, 58

E
Eaton, Howard, 57
"Ecological Future of the North American Bison, The" (Carter, et. al.), 95
1891 federal Forest Reserve Act, 26
Eising, Kaja, 156–157
Elder Dialogues, 115, 122
Eleonorenwald project, Germany, 163
elephants, 193–194, 213
elk, 176–177, 183, 215
Elk Island National Park, Canada, 136, 137, 140, 145
Endangered Species Act, 49, 133
European Bison Conservation Center, 151
European Bison Pedigree Book, 150–151
European Endangered Species Programme, 151, 162
Extermination of the American Bison, The (Hornaday), 19, 43–44, 47

F
Federal Aid in Wildlife Restoration Act of 1937, 84
Ferguson, Rob, 93–94
First National, Canada, 142–144
Flathead Indian Reservation, 57, 58, 134, 135
Flathead Indians, 56, 71, 74
Forest Reserve Act of 1891, 51, 78, 85
forest reserves, 51

Forest Service Organic Administration Act of 1897, 51, 85
Fort, Representative Greenbury, 46–47
Fort Keogh, 37–38, 39, 134
Fort Niobrara National Wildlife Refuge, 76, 87
Fort Peck, 115
Fort Peck Assiniboine Tribe, 187–188

G
Game Management (Leopold), 82–83, 84
Gandl, Nina, 157–159
General Allotment Act of 1887, 73
George, Jason, 120
geysers of Yellowstone National Park, 27
Gianforte, Governor Greg, 210
Glacier National Park, 79
Goode, G. Brown, 42
Goodnight, Charles, 60, 74, 90, 173, 199, 200
Goodnight, George, 60
Goodnight, Mrs. Mary, 62
Goodnight Jr., Charles, 60, 61–63
gorillas, 192–193
Grant, Madison, 54
Grant, President Ulysses S., 33, 46, 47
Greater Wood Buffalo National Park, 141
Grinnell, George Bird, 21–25, 27, 29, 32, 33, 36, 45, 48, 53–54, 77

H
Haley, J. Evetts, 60–61, 63–64
Harris, Captain Moses, 25, 28, 29
Harrison, President Benjamin, 26
Hay-Zama herd, 143
Hearst, William Randolph, 58
Hedley, George, 41, 42–43
Heidelberg, Aurel, 161, 162, 165
Heising, Kaja, 166
herds
  See also specific herd
  conservation, 104
  lost Canadian, 134–145
  lost Mexican, 125–134
  private, 89–107
  tribal, 107
hide hunters, 14–16
Hill, Louis, 79
hormones, growth, 91
Hornaday, William T., 15, 18–19, 29, 34, 36, 37–40, 41, 42–44, 47–48, 49, 52, 53, 55, 56, 68, 71, 74, 77, 81, 82, 101, 109, 123, 135, 200
horses, and bison-hunting, 13–14, 109–110
Hough, Emerson, 32, 34
Howell, Edgar, 30, 31–32, 33–34, 35–36
hunting of bison
  restrictions, 47–48
  techniques of Plains Indians, 13–14
  unregulated, 142
Hunting Trips of a Ranchman (Roosevelt), 21, 23, 38

I

Iinnii Days (Blackfeet buffalo celebration), 123
Iinnii Initiative, 122
Indian Rights Association, 73
Indians. *See* Plains Indians *and specific tribe*
InterTribal Bison Cooperative (ITBC), 114–115, 207
InterTribal Buffalo Council, 181

J

Janos Biosphere Reserve, 130, 132
Janos herd, 129–130
Janos-Hidalgo herd, 128
Jones, Charles "Buffalo," 57, 60, 63–64, 77, 90, 98, 112, 135, 200
Jones, Charles Jesse, 64–67
Jones, Lee C., 183, 201, 202, 204
Joseoph H. Williams Tallgrass Prairie Preserve, Oklahoma, 100

K

Kamoto, Sam, 193
Knieriem, Andreas, 161
Kossler, Mark, 104–106

L

Lacey, Representative John, 34, 36, 44, 47–48, 49, 50, 75–76, 98–99, 199
Lacey Act of 1900, 49
Lakota (Sioux), last bison hut, 15
Lakota (Sioux) tribe, 124
Lakota Belief and Ritual (Walker), 108
Lamar herd, 174–175
Lane, Franklin, 79, 80
Langley, Samuel, 42
Latatitsa (Little Peregrine Robe), 135
Leakey, Richard, 213
Leopold, Aldo, 81–83
Leopold, Starker, 84
Lewis and Clark, 14
Lincoln, Abraham, 64
List, Rurik, 128, 129, 131, 133, 134
Little Thunder, Rosalie, 182
Livingston (MT) Enterprise, 28–29
Locke, Harvey, 205
Loring, J. Alben, 55, 75
lowland bison, 148
Ludlow, Colonel William, 23, 27–28

M

Mackenzie Bison Sanctuary, 140, 144
Malawi's Kasungu National Park, 193
Malawi's Liwonde National Park, 193
Malone, John C., 104
Manifest Destiny, 20
map of bison ranges, 6
Marine Mammal Protection Act, 49
Marsh, O. C., 22
Mather, Stephen Tying, 79, 80
Mayer, Frank, 12, 14, 63, 110, 111, 112
McCormick, Representative R. C., 46
McKay, James, 59–60

McKinley, President William, 26, 49, 67, 85
Meagher, Mary, 173, 174–175, 180
Mease, Mike, 175, 182, 184–185, 187, 189–190, 215–216
Mètis annual hunting expedition, 59
Mexican Game Trails: Americans Afield in Old Mexico, 129
Mexican lost herd, 125–134
Mexican Revolution of 1910, 130–131
microchips, 87
microhabitats created by bison, 11–12
Miller, Mary, 100
Mitchell, H. Raymond, 69, 76
Montana expedition, 37–39
Montana national bison range, 71
Montana Wild Bison Restoration Coalition, 210
Mornorunni, Cristina, 115–116, 118–119, 121, 122–123
mountain gorillas, 192–193
Muir, John, 28, 85

N

National Audubon Society, 22, 213
National Bison Association, 89–90, 93
National Bison Legacy Act, 95
National Bison Range, 72, 103–104, 123
National Environmental Policy Act, 78, 133
National Park Protective Act of 1894, 34–35, 53, 185
National Park Service, 79, 80, 81, 84, 177, 182, 186, 189, 203, 209
National Wildlife Refuge System Improvement Act, 210
National Zoo, 55
Nature Conservancy, The, 93, 99–100, 120
New York Zoological Park, 56
New York Zoological Society, 54
Nez Perce Tribe, 181
Northern Buffalo Management Board, 144
Northern Pacific Railroad, 15, 44–45, 74
notes to this book, 221–238

O

Obama, President Barack, 95
Olech, Wanda, 151, 153–154, 157, 166
Olson, Wes, 137, 139–140, 143, 144–145
Ordway Preserve, 100
Osage Nation, 119–121
Osborn, Henry Fairfield, 54
Outdoor Pastimes of an American Hunter (Roosevelt), 26

P

Pablo, Michel, 57, 67, 135
Pablo herd, 136
Pablo-Allard herd, 72, 123, 134, 173
Panic of 1873, 61–62
Parker, Quanah, 69–70
Philip, James "Scotty," 58
Pinchot, Gifford, 85
Pine Ridge Lakota Indians, 76
plains bison, 10, 138–139, 140, 199
Plains Indians, 22, 207
    and bison restoration, 116–124
    bison's symbolic value, 9–10
    hunting techniques, 13–14
    InterTribal Bison Cooperative (ITBC), 114–115

relationship with bison, 108–113
Plumb, Glenn, 97, 204, 207
poaching of bison, 10, 28–29, 30–34, 35, 193–194, 213
Popper, Deborah and Frank, 206–208
prairie dogs, 127–128, 131
private herds, 89–107

R
radio telemetry, 83–84
railroads and the bison, 44–45
Recovery Strategy for the Wood Bison, 141
Red Cloud (Lakota chief), 113
resources, 245–250
restoration of the bison, 95–98, 116–124, 133–134, 141–142, 145, 163–166, 172–175, 189, 205, 210–212, 216–217
Rewilding Europe, 152
Rocky Boy's Reservation, 116
Rocky Mountains Park, Canada, 136
Roosevelt, President Theodore, 50–52, 53, 54–55, 69, 72, 75, 77, 78
Roosevelt, Theodore, 18, 19–21, 23, 24, 25, 36, 38, 42, 43, 45, 72, 200
Rosenquist, Eric, 100
Rush, Frank, 69, 70, 76

S
Samuel H. Ordway Jr. Memorial Preserve, 99
Sanderson, Eric W., 198
Sandoval, Andrew, 125–126, 127
Sandy the bison calf, 41, 42
Sargent, Charles Sprague, 85
Saskatchewan's Grasslands National Park, 169–170
Schafer, Governor Edward, 207
Secretary of the Interior, 29, 30, 34, 45, 68
Shahdag National Park, Russia, 160, 162–163
Sheridan, General Philip, 111
Sherman, General William Tecumseh, 111
Sicks, Florian, 151–152, 153, 161, 163–164, 165, 166
Simpson, Sir George, 59
Sitting Bull (Tatanka Iyotanka), 123–124
Smith, Sir Donald, 60
Smithsonian Institute, 37, 42
Soper, J. Dewey, 139
Species at Risk Act, Canada, 144
Sport Fish Restoration Act of 1950, 84
Standing Bear, Luther, 109, 110
sun dance, 117
Sztoleman, J., 150, 151

T
Tallgrass Prairie National Preserve, Kansas, 133
Tatanka (Lakota's buffalo god), 108
Theodore Roosevelt National Park, 113
Treviño, Jose "Pepe," 125, 126, 127
tribal herds, 107
Troike, Private, 30, 31
Trump's border wall, 132–133
Tsars Alexander I, II, 147
Tsar Paul I, 147

Turner, Ted, 96, 97, 103–107, 119, 209, 216
2008 Bison Conservation Initiative, 98

U
Ujscie Warty National Park, Poland, 158
Upper Missouri River Breaks National Monument, 101
US Fish & Wildlife Service, 77, 78, 194–195, 203, 210, 211
US Forest Service, 54

V
Vanderbilt, Cornelius, 21
Vermejo Park Ranch, New Mexico, 63
Vermejo Statement, 96–97, 198
Vest, Senator George, 44, 45
Virginia Bison Company, 92, 93, 94

W
Wallace, General Lew, 128–129
Wallen, Rick, 169, 183, 186, 187, 188–189, 190, 208–209, 214–215
wallows, bison, 11–12, 149
Ward, Henry Augustus, 39
Warren, Senator Francis, 45
Watkins, T. H., 73
Welsh, Herbert, 73
Wenk, Daniel N., 190
Wichita Forest Reserve, 52, 68
Wichita Mountains National Wildlife Refuge, 120
Wild Life Conservation in Theory & Practice (Hornaday), 82
Wildlife Conservation Society (WCS), 96, 121
wildlife corridors, 208
Wilson, Alexander, 40
Wilson, President Woodrow, 80
Wilson, Senator Henry, 46
Wind Cave National Game Preserve, 76, 87
Wind Cave National Park, 75–76, 93, 99, 115, 130
wisent (European bison), 10, 146–166
Wisent-Welt-Wittgenstein, 155–157
Wolakota Buffalo Range, 203
wolves, 13
wood bison, 10, 138–139, 140
Wood Buffalo National Park, Canada, 138, 139, 141, 143, 144
Wright, George, 80–81, 84

Y
Y2Y Yellowstone to Yukon corridor, 208
Yellowstone Bison: Conserving on American Icon in Modern Society, 170, 176, 190–191, 206, 212
Yellowstone National Park, 12, 19, 33, 35, 44, 45, 67, 79, 85, 98, 167–169, 174, 180, 182, 185, 188, 196, 197, 205, 209, 212, 215
Yellowstone National Park herd, 198
Yellowstone National Park Timberland Reserve, 26
Young, Colonel Samuel, 35–36

Z
Zontek, Ken, 143–144

About the Author

Roger L. Di Silvestro has worked as a writer, magazine editor, communications director, television-documentary producer, and book editor for wildlife conservation groups such as the National Audubon Society, Defenders of Wildlife, the National Parks Conservation Association, and the National Park Foundation. He is the author of eleven books, including *In the Shadow of Wounded Knee: The Untold Final Chapter of the Indian Wars* and *Theodore Roosevelt in the Badlands: A Young Politician's Quest for Recovery in the American West*.

At the start of his career, he served as a general curator for a private zoo and as a naturalist for a city park. He lives in Virginia.

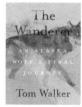